Bones

WILLIAM MORROW

An Imprint of HarperCollins*Publishers*

Bones

Recipes, History, and Lore

Jennifer McLagan

HarperCollins books may be purchased for educational, business, or sales promotional use. For information please write: Special Markets Department, HarperCollins Publishers, 10 East 53rd Street, New York, NY 10022.

FIRST EDITION

Designed by Leah Carlson-Stanisic
Prop styling by Catherine MacFadyen
Food styling by Jennifer McLagan

Printed on acid-free paper

Library of Congress Cataloging-in-Publication Data

McLagan, Jennifer.
    Bones: recipes, history, and lore / Jennifer McLagan.—1st ed.
       p.   cm.
    Includes bibliographical references and index.
    ISBN-10: 0-06-058537-4   ISBN-13: 978-0-06-058537-2
    1. Cookery (Meat) 2. Bones. I. Title.
  TX749.M217   2005
  641.6'6—dc22

                       2005040372

05 06 07 08 09   WBC/QWV   10 9 8 7 6 5 4 3 2 1

For Haralds, love you to the bones

Contents

Acknowledgments

L ooking back to my childhood, I don't remember either of my grandmothers ever cooking a single meal, but I do remember eating and I know that the appreciation of good food, all the way down to its bones, began early for me. Meal times were important and the food was plain but good. My mother, Claudine, and her sisters, my aunts, Pat and Joyce, cooked because that's what wives and mothers did. They were frugal, able to make a meal out of almost nothing. From them, right from the start, I learned that food was valuable and not to be wasted, an important lesson, and I thank them for that.

As a professional cook, I have been influenced by a host of chefs, cooks, and food writers whom I've met through my work, in my travels, and through reading their books. Special thanks go to Chris McDonald of Avalon restaurant, and Andrew Milne-Allan and Louis Alves of Zucca restaurant.

A cook is nothing without quality products. Writing this book and testing recipes, I relied on old friends and discovered new ones: Leila Batten and Stanley Janecek at Whitehouse Meats, John Rietkerk at Second Wind Elk, Elizabeth and Peter Bzikot and their sheep, Chang Lin at Pisces Fish, and Mary Lou Dolan at Beretta Organic Farms. My butcher in Paris deserves special mention. Watching Joël Lachable work is a joy and an education. It reveals the art form that is good butchery. I often don't want to cook the meat he has prepared; I am content to just to admire its beauty.

Writing is a solitary task, so the help and encouragement of friends is invaluable. Pat Holtz, who always encourages me and even manages to write wonderful words about me; Miriam Rubin, who tested, read, edited, and explained American idiosyncrasies; and Heather Trim, who gave valuable advice and tested my recipes. Thank you.

Many people volunteered to taste my cooking and they deserve thanks. It is not always an enjoyable task or easy pinpointing why you like or dislike a recipe. I have many friends with fine palates, who, even more important, are not afraid to criticize. Those who know me well realize just how brave these individuals are. Thank you to Karen Lim and Vincent Wong, François and Caroline Gerard, Val and Ilze Lapsa, Eric and Marie-line Incarbona, Nancy Shanoff and Peter Weis, David Field, Jacques Fortier, and Oksana Slavyutch, who all happily ate anything I put in front of them and told me exactly what they thought of it.

Other friends discovered unusual bone facts, researched information, and passed on recipes. Francois Gerard; Hiroko Sugiyama; David Field; Laura de Turckheim; Melinda Leong, her colleagues at the Deutsche Gesellschaft für Technische Zusammenarbeit (German Technical Cooperation), and her mother Ruby Leong; James Tse; Sally Coles; Robyn McAlister; and Uta Taylor, to all of you I am grateful.

You meet lots generous people in food writing and I would like to express my gratitude to my editors, Amy Albert, Jody Dunn, and Pat Holtz, and to authors Jeffery Alford, Naomi Duguid, and Rosie Schwartz. All of them supported me and provided good sound advice.

I am grateful to those who didn't know me but sent information and answered my questions after we met via the Internet: Barbara Ketcham Wheaton, Andrew Smith, and Bruce Aidells.

Merci beaucoup Laura Calder. Laura and I both began writing book proposals at the same time. Laura finished her proposal and book long before me, however, and then shared with me much useful insider information. She cheered me on throughout and even introduced me to Harriet Bell before my agent had a chance to do so.

As I have no platform or a line of cookware to my name I would not have had a chance to write this book without the foresight and risk-taking of my agent, Rebecca Staffel of the Doe Coover Agency. Thank you Rebecca and Doe, who took up the torch from Rebecca partway along.

Perhaps even braver was Harriet Bell, editor at William Morrow. Right from that first breakfast in Montréal she was enthusiastic about this project.

As time passed we discovered friends and interests we shared, especially a love of France. Without Harriet's support, honesty, and patience, I would never have arrived here, and for that I am very grateful. All the team at HarperCollins deserves praise, especially Lucy Baker, Leah Carlson-Stanisic, and Carrie Bachman and Judith Sutton.

The visuals of this book were extremely important to me. Luckily, over the years I have met and become friends with many very talented designers, photographers, and stylists who have become my friends. Thank you to Lim Graphics, especially Karen Lim and Paola Beltrame, for helping to clarify my ideas. I was thrilled when photographers Rob Fiocca and Colin Faulkner agreed to work on *Bones*. To them and their coworkers, Jim Norton, Irene Hullah, Daniela Fiocca, and Julia Francisco, without whom neither of them could function, a sincere thank-you. The prop stylist is the unsung hero of a photography shoot, especially when working with a small budget. The artistic, resourceful Catherine MacFadyen worked wonders for this book, even cajoling her family into helping, so thank you to her and to her daughter Piper, who carried props back on the train from Montréal.

I wanted people to understand animal skeletons, but I wanted the illustrations to be fun as well as informative. So I turned to my friend Rene Zamic; a brilliant illustrator, Rene took on the project with enthusiasm. Suffice it to say, he is now an expert on any bone he finds on his plate.

I am saving until last the person to whom I am most grateful, my husband, Haralds Gaikis. It is not easy to live with someone writing a book, especially when you are asked to regularly criticize and comment on what your partner is doing. Haralds willing ate his way through the recipes, daring to critique what was presented and so improved the final result.

Most important, he never doubted my ability to do it. Thank you Haralds, thanks for the twenty-five years we have shared. I look forward to the next twenty-five.

Toronto 2005

Author's Note

Cooking is an art, not an exact science. It is and should be open to interpretation and personal taste. Ingredients and equipment will never be exactly the same. While great care has been taken to test all the recipes in this book, the timing will fluctuate and portion size will be a matter of personal preference. All recipes must be approached with a good dose of common sense.

Kosher salt is specified in most of the recipes; make sure that yours is additive free.

Many kosher salts are not as pure as they could be. If you use another type of salt, the amounts will vary. All the herbs used are fresh unless indicated. It is assumed that you will peel the onions, shallots, and garlic unless directed to do otherwise.

Introduction

The connection between flesh and bone is primordial and fundamental. Yet today, bones have fallen out of favor. We are all familiar with the expression, "The nearer the bone the sweeter the meat," but we demand everything precut and prepackaged, and that is, increasingly, all we can buy. Our world is full of recipes for boneless, skinless (and often tasteless) pieces of meat, chicken, and fish, and we scarcely recognize whole fish or birds. We have become so obsessed with ease of preparation and speed that we have lost touch with the visceral appeal of cooking with—and eating—bones. No carcass to cut around, no whole fish to fillet awkwardly. When was the last time, other than Thanksgiving, you ate a meal that was carved at the table? Carving has become a lost art.

My passion for bones was rekindled during a wedding anniversary dinner several years ago, at a well-known Paris restaurant. The evening began tentatively, with my furtive glances at the man seated at the next table. No, I wasn't plotting a change of mate, I was envious. Envious of this stranger's bones: a plate of three towering marrow bones, each crowned with a different topping. I wanted those bones. Luckily, my husband is patient man who shares my passions. There was no need to stray, we celebrated with our own plate of bone towers. As we scooped their soft, creamy centers onto toast, dusting them with salt, I reflected sadly on how such a simple, indulgent pleasure was vanishing.

Not just marrow bones, but all bones are disappearing from our kitchens. As bones fade from our consciousness, the ways in which they enhance and improve the food we eat are forgotten and ignored. But bones play an integral role in the art of cookery, adding taste and texture while enhancing the presentation of the food. Think of osso buco, rack of lamb, fish grilled on the bone, spareribs, roast chicken.

The food of my childhood was enriched by bones. Every Friday morning, my mother and I crossed the butcher's sawdust-covered floor, joking with the ensemble of jolly, big men in long white aprons. We passed the refrigerated counter, with its carefully arranged cuts of meat, and headed directly for a side room where whole animals hung suspended by metal hooks. Entranced, I watched as the butcher skillfully cut an animal into more familiar pieces. After much earnest discussion, we would leave with an assortment of meat with its bones. Once home, bacon bones were transformed into thick pea soup, while oxtail was slowly braised with red wine until the sauce was so rich and sticky it glued your lips together. Irish stew was made with lamb shoulder chops layered with thickly cut potatoes, which readily absorbed the lamb's flavor and fat.

Once I began to travel, I discovered more exotic bones. A warming bowl of *pho*, beef soup, shared with three old Vietnamese women on a rainy, damp market day in Hue, brimmed with the aromas of long-cooked beef bones and star anise. In Italy, I relished a tiny songbird, bones and all, much to the horror of my companions. The little bird, impaled with toothpicks to a piece of toast, had been deep-fried until the bones were so soft they dissolved in my mouth. All that remained uneaten was its beak. In Berlin, fork-tender, juicy *Eisbien* (pork hock) crowned a massive platter of sauerkraut.

I am often in France, where bones are still revered. I eat lip-smacking pig's feet, sucking the meat from the many small bones. In the spring on the banks of the Sâone, in Burgundy, tiny fish are passed quickly through flour and hot oil, eaten like French fries, their bones so tiny you simply crunch them up. The highlight of a stay in Provence is whole rougets grilled with wild fennel.

So appreciated worldwide, bones and many of the cuts containing them are often overlooked in North America. The pig's feet at my local Toronto farmers' market spark only the interest of recent immigrants, and my butcher gives away his veal bones. (He confides to me with regret that he rarely buys whole animals anymore because he can't sell the "odd parts.") Why don't we buy these tasty, often cheap, cuts? Because we no longer know how to cook them and have forgotten the recipes for them. I had to write a book to help solve the problem.

Restoring bones to their deserved place in our kitchens will not be easy. First, we must fight against the current fascination with fast and quick, boneless food. Then we need to familiarize ourselves with the whole animal, its essential structure. When we understand where the bones are, we will be able to cook the meat attached to them. And, in a world where resources are increasingly limited, we must learn to value the entire animal. A cow isn't just tenderloin steaks, and there is more to a chicken than boneless breasts. We pay for the bones that are, or were, part of each piece of meat, poultry, or fish we buy, whether we use them or not, so why not benefit from them? Finally, we must seek out knowledgeable, caring suppliers and support them, badger them, and implore them. The more we ask for different cuts, the more they will become available again.

Chicken soup is a simple example of the importance of bones. With only a chicken, a few vegetables, and water, you can make a rich, nourishing broth that jells as it cools. Why? The chicken's bones. Those bones add body and substance to the soup, as well as taste. Likewise, bones are the starting point of stock, an essential building block in the kitchen. While it's true that stock is not quick to make, it essentially cooks itself. Preparing your own stock gives you control over the ingredients, and the results are far superior to anything you can buy. Stock can be made ahead and frozen, and it can be concentrated, so that it is easy to store. With stock on hand, you have the foundation of delicious sauces and great soups.

Cooking with bones can be homey and reassuring or challenging and inspiring, and I've included recipes here to suit every palate and skill level. The adventurous can tackle marrow bones and pigs' feet, or discover a classic dish with a modern twist, perfect for a dinner party. The occasional cook will find easy, slow-cooked comfort food, and a use for that leftover poultry carcass she or he might otherwise be inclined to toss. There are practical advance-preparation tips, and suggestions for alternative flavorings that make the recipes flexible.

When you cook with bones, you will be rewarded with a wonderful aroma permeating your kitchen, a delicious meal, and the accolades of your guests or family. An added benefit is that many of the dishes improve with keeping and reheat well.

Bones connect me to my childhood, and they link all of us to our past. As I researched this book, I discovered that bones have played an essential role in the history of mankind. They were practical, providing the material for tools. They were powerful, enabling people to foretell the future and ward off evil. They were decorative, fashioned into beautiful objects and jewelry.

They were a source of entertainment used to make music and to play games. Bones and their symbolism pepper our language and literature. We still rely on bones in many ways in the modern world; they are in our bone china, in bone-meal fertilizer, and in many other products. Bones sustain man on many levels, and you will find their history and folklore on these pages.

I hope this book helps you rediscover bones and, most important, brings them back into your kitchen.

Bones

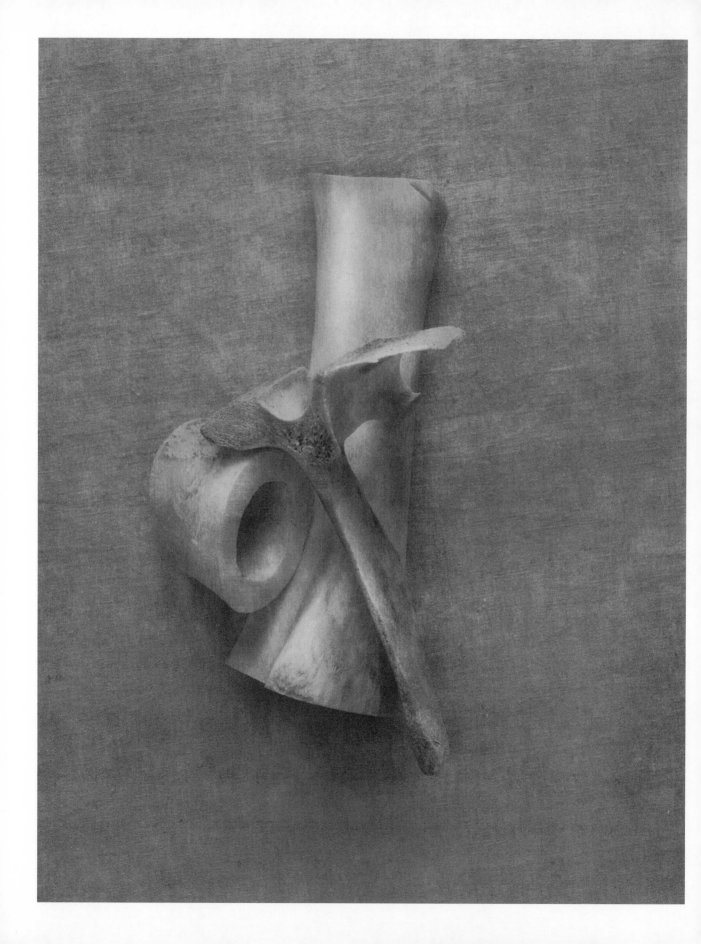

Beef and Veal

From the bone dividing a juicy porterhouse steak to those supporting a prime rib roast, beef bones add flavor to the meat that surrounds them. Steak on the bone and bone-in roasts are always juicier and tastier than their boneless counterparts. And once the meat is eaten, you're left with the bones to gnaw on.

Cows are large animals, and their size limits the number of bone-in cuts that are practical for the home cook. A whole beef leg or shoulder, for example, won't fit in a home oven. But there are many other excellent choices, beyond steaks and roasts. Short ribs, with their intense beefy taste, turn a simple stew into a meat lover's delight. Shanks and oxtails, slowly braised, surround themselves with a rich unctuous sauce.

Veal comes from young beef calves fed a special diet. While veal cuts are similar but smaller and more manageable than beef cuts, veal can't be substituted in all beef recipes. Veal lacks the fat and marbling of beef, which comes with age, so it needs careful handling, especially when grilling or roasting, to prevent the meat from drying out. Here is where bones come in, by keeping the meat juicy. Veal's youth makes it more suitable to braising, because its mild meat easily absorbs flavors.

Beef and especially veal bones are loaded with collagen, a protein that dissolves into gelatin when cooked, thickening and enriching sauces, and veal bones make rich full-bodied stocks. The richest source of this transforming collagen is calves' feet; just one added to stock will immensely improve its flavor and body.

Both veal and beef bones hold a hidden treasure, the marrow. All animal bones contain marrow, but the shank bones of beef and veal hold an especially high proportion of marrow and are the most prized. Marrow bones are often added to enrich stews, but these same bones can be either roasted or poached and eaten simply for the marrow they contain. These bones and their marrow also have some unexpected uses (see Bonelogue, page 239).

Don't buy your beef and veal just anywhere. A good butcher, or a local small producer, can ensure the provenance of your meat and guarantee that your veal is humanely raised. The tenderness of beef cuts can't be judged by simply looking at them: a good butcher carefully ages his meat to ensure its flavor and tenderness. With these large animals, knowing where the bones and the meat that surrounds them are found will dictate how they are cooked, so it is helpful to familiarize yourself with their skeletal structure.

The Front End

When beef and veal are butchered, the shank is removed from the front leg (see "The Extremities"). The remaining arm and shoulder are called the chuck or the blade. This section provides flavorful, well-marbled cuts made up of several muscles and connective tissue. Blade roasts and cross rib roasts come from here, as do short ribs. Whole or cut into steaks, they are ideal for pot-roasting and braising.

Veal yields similar but smaller cuts. Bone-in veal shoulder roasts, also called blade or arm roasts, are full of collagen and produce rich sauces when pot-roasted or braised.

The Middle

The muscles in this part of the animal do the least physical work, so the meat is very tender. For both beef and veal, the midsection is divided into two parts, the rib and the loin.

The rib section is where the classic beef roast comes from, often called a standing rib roast because it comes with its own built-in roasting rack. A whole rib roast has up to eight ribs, but these are more often divided into two-, three-, or four-rib roasts. If you are buying one of these smaller roasts, ask your butcher to cut it from the loin end, where the meat is a single muscle and more tender, rather than the shoulder end. The same applies when buying bone-in rib steaks.

What I love about these braised items is that they're not just sauté-and-serve. The process behind them requires more thought on the part of the cook, and technique to create something more that what you started with. A filet mignon is a filet mignon—there's little difference between the raw meat and the cooked meat. But short ribs, veal breast—they become completely different entities after they're cooked. They transcend themselves, developing a full, complex, satisfying aroma.

—THOMAS KELLER,
The French Laundry Cookbook

To T-bone is to hit from the side, often used when describing a car accident.

There is a universal understanding that bones and meat are inseparable.
Yiddish: Bones without meat are possible, meat without bones is not possible.
Hebrew: There is no such thing as boneless meat.
Greek: Meat is sold with bones.
Norwegian: He who buys the meat has to take the bone with it.
English: Bones bring meat to town.
He who eats the meat let him eat the bones.
You buy the land you buy the stones: you buy the meat you buy the bones.

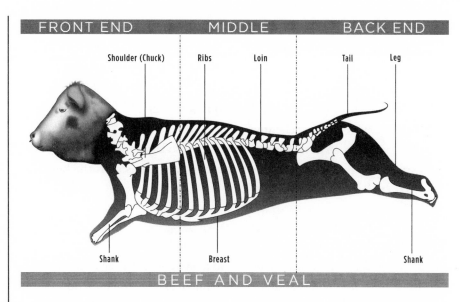

FRONT END   MIDDLE   BACK END

Shoulder (Chuck)   Ribs   Loin   Tail   Leg

Shank   Breast   Shank

BEEF AND VEAL

Ask your butcher for racks of beef rib bones left from cutting boneless steaks. With just enough meat clinging to the bones, they are tender enough to be grilled or roasted, whole or individually, without any preliminary cooking.

The beef loin is always cut into steaks, with or without bones: loin, tenderloin, sirloin T-bone, and porterhouse. For the bone lover, the choice, closest to the ribs, is the short or top loin steak. Next, where the tenderloin appears on one side of the bone, are the T-bone and porterhouse steaks. The first cut is the T-bone with its piece of loin on one side of the bone and a small piece of tenderloin on the other. As the butcher cuts toward the back end of the animal, the size of the tenderloin increases, yielding porterhouse steaks. When thickly cut these big steaks can serve two or three people.

Short ribs may be cut from the ends of the rib roast through to where the ribs form the animal's chest. These ribs have a good covering of fat and are best braised.

Veal can also yield an eight-rib roast, smaller than one from beef, of course. The meat-to-bone ratio is lower, and the bones are usually frenched (see page 108) for presentation. As with beef, the roast can be cut into thick individual rib chops.

The veal loin is sold either whole as a roast or cut into chops that resemble small T-bone steaks. Both rib and loin chops are lean, so it's best to have them cut 1½ to 2 inches (4 to 5 cm) thick. Grill or panfry them, and take care not to overcook them, serving them medium-rare or medium.

The veal breast, layered with bones and fat, is cut from where the ribs form the chest. Whether sold as one piece or cut into individual ribs, veal breast should be braised.

The Back End

In butchering the back section, the tail and shank of beef and veal are removed (see "The Extremities"), leaving the leg. The large beef leg is in turn cut into sections, the rump, round, and tip. These pieces yield steaks and roasts that are usually boneless. The bone lover should look for bone-in round steaks, which are excellent when braised.

While smaller than that of beef, a veal leg is also large and is cut into bone-in roasts and steaks. These cuts are lean, though, so braising is the best way to keep them juicy.

The Extremities

The shanks come from both the back and front legs, with the back ones being larger. Both beef and veal shanks (osso buco) can be bought whole or cut crosswise into thick pieces. With the marrow-filled leg bone these cuts are ideal for slow-cooking. Marrow bones, free of meat, are also sold separately. Ask that the bones be cut from the center section of the leg and sawed into 3- to 4-inch (7.5- to 10-cm) lengths so that you can get at the marrow. At the ends of the bone, there is less marrow proportionately; these bones should be reserved for the stockpot.

Despite the name, today oxtail comes from cows, not just oxen or castrated beef. An oxtail can be bought as one piece or sliced into thick pieces, which become progressively smaller as the tail tapers toward its end. The smallest pieces have more bone than meat and are more useful for stock. Larger pieces are best braised. I have asked my butcher for veal tails, but it appears they do not leave the abattoir.

If you are lucky enough to be able to get a calf's foot, you'll want to add it to your stockpot. Ask your butcher to split it in two and then cut it into smaller pieces. A very rich source of gelatin, one calf's foot is enough to set 2 cups (500 ml) of liquid.

Buffalo, Bison, and Beefalo

Yes, buffalo is the shaggy beast of the Great Plains—but its correct name is bison. Now farm-raised, bison has lean, dense meat that is richer in taste than its cousin the cow. It is increasingly available at specially butchers and through mail-order.

With its hump, big head, and broad shoulders, the bison is "front heavy," resulting in less weight proportionately in the middle region where the prime cuts are located—the reason why bison is more expensive than beef. The meat is darker in color than beef because of its higher iron content. Bison is low in

"Have you got nothing else for my breakfast, Pritchard?" said Fred to the servant who brought in coffee and buttered toast; while he walked around the table surveying the ham, potted beef, and other cold remnants, with an air of silent rejection, and polite forbearance from signs of disgust.

"Should you like eggs, sir?"

"Eggs, no! Bring me a grilled bone."

"Really, Fred," said Rosamond when the servant had left the room, "if you must have hot things for breakfast, I wish you would come down earlier. You get up at six o'clock to go out hunting; I cannot understand why you find it so difficult to get up on other mornings."

"That is your want of understanding, Rosy. I can get up to go hunting because I like it."

"What would you think of me if I came down two hours after everyone else and ordered grilled bone?"

fat, with little marbling, so it needs more careful cooking than beef. Treat it like venison instead, which is also low in fat; marinate it or wrap in a protective coating of fat before cooking. Bison is best eaten rare or medium-rare.

Beefalo is a cross between beef and bison. It is leaner than beef but has more marbling than bison, making it less likely to dry out. It tastes like beef and can be cooked the same way.

Beef and Veal Cooking Temperatures

The simplest way to determine if the meat is cooked is with an instant-read thermometer. Instant-read thermometers have almost become standard issue for the serious cook. These thermometers aid the experienced and novice cook alike. Inserted into meat (away from the bone or fat for an accurate measure) toward the end of cooking they display the internal temperature of the meat either on a dial or with digital readout. The newest thermometers have a probe that is inserted into the meat before it goes in the oven. The internal temperature of the meat is signaled on a digital readout and also by an alarm. While thermometers are a great help to the cook, remember they are not infallible.

The temperatures below serve as a guide when using a thermometer. Remember to allow the meat to rest at least 10 to 15 minutes, during which time the internal temperature will rise by up to 5°F (2°C).

Beef and Veal

Rare	125°F (51°C)
Medium-rare	130°F (54°C)
Medium	140°F (60°C)

While the same internal temperatures apply to veal cuts, the roasts and chops are juicier when cooked to medium-rare or medium, rather than rare. When braising, cook the veal or beef until fork-tender and almost falling off the bone.

Veal

Veal has always been a popular meat in Europe, especially in Italy, where its mild delicate flavor is much appreciated. Calves are essential to maintain the cows' milk production. Despite arguments to the contrary, veal can be humanely raised with the animals allowed to move around freely and feed on milk, or a combination of milk and grain until slaughter. Their meat is pale and mild. Veal allowed to graze on pasture produce meat that is a redder color and has a more robust flavor.

Brown Stock

Stock is very simple to make, as most of the cooking time is unattended. A good stock is very useful to the cook; it is the foundation of soups and sauces and it adds depth of flavor to braised meats and other dishes. The recipes here are for brown beef stock and white veal stock, but you can, of course, make a white beef stock or a brown veal stock following the same methods. When making beef stock, add some veal bones if you can, because they contain more collagen and will result in a richer, more gelatinous stock. A split calf's foot is ideal, but not easy to find.

Brown stock is made by roasting the bones before cooking them in water. The result is a darker, stronger flavored stock that is a great addition to slow-cooked beef dishes and sauces for roast beef, as well as with game when game stock isn't available.

Stock can be made in almost any quantity. I find this amount fits easily into my stockpot, but the recipe can be doubled. The stock can be refrigerated or frozen; if room is tight in the freezer, the stock can be concentrated before freezing (see page 14).

2 carrots, sliced
1 large onion, unpeeled, cut into wedges
1 celery stalk, sliced
1 leek, trimmed and quartered lengthwise
4½ pounds (2 kg) mixed beef and veal bones, cut into 2- to 3-inch (5- to 7.5-cm) pieces
1 large tomato, halved
6 garlic cloves
Mushroom trimmings, optional
1 bay leaf
3 thyme sprigs
3 flat-leaf parsley stems
¼ teaspoon black peppercorns
Kosher salt, optional

1. Preheat the oven to 425°F (220°C). Scatter the carrots, onion, celery, and leek over the bottom of a large roasting pan. Rinse the bones well under cold running water, pat bones dry, and place them on top of the vegetables.

2. Roast, turning the bones once or twice, for 1 hour, or until the bones are well browned.

3. Using tongs, transfer the bones and vegetables to a large stockpot. Discard any fat from the roasting pan. Add 2 cups (500 ml) water to the pan and bring to a boil over medium heat, deglazing the pan by scraping up the browned bits from the bottom. Add this liquid to the stockpot, along with the tomato, garlic, mushroom trimmings, if using, bay leaf, thyme, and parsley. Pour in 10 cups (2.5 l) cold water, or enough to cover the bones, and bring slowly to a boil. As soon as the stock begins to boil, reduce the heat so that it simmers. Using a soup ladle, skim off any scum that has risen to the surface (rotate its bowl on the surface of the stock to make ripples: these will carry the scum to the edges of the pot, and you can then use the ladle to lift it off). Add the peppercorns and simmer, uncovered, for 5 hours, skimming from time to time.

4. Strain the stock through a sieve into a large bowl. Discard the debris left in the sieve, and cool the stock quickly by placing the bowl in a larger bowl or sink filled with ice water; stir occasionally as it cools. When you taste the stock, you will notice that something is missing—the salt. Once you add it, the flavor will sparkle. But it was deliberately left out so that you can reduce the stock if desired, without any fear that it will become too salty. If you are not reducing the stock, add about 1 teaspoon salt.

5. Refrigerate the stock for 6 hours, or overnight, to allow the fat to rise to the top of the stock and the debris to sink to the bottom. Remove the fat before using (and discard the debris at the bottom of the bowl). Divide into 1-cup (250-ml) quantities and refrigerate up to 3 days or freeze for up to 6 months.

White Veal Stock

○ White veal stock can be used in any veal dish as well as in place of poultry or pork stock.

○ Use only veal bones rather than a mixture of beef and veal bones. Do not roast the bones or vegetables. Place the bones and vegetables in the stockpot, along with the tomato, garlic, optional mushroom trimmings, bay leaf, thyme, and parsley, and add 12 cups (3 l) cold water. Proceed as for brown stock, adding the peppercorns after skimming.

Concentrated Brown or White Veal Stock

Often I don't have room for one more container of stock in my freezer, so I make easy-to-store frozen concentrated stock cubes. As the stock boils, the water evaporates, concentrating the stock's flavor and making what is called a *demi-glace*. (This technique of boiling to reduce the liquid is also a way to boost the flavor of an insipid stock—but only if there is no salt in it.) The wider the saucepan, the faster the liquid will evaporate, but it will still take at least 15 to 20 minutes. The saucepan must be deep enough to prevent the stock from boiling over. Watch the stock carefully toward the end of the cooking time, as it can boil up quite dramatically.

6 cups (1.5 l) unsalted Brown Stock or White Veal Stock (pages 12–13)
Kosher salt

1. Before starting, pour 1½ cups (375 ml) water into the saucepan you plan to use. This will show you the quantity of the concentrated stock you're aiming for. Discard the water.

2. Pour the stock into the pan and bring to a boil. Continue to boil until it is reduced by about three-quarters, about 15 minutes. Pour the stock into a glass measuring cup to see if it has reduced to 1½ cups (375 ml). If not, return it to the saucepan and continue to boil to reduce it further. The stock will become syrupy and turn darker.

3. Pour the reduction back into the measuring cup and add a good pinch of salt. Taste for seasoning, and allow to cool slightly. Then pour the stock into ice cube trays and place in the refrigerator. (I usually end up with twenty-four cubes, each about 1 tablespoon.) When cold, the cubes will set like jelly and can be popped out of the trays and stored in bags in the freezer.

4. These stock cubes are four times as strong as the original stock. You can use them to boost the flavor of soups and sauces. Or, to reconstitute them to use in place of stock, add 3 tablespoons water along with each cube.

TIP If you reduce the stock too much, just add a little water.

Beef Consommé

Beef consommé is beef essence in a bowl. Consommé makes the perfect starter for an elegant winter dinner party, with a garnish of blanched julienned root vegetables, or chilled and lightly set in summer with a garnish of diced tomato.

6 cups (1.5 l) Brown Stock (page 12)
1 small leek, trimmed and chopped
1 small carrot, peeled and chopped
3 flat-leaf parsley stems
6 ounces (175 g) diced or ground lean beef
2 egg whites
Kosher salt

○○○

1. Place the cold stock in a large saucepan and heat it just until it liquefies. Remove the saucepan from the heat.

2. Place the leek, carrot, and parsley in a food processor and process until finely chopped. Add the beef, egg whites, and 2 tablespoons water and blend until well mixed. Stir this mixture into the stock and bring to a boil over medium-high heat, stirring constantly with a spatula or wooden spoon, scraping the bottom of the saucepan to prevent the egg white from sticking. As the liquid approaches a boil, it will appear to curdle; don't panic, that is what you want. As soon as the stock begins to boil, stop stirring, and remove the saucepan from the heat. The whites will form a congealed mass on the surface, which will puff up and then crack as the steam escapes.

3. Reduce the heat to very low and return the saucepan to the heat, making a larger hole in the egg white mass with a spoon to allow the steam to escape. Simmer very gently—you want to see small bubbles of steam break through the hole in the egg white mass—for 45 minutes. Remove the saucepan from the heat and let stand for 5 minutes.

4. Line a sieve with a double thickness of damp cheesecloth or a dampened thin cotton tea towel, and place over a bowl. Using a skimmer or large slotted spoon, carefully lift off as much of the egg white mass as you can and set aside in another bowl. Ladle the consommé into the sieve and allow it to drip slowly through the cloth. As you get closer to the bottom of the saucepan, you might notice that the clear consommé is muddied by bits of egg white. Don't worry, just add it to the sieve. Check the bowl with the egg white debris and pour any liquid that has escaped from it into the sieve. Allow all the liquid to drip slowly through the sieve; don't be tempted to press on the egg whites, as that would cloud the consommé.

5. You will have about 5 cups (1.25 l) clear consommé in the bowl and a mess of congealed egg white to discard. Season the consommé with about ¼ teaspoon salt. Serve hot, or allow it to cool, then chill and serve cold. If serving cold, you will probably need to boost the seasoning, as cold dulls the flavor.

Oxtail Consommé with Sherry

This rich beefy oxtail consommé takes two days to prepare, as the oxtail stock must be refrigerated overnight. But don't be put off, because for most of the time, it cooks itself, and only the final step of clarification needs attention. In fact, if you choose to skip the clarification, you will end up with a fine oxtail soup. If you do clarify the stock, your perseverance will be rewarded with a stunning golden broth with an intense beef flavor. You can use large oxtail pieces, or use up all those small pieces from the ends of oxtails that you have stored in the freezer.

Dry sherry is the classic drink pairing for consommé.

2 carrots, sliced
2 celery stalks, sliced
1 onion, unpeeled, cut into wedges
4½ pounds (2 kg) oxtail pieces
½ cup (125 ml) dry sherry
2 thyme sprigs
1 bay leaf
¼ teaspoon black peppercorns

FOR CLARIFYING
1 small carrot, diced
1 celery stalk, diced
1 small leek, diced
6 ounces (175 g) lean ground beef
2 egg whites
Kosher salt

Extra dry sherry, if serving the consommé hot

1. Preheat the oven to 425°F (220°C). Scatter the carrots, celery, and onion over the bottom of a large roasting pan. Rinse the oxtail pieces well under cold running water and pat dry, then place them on top of the vegetables. Roast for 1 hour, turning the oxtail pieces after 30 minutes.

2. Using tongs, transfer the oxtail and vegetables to a large stockpot. Discard any fat from the roasting pan. Add the sherry with 2 cups (500 ml) water, place over medium-low heat, and bring to a boil, deglazing the pan by scraping up the browned bits from the bottom. Pour this liquid into the stockpot and add 10 cups (2.5 l) cold water. Bring just to a boil, then reduce the heat so that the liquid simmers, and skim off the foam. Add the thyme sprigs, bay leaf, and peppercorns and simmer gently for 5 hours, skimming from time to time.

3. Strain the stock through a sieve into a large bowl. Discard the debris left in the sieve and cool the stock quickly by placing the bowl in a larger bowl or sink filled with ice water; stir occasionally as it cools, then refrigerate overnight.

4. The next morning, you will have a jellied liquid topped with fat. Remove the fat and discard the debris at the bottom of the bowl. You should have about 6 cups (1.5 l) stock; if you have more, reduce it by boiling, then allow to cool. To clarify it, the stock must be cold but not jelled. Reheat gently to liquefy if necessary.

5. Place the diced carrot, celery, and leek in a food processor and process until finely chopped. Add the meat, egg whites, and 2 tablespoons of water and blend until well mixed. Stir this mixture into the stock and bring to a boil over medium-high heat, stirring constantly with a spatula or wooden spoon and scraping the bottom of the saucepan to prevent the egg white from sticking. As the liquid approaches the boil, it will appear to curdle; don't panic, that is what you want. As soon as the stock begins to boil, stop stirring, and remove the saucepan from the heat. The whites will form a congealed mass on the surface, which will puff up and then crack as the steam escapes.

6. Reduce the heat to very low and return the saucepan to the heat, making a larger hole in the egg white mass with a spoon to allow the steam to escape. Simmer very gently—you want to see the small bubbles of steam break through the hole in the egg white mass—for 45 minutes. Remove the saucepan from the heat and let stand for 5 minutes.

7. Line a sieve with a double thickness of damp cheesecloth or a dampened thin cotton tea towel, and place over a bowl. Using a skimmer or large slotted spoon, carefully lift off as much of the egg white mass as you can and set aside in another bowl. Ladle the consommé into the sieve and allow it to drip slowly through the cloth. As you get closer to the bottom of the saucepan, you might notice that the clear consommé is being muddied by bits of egg white. Don't worry, just add it to the sieve. Check the bowl with the egg white debris and pour any liquid that has escaped from it into the sieve. Allow all the liquid to drip slowly through the sieve; don't be tempted to press on the egg whites, as that would cloud the consommé.

8. You will have about 5 cups (1.25 l) clear consommé in the bowl and a mess of congealed egg white to discard. Season the consommé with about ¼ teaspoon salt. Serve hot, or allow to cool, then chill and serve it cold. If serving hot, pour 1 tablespoon dry sherry into each bowl before ladling in the consommé. If you serve it cold, you will probably need to boost the seasoning, as cold dulls the flavor.

Garnishes for Beef (and Oxtail) Consommé

○ Consommé speaks for itself, but if you wish to add something, keep it simple so that the consommé isn't overpowered by the garnish.

o Julienned root vegetables, carrots, parsnips, and celeriac (celery root), blanched in salted water, can be added to the warmed soup bowls before ladling in the consommé. Thinly sliced celery and shredded green onions, lightly blanched, are also good. You can prepare all of these garnishes ahead of time and refrigerate until ready to serve.

o For oxtail consommé, fill wonton wrappers with diced cooked oxtail and minced flat-leaf parsley (brush the edges with beaten egg white to seal). Cook these separately, by steaming them for 10 minutes, so they don't cloud your crystal-clear soup.

o Chopped fresh herbs such as chervil, chives, savory, or thyme are a good addition to hot or chilled consommé, about ½ teaspoon per serving. A spoonful of peeled, seeded, and finely diced tomato is also good, especially with chilled consommé.

Veal Shoulder with Salsa Verde

Veal shoulder gently braised yields succulent meat. Cooking the meat in an aromatic liquid and a tightly covered pot ensures that it won't dry out, and you end up with a rich sauce. The salsa verde, green sauce, both reinforces the fresh herb marinade used on the veal and adds some needed punch to the veal's mild taste. Vary the mixture of herbs in the marinade and sauce as you like, but be sure to include lots of parsley. Arugula adds a peppery touch and counteracts the saltiness of the anchovies and capers.

Serve the sliced veal with a few spoonfuls of the cooking juices and the green sauce. It is also delicious cold. To serve cold, thickly slice the braised veal, layering the slices on a serving dish with a lip. Cool the braising liquid until it just starts to thicken, then pour it over the meat and refrigerate. The liquid will set into a light jelly. A perfect dish for a summer's night. Serve with the salsa verde.

The veal needs a good twelve hours in the herb marinade, so begin this dish a day in advance.

1 bone-in veal shoulder roast, about 5 pounds (2.5 kg)
2 cups (500 ml) flat-leaf parsley leaves
¼ cup (60 ml) chopped chives
20 large basil leaves
10 sage leaves
2 tablespoons oregano leaves
1 tablespoon thyme leaves
¼ cup (60 ml) plus ⅓ cup (75 ml) extra virgin olive oil
Kosher salt and freshly ground black pepper
1 tablespoon (15 g) unsalted butter
1 onion, diced
1 small carrot, peeled and diced
3 garlic cloves, halved
1 cup (250 ml) White Veal Stock (page 13)
½ cup (125 ml) dry white vermouth
3 cups (750 ml) arugula, coarse stems trimmed
2 tablespoons capers, preferably salt-packed, rinsed
6 cornichons, rinsed
4 anchovy fillets, rinsed
1 tablespoon chopped shallot
1 tablespoon freshly squeezed lemon juice

1. Pat the veal dry and place in a dish. Place 1 cup (250 ml) of the parsley leaves, the chives, basil, sage, oregano, and thyme in a food processor and process until pureed. Add 3 tablespoons of the olive oil, a pinch of kosher salt, and a few grindings of pepper, and blend well. Coat the veal all over with this mixture. Cover and refrigerate for 12 hours.

2. One hour before cooking, remove the veal from the refrigerator. Preheat the oven to 300°F (150°C).

3. In a Dutch oven or flameproof casserole, heat 1 tablespoon of the olive oil and the butter over medium heat. Add the onion and carrot and cook gently for 5 minutes. Season the veal well with salt and pepper and place on top of the vegetables, the large flat side down. After 3 minutes, turn the veal over so that the second large side sears; but does not brown. Add 2 of the garlic cloves, ½ cup (125 ml) of the stock, and all but 1 tablespoon of the vermouth and bring to a boil.

4. Remove from the heat and cover with a damp piece of parchment paper and then the lid. Braise in the oven for 1 hour.

5. Turn the veal over, cover again with the parchment paper and the lid and cook for another 1½ to 2 hours or until internal temperature of the veal registers 155°F (68°C) on an instant-read thermometer.

6. While the veal is cooking, make the sauce: Place the remaining 1 cup (250 ml) parsley leaves and garlic, the arugula, capers, cornichons, anchovies, shallot, and lemon juice in a food processor and process until well blended. With the motor running, add the remaining ⅓ cup (75 ml) olive oil. Spoon the sauce into a bowl and season with salt and pepper. Cover by pressing plastic wrap directly onto the surface of the sauce to keep it green, and refrigerate. (The sauce can be made up to a day in advance.)

7. Transfer the cooked veal to a warmed platter and let it rest, loosely covered with aluminum foil, for 15 to 20 minutes. Remove the salsa verde from the refrigerator. Strain the veal braising liquid into a large glass measuring cup or a bowl and let the fat rise to the top (set the pot aside).

8. Skim off the fat from the braising liquid and discard; you will be left with about 3 cups (750 ml) liquid. Stir ¼ cup (60 ml) of this liquid into the salsa verde and set aside. Pour the rest of the liquid back into the pot, add the remaining ½ cup (125 ml) stock, and bring to a boil. Boil for about 10 minutes, or until the liquid reduces to 2 cups (500 ml) and feels slightly sticky on the tongue. Add the remaining tablespoon of vermouth and check the seasoning.

9. Carve the meat from the bones in one or two pieces, then thickly slice the meat. Serve in shallow bowls with a ladle of reduced braising liquid spooned over the top, and pass the salsa verde.

Carving Veal Shoulder

Don't expect to get perfect slices from this cut. The bone structure will vary depending on the section of shoulder you have. With the upper shoulder, the blade bone divides the roast in two sections, while in the lower section, the arm bone does the same. So what you will have is half-slices. First, cut away any rib neck bones. Then place the meat fat side up and slice down until you hit the bone. Cut along the bone to free each section.

Roasted Veal Chops with Madeira and Parsnips

Madeira is a Portuguese fortified wine from the island of the same name. For this recipe, choose a medium-dry one. It adds depth to the mild veal and enhances the natural sweetness of the parsnips.

A large frenched veal chop is an impressive piece of meat that cooks quickly. But veal chops are lean, so careful cooking is necessary to keep them from drying out. This combination method of searing them, then cooking them in the oven solves the problem. Veal chops are best cooked medium-rare to medium.

2 veal rib chops, 2 inches (5 cm) thick, frenched
4 medium parsnips, peeled and halved
Kosher salt
½ cup (125 ml) plus 2 tablespoons, medium-dry Madeira
2 tablespoons olive oil
1 tablespoon sugar
Freshly ground black pepper
½ cup (125 ml) White Veal Stock (page 13)

1. One hour before cooking them, remove the chops from the refrigerator. Preheat the oven to 425°F (220°C).

2. Place the parsnips in a saucepan, cover with cold salted water, and bring to a boil, then reduce the heat and simmer for 7 to 10 minutes. The parsnips should be barely tender. Drain and pat them dry.

3. Toss the parsnips with 2 tablespoons Madeira, 1 tablespoon of the olive oil, and the sugar, and arrange them rounded side down in a roasting pan large enough to hold the veal chops comfortably. Season well with salt and pepper, and roast for 10 minutes.

4. Meanwhile pat the veal chops dry and season with salt and pepper. In a large frying pan, heat the remaining tablespoon oil over medium high heat and brown the chops, about 2 minutes on each side. Transfer the chops to a plate and discard any fat from the pan. Pour in the remaining ½ cup (125 ml) Madeira; *be careful* as it may catch alight. Bring to a boil, deglazing the pan by scraping up the browned bits from the bottom. Add the veal stock and continue to boil until the liquid is reduced to ½ cup (125 ml), about 3 minutes. Remove from the heat.

5. Remove the roasting pan from the oven, turn the parsnips over, and place the veal chops on top. Pour over the reduced liquid from the pan. Cook for another 10 to 15 minutes, until the chops and parsnips are cooked. Check the internal temperature of the veal with an instant-read thermometer: it should read 130°F to 135°F (54° to 57°C).

6. Transfer the chops to a plate, cover loosely with foil, and let them rest for 5 minutes.

7. Serve the chops with the parsnips and the pan juices spooned over them.

Double-Bone Beef with Red Wine Sauce

For any bone lover, what could be better than two bones—rib and marrow—in one dish? A standing rib roast is great for a crowd but impractical for two people. This recipe is the perfect way to enjoy a rib of beef without buying the whole roast. Begin this recipe a day in advance, as the marrow bones must be soaked to remove the blood. You can make the sauce ahead of time and reheat it while the beef is cooking.

2 marrow bones, about 2 inches (5 cm) long
Kosher salt
1 cup (250 ml) dry red wine
2 shallots, diced
1 small carrot, peeled and diced
1 large thyme sprig
1 small bay leaf
¼ teaspoon white peppercorns, crushed
1 cup (250 ml) Brown Stock (page 12)
One 2-inch (5-cm)-thick 2¼ pounds (1 kg) bone-in rib steak
1 tablespoon vegetable oil
Freshly ground black pepper
Fleur de sel

1. Place the marrow bones in a bowl of ice water to cover and add 2 tablespoons salt. Refrigerate them for 12 to 24 hours, changing the water 4 to 6 times and adding 2 more tablespoons salt to the water each time.

2. Place the red wine, shallots, carrot, thyme, bay leaf, and peppercorns in a small saucepan and bring to a boil. Reduce the heat to a simmer and cook until the wine is reduced to ⅓ cup (75 ml), about 15 minutes. Add the stock and simmer until reduced by half. Strain through a sieve, pressing hard against the solids to extract all the liquid; discard the debris in the sieve. Set the sauce aside, or refrigerate if making ahead (the sauce can be made up to 1 day ahead).

3. One hour before cooking remove the rib of beef from the refrigerator. Preheat the oven to 450°F (230°C).

4. Heat the oil in a large overproof frying pan over medium-high heat. Pat the steak dry and season with salt and pepper. Brown the meat, about 4 to 5 minutes on the first side, then 2 to 3 minutes on the other side. Transfer the pan to the oven and roast for 25 minutes, or until an instant-read thermometer inserted in the center of the meat registers 125°F (51°C), for medium-rare.

5. While the meat is cooking, drain the marrow bones. Bring a medium saucepan of salted water to a boil, add the bones, and lower the heat to a gentle simmer. Cook until the marrow sets and shrinks away from the bone and gives no resistance when pierced with a thin metal skewer, 10 to 12 minutes; the skewer should be warm when removed from the center of the marrow. Remove the bones from the water, drain well on paper towels, and keep warm.

6. When the steak is cooked, transfer the meat to a warm plate. Let rest, loosely covered with aluminum foil, for 10 minutes.

7. Meanwhile, remembering that *the pan handle will be very hot*, discard any fat from the pan. Add the sauce to the pan and deglaze by scraping up the browned bits from the bottom.

8. Cut the meat from the bone and slice it. Serve with the sauce, marrow bones, and a sprinkling of fleur de sel.

Beefsteak Fiorentina

ooooooooooooooooooooooooooooooooooooooooooooooooooooooooooooooooooooooooooooooo { SERVES 2 TO 3 } ooooooooooo

A specialty of Tuscany, where the local Chianina beef is known for its succulence, beefsteak fiorentina is simply a thickly cut porterhouse steak grilled over hot coals and bathed in the best-quality extra virgin olive oil fragrant with herbs. My husband and I ate our first one more than fifteen years ago in a nondescript restaurant in a little town outside of Florence. The town had a bakery, a butcher, and a café/bar with a small dining room. The menu was short, and there was no wine list; you chose your wine from a selection displayed on the shelf behind the bar. Neither of us knew much about Italian wine at the time, so I made my husband choose. Being an artist, he picked the one with the label he liked best—Tignanello. Now I always let him choose the wine.

1 porterhouse steak, 2 inches (5 cm) thick, about 3½ pounds (1.35 kg)
½ cup (125 ml) extra virgin olive oil
1 teaspoon rosemary leaves
1 tablespoon marjoram leaves
10 sage leaves
2 garlic cloves, sliced

1. One hour before cooking, remove the steak from the refrigerator.

2. Heat the oil in a small saucepan until hot. Remove from the heat, add the rosemary, marjoram, sage, and garlic, and stir to mix. The moisture in the herbs will cause the oil to sizzle. Set aside to cool.

3. Preheat a grill or broiler to high. Grill or broil the steak to rare or medium-rare (see page 25), turning once. Place it a shallow dish, pour over the herb-infused oil, and turn to coat. Let the steak rest in the oil bath for 5 to 7 minutes.

4. Remove the steak from the oil and cut the meat off the bone in two pieces. Cut into thick slices, then drizzle with the flavored oil, making sure each person gets some meat from both sections of the steak.

Carving Porterhouse Steak

This steak is removed from the center bone in two sections, then carved into slices or thick pieces. Place the steak on the carving board and cut along either side of the T-bone to remove the meat. Slice the tenderloin and the loin, and make sure each person receives meat from both sections.

Two things contribute to the success of grilling bone-in steaks. First is the thickness of the steak. T-bone steaks should be at least 1 inch (2.5 cm) thick, and porterhouse and bone-in rib steaks are best if they are at least 2 to 3 inches (5 to 7.5 cm) thick. This allows you to test the internal temperature with an instant-read thermometer.

The second thing is the temperature of the grill. Make sure the grill is very hot, and sear the steak for 1 minute on each side. Then lower the heat or move the grill rack farther away from the heat and continue cooking the steak. For medium-rare steak, cook T-bone steaks for a total of 7 to 10 minutes longer and porterhouse and bone-in rib steaks for 10 to 14 minutes, or until an instant-read thermometer inserted into the meat away from the bone registers 125° to 130°F (51° to 54°C).

Millennium Rib Roast

My New Year's Eve dinner for the millennium was a long time in the planning. We had just finished the renovations on our apartment in Paris and guests would be coming from as far away as Australia. The menu was hotly debated for weeks. Finally I settled on a standing rib roast of beef for the main course. Impressive, simple to carve, and delicious hot, warm, or even at room temperature, depending how the dinner progressed and how much the cook celebrated. I left Canada on Christmas Day, armed with a terrine of Canadian foie gras, to show the French that we could do it as well as them, and a vacuum-sealed rib roast. (Although the meat in France is excellent, I was worried that during the holiday season, our Paris butcher might be closed or not have the size of roast I needed.)

Knowing that I had dinner with me, I relaxed as we took off. The next morning, the pilot woke the passengers with an announcement that we would be arriving an hour early, thanks to extremely strong tailwinds; all was going well. Five minutes later, he informed us that the Paris airports were closed and the plane was detoured to Heathrow. It was the night of *La Grande Tempête*, the huge windstorm that struck Paris and destroyed thousands of trees in the city, parks, and, most notably, at Versailles. I spent many fretful hours at Heathrow worrying about the contents of my luggage, but when we finally arrived in Paris, after a very bumpy flight across the Channel, the roast and terrine were both still cold and unharmed by their long voyage. At last, we made our way to Paris. Our taxi ride revealed the extent of the devastation.

This recipe began with one in *Gourmet* magazine that has evolved over time. By the way, our French dinner guests were very impressed by the Canadian foie gras.

One 4-rib standing rib roast, 8 to 10 pounds (3.5 to 4.5kg)
Kosher salt and freshly ground black pepper
3 tablespoons green peppercorns, coarsely ground
1 teaspoon black peppercorns, coarsely ground
1 teaspoon white peppercorns, coarsely ground
1 tablespoon allspice berries, coarsely ground
3 tablespoons (45 g) unsalted butter, softened
2 tablespoons flour
1 tablespoon brown sugar
1 tablespoon grainy mustard
1 shallot, finely diced
1 cup (250 ml) dry red wine
2 cups (500 ml) Brown Stock (page 12)
2 teaspoons cornstarch
1 tablespoon red wine vinegar

1. Two hours before you plan to cook it, remove the roast from the refrigerator. Preheat the oven to 450°F (230°C).

2. Pat the beef dry and season with salt and pepper. Place the beef, bones down to form a natural roasting rack, in a roasting pan and roast for 30 minutes.

3. While the beef is roasting, mix all the peppercorns and the allspice berries in a small bowl. Add 2 teaspoons salt, the butter, flour, sugar, and mustard and blend to a paste.

4. Remove the beef from the oven and reduce the oven temperature to 325°F (160°C). Transfer the beef to a platter and discard the fat from the roasting pan. Spread the fat side of the beef with the peppercorn paste and return it to the pan. Roast for another 2 to 2¼ hours, or until an instant-read thermometer inserted into the meat, away from the bone, registers 125°F (51°C).

5. Transfer the roast to a warm platter, cover it loosely with aluminum foil, and allow it to rest for 30 minutes before carving. During this time, the internal temperature of the roast will rise to 130°F (54°C), for medium-rare.

6. While the roast rests, discard the fat from the pan and place the pan over medium heat. Add the shallot and cook, stirring, until softened, about 2 minutes. Pour in the wine and bring to a boil, deglazing the pan by scraping up the browned bits from the bottom. Continue to boil until the wine reduces by half, then add the stock and boil for another 5 minutes. If you prefer thicker gravy, mix the cornstarch with the vinegar, whisk into the sauce, and continue to whisk until the sauce has thickened slightly. If not, add the vinegar alone. Strain into a sauceboat.

7. Carve the beef into thick slices, and serve with the sauce.

═══════════════════════ Carving a Rib Roast ═══════════════════════

Carving a rib roast is straightforward, since your butcher will have removed the chine, or backbone. Stand the roast on its bones, with the meat side facing you. Run the carving knife between the meat and the feather bones on the thick side of the roast, at right angles to the rib bones. Slice off any excess fat from the top of the roast, and turn the roast on its side, so that the ribs are to one side and the meat is facing down. Cut the meat into thick slices from the fat side to the rib bone, cutting along the rib bone to release each slice. Once the rib bone is exposed, you can cut it free from the roast and continue carving. Serve the ribs with the roast or set them aside for Deviled Bones (page 28).

Deviled Bones

The trick to this recipe is hanging on to those prime rib roast bones—bone lovers usually polish them off with the roast. My friend Miriam sent me James Beard's recipe, and I found another recipe reputed to have been served in 1923 for breakfast at the famous London club Boodles. It's not my sort of breakfast, but I could eat a couple of rib bones with a good green salad for lunch or dinner. Both those recipes are based on coating the bones with spices and bread crumbs, as I do here. Some recipes just grill the leftover bones and serve them with a spicy butter.

I prefer my bones simple, but if you fancy a sauce, try the Mustard Sauce (page 62), replacing the Pork Stock with Brown Stock (page 12).

⅓ cup (80 g) unsalted butter
1 teaspoon dry mustard
1 teaspoon dry cayenne
1 teaspoon Worcestershire sauce
Kosher salt and freshly ground black pepper
4 leftover beef rib bones
1 cup (80g) fresh bread crumbs

1. Preheat the broiler or grill to high. Melt the butter in a small saucepan. Remove from the heat and stir in the mustard, cayenne, and Worcestershire sauce. Season with salt and pepper.

2. Brush the ribs with the spiced butter, then roll them in the bread crumbs, coating well. Broil or grill, turning occasionally and basting them with any remaining butter, until golden brown, 12 to 15 minutes.

Beer-Glazed Beef Ribs

Perfect for the grill, beef ribs are more readily available in summer—when the demand for boneless steaks increases. I actually prefer them to a steak, because there's a bit of meat and all that bone to chew on. They are sold in racks or cut into individual ribs; ask your butcher for meaty ones. This is serious finger food. Grill them rare or medium-rare, but don't go past that.

8 meaty beef ribs, about 2 pounds (1 kg)
⅓ cup (75 ml) hoisin sauce
⅓ packed cup (70 g) brown sugar
2 tablespoons rice wine vinegar
1 cup (250 ml) lager beer
1 tablespoon finely chopped fresh ginger
2 garlic cloves, finely chopped
1 teaspoon soy sauce
⅛ teaspoon five-spice powder

1. If the ribs are still joined together, cut them into individual pieces. Place them in a shallow baking dish, meat side down.

2. Mix the hoisin sauce, sugar, and vinegar in a bowl. Gradually stir in the beer, then add the ginger, garlic, soy sauce, and five-spice powder and mix well. Pour the marinade over the ribs, turning them to coat, then turn them meat side down again. Cover and refrigerate for 8 hours. One hour before cooking, remove the ribs from the refrigerator. Preheat the grill or broiler to high.

3. Transfer the ribs to a platter, and pour the marinade into a small saucepan. Bring to a boil and boil for 12 to 15 minutes, until reduced to 1 cup (250 ml).

4. Grill or broil the ribs, turning to cook on all four sides and brushing them with the reduced marinade, for 4 to 5 minutes on each side, 16 to 20 minutes total. Serve any remaining marinade as a dipping sauce.

Spiced Roasted Rack of Ribs

Beef ribs cook in about half the time pork and lamb ribs take, and they have less fat. Here they are rubbed with spices before being roasted, and a glaze is added during the final fifteen minutes of cooking. The glazing also can also be done on the grill. Look for a complete rack, as meaty as possible.

1 dried ancho chile
1 small dried red chile
1 teaspoon sugar
1 teaspoon coriander seeds
½ teaspoon kosher salt
2 racks meaty beef ribs, 4 to 5 pounds (1.8 to 2.25 kg)
½ cup (125 ml) ketchup
2 tablespoons Worcestershire sauce
2 tablespoons red wine vinegar
1 tablespoon corn syrup
½ teaspoon dry mustard
1 tablespoon vegetable oil
1 small onion, finely chopped
1 garlic clove, finely chopped

1. Discard the stem and seeds from the chiles and tear the chiles into small pieces. Place them in a spice grinder, along with the sugar, coriander seeds, and salt and grind until powdery.

2. Remove the opaque membrane from the bone side of the ribs by loosening it with a sharp knife, then pulling it off. Pat the ribs dry and place them in a dish. Two hours before you wish to cook the ribs, coat them with the spice rub, patting the rub so that it adheres. Cover and refrigerate.

3. Mix the ketchup, Worcestershire sauce, vinegar, corn syrup, and mustard with ½ cup (125 ml) water in a small bowl. In a small saucepan, heat the oil over medium-low heat. Add the onion and cook for 5 minutes, or until softened. Add the garlic and cook for 1 minute longer. Pour in the ketchup mixture and bring to a boil, stirring. Boil gently, stirring from time to time, for 10 minutes, or until the glaze is slightly thickened. Remove from the heat, add a pinch of salt, and allow to cool. You will have about 1 cup (250 ml) glaze.

4. Thirty minutes before cooking, remove the ribs from the refrigerator. Preheat the oven to 350°F (175°C).

5. Place the ribs in a roasting pan and roast for 45 minutes. Remove the ribs from the oven and brush the meaty side with the glaze. Increase the heat to 400°F (200°C) and cook the ribs for 15 minutes more, or until the ribs remain rare at the bone. Let rest for 10 minutes.

6. Cut into individual ribs to serve, and pass plenty of paper napkins.

Variations

- Both the rub and the glaze can be used on pork ribs or chicken wings.

- Omit the rub and replace the glaze with the Mustard Oregano Glaze (page 111) or the Tamarind Chile Glaze (page 229).

BONES AND THE ARTIST

○○

Bones are the framework of the human body, and they have inspired many artists, including Henry Moore, a celebrated sculptor of the twentieth century. As a student Moore collected all sorts of bones from the beach and his stew pot. Fascinated with bones and their importance in the structure of animal and human form, he spent hours in the British Natural History Museum studying and drawing bones.

During World War II, after his London studio was bombed, Moore moved to a seventeenth-century farm house on a former pig farm known locally as Hoglands. The farm provided Moore with a place to work and the English countryside became a source for bone foraging. Photographs of his studio show his large collection of animal bones. He was intrigued by the lightness and flexibility of bones, which belied their strength, and they influenced his sculptures, such as "Knife's Edge," a large bone with a head attached.

Moore also had fun with bones. He made a model of a maze using plaster casts of beef bones, "Stone Maze Project for Hill Monument 1977." He had the model photographed to make it appear to be a full-size, monumental, and imposing maze.

The sun-bleached bones of deer, cows, and horses that litter the New Mexico desert were inspiration for American artist Georgia O'Keeffe. Famous for her huge paintings of flowers, she was also captivated by the desiccated bones, and she juxtaposed dry hard bones with soft delicate flowers in her work.

Bones have inspired many artists, not just sculptors and painters. Several typefaces are styled after bones. You don't find them in everyday use, but they are popular at Halloween.

Braised Short Ribs

There are two different cuts of short ribs. Larger ones are cut into individual pieces between the bones. Cross-cut ribs, or flanken, are strips cut across the bones against the grain. For this recipe, I used cross-cut ribs and cut them into rectangular pieces, each with a piece of bone.

I make this dish ahead and chill it so you can easily remove any fat from the top of the sauce. The flavor improves with reheating, but add the chopped herbs just before serving, so they don't lose their freshness.

3½ pounds (1.5 kg) cross-cut short ribs, cut into pieces
Kosher salt and freshly ground black pepper
2 tablespoons olive oil
2 large onions, diced
1½ cups (375 ml) dry red wine
3 large carrots, peeled to cut in 1-inch (2.5-cm) pieces
6 large garlic cloves, peeled
1 serrano chile, stem removed
One 14 ounce (398 ml) can whole tomatoes
3 flat-leaf parsley sprigs, plus ⅓ cup (75 ml) chopped parsley
1 large basil sprig, plus, ⅓ cup (75 ml) slivered basil leaves
1 large thyme sprig
1 bay leaf

1. Preheat the oven to 300°F (150°C). Pat the ribs dry and season with salt and pepper. In a Dutch oven or flameproof casserole, heat the oil over medium heat. Brown the ribs on all sides, in batches if necessary. Transfer the browned ribs to a plate.

2. Add the onion to the pot and cook for 5 minutes, or until slightly softened. Pour in the red wine and bring to a boil, deglazing the pot by scraping up the browned bits from the bottom. Add the carrots, garlic, chile, and tomatoes, with their juices. Bring to a boil, then add the ribs, with any juices, the parsley, basil, and thyme sprigs, and the bay leaf.

3. Remove the pot from the heat and cover with a damp piece of parchment paper and then the lid. Transfer to the oven and cook covered for 1½ hours.

4. Remove the lid and parchment paper and cook the ribs for another 1½ hours, or until very tender.

5. If making ahead, let the ribs cool, then refrigerate overnight. The next day, remove the layer of fat and discard the herbs sprigs and chile. Reheat, covered, in a 300°F (150°C) oven for about 1 hour, or until heated through. Sprinkle with the chopped herbs, check the seasoning, and serve.

6. If serving the ribs immediately, tip the pan and skim off as much fat as possible. Remove the herb sprigs and chile pepper, sprinkle with the chopped herbs, and check the seasoning.

Short Ribs in Wine and Balsamic Sauce

I wanted to dress up my short ribs and highlight their rich beefy flavor. These impressive ribs with balsamic wine sauce are worthy of a fancy dinner. I used the large short ribs cut between the bone, with a hefty chunk of meat attached, giving me individual ribs with a bone 4 inches (10 cm) long, but the recipe will work equally well with cross-cut ribs (flanken).

1½ cups (375 ml) dry red wine
1 carrot, peeled and sliced
1 leek, trimmed and sliced
1 celery stalk, sliced
2 garlic cloves, halved
6 black peppercorns
1 clove
2 flat-leaf parsley stems
1 rosemary sprig
3 pounds (1.35 kg) large short ribs, cut into 6–8 pieces
¼ cup (30 g) flour
Kosher salt and freshly ground black pepper
2 to 3 tablespoons vegetable oil
1 to 1¼ cups (250 to 310 ml) Brown Stock (page 12)
2 tablespoons balsamic vinegar

1. Add the wine, carrot, leek, celery, garlic, peppercorns, and clove to a medium saucepan and bring to a boil. Reduce the heat so the wine bubbles gently, then tip the saucepan slightly away from you and, using a long match, *carefully* light the wine. Let the wine bubble and burn until the flames die out, then light again and let it burn out. Continue lighting the wine until it no longer burns. (This method burns off the alcohol in the wine.) Pour the marinade into a large glass measuring cup or a bowl, add the parsley stems and rosemary, and leave it to cool.

2. Place the ribs meaty side down in a nonreactive container and pour the cooled marinade over them. Cover and refrigerate for 8 to 12 hours, turning the ribs from time to time.

3. Preheat the oven to 300°F (150°C). Remove the ribs from the marinade, drain them well, and pat dry; reserve the marinade. Season the flour with salt and pepper, then dredge the ribs in the flour, brushing off any excess. In a Dutch oven or flameproof casserole that will hold the ribs snugly in one layer, heat the oil over medium heat. Brown the ribs on all sides, in batches if necessary, transferring them to a plate as they brown.

4. Pour the marinade, with all the vegetables and seasonings, into the pot and bring to a boil, deglazing the pot by scraping up the browned bits from the bottom. Return the ribs to the pot and add enough stock to almost cover the ribs. Cover with a damp piece of parchment paper, then the lid. Transfer to the

oven and cook for 3 hours, or until the ribs are very tender and almost falling off the bone. Transfer them to a baking dish and keep warm, loosely covered with aluminum foil.

5. Strain the braising liquid through a sieve into a glass measuring cup, and discard the vegetables, herbs, and spices. Skim off the fat, then return the liquid to the pot and bring to a boil. Boil until reduced to 1 cup (250 ml), 3 to 4 minutes. Add the balsamic vinegar and check the seasoning.

6. Pour the braising liquid over the ribs and return them to the oven, cook uncovered, 10 to 15 minutes, until hot and glazed.

Breast of Veal

When I considered cooking a breast of veal, the late Laurie Colwin's words rang in my ears: "Stuffed breast of veal: a bad idea." Well, her experience was with a stuffed boneless breast; I definitely wanted my breast with bones. When I looked at the cut, I couldn't imagine boning it or taking the time to stuff it. So much better, I thought, to braise it slowly and let all the natural collagen from the veal and its bones thicken and enrich my sauce. The flavor of the vegetables in the braising liquid is enhanced by the shredded peppery arugula added at the last minute, while the wine and lemon cut through the richness. The prosciutto topping adds a crisp texture to the final dish.

Now, despite what other recipes may tell you, breast of veal isn't usually manageable whole, at least not for me. I don't have a roasting pan that big. Much better to have your butcher cut it in half. (If he requires you to buy the whole thing, freeze the other half.) The thicker half of the breast will take about an extra half hour longer to cook than the thinner half. Because veal breast contains bones and cartilage, despite its size, this wide, flat piece of meat will feed fewer people than you think.

½ veal breast, about 5 pounds (2.25 kg)
Kosher salt and freshly ground black pepper
3 tablespoons vegetable oil
2 Vidalia or other sweet onions, sliced
3 celery stalks, sliced
2 carrots, peeled and sliced
1 leek, trimmed and sliced
4 garlic cloves, peeled
1 cup (250 ml) dry white wine
1 cup (250 ml) White Veal Stock (page 13)
8 to 10 thin slices prosciutto
1 bunch arugula, shredded
1 lemon
2 teaspoons cornstarch

1. Preheat the oven to 300°F (150°C). Pat the veal breast dry and season with salt and pepper. Heat 2 tablespoons of the oil in a large roasting pan over medium-high heat and brown the veal on both sides. Transfer to a platter.

2. Lower the heat, add the remaining 1 tablespoon oil, the onions, celery, carrots, and leek and cook, stirring often, for 10 minutes or until the vegetables are softened and just beginning to color.

3. Season with salt and pepper, then add the garlic, wine, and stock and bring to a boil. Remove from the heat.

4. Place the veal on top of the vegetables, bone side down. Cover the veal with a damp piece of parchment paper and then cover the pan with aluminum foil. Place in the oven and cook for 2½ to 3 hours.

5. Uncover the veal and place the prosciutto slices on top of the meat, overlapping them slightly if necessary. Increase the oven temperature to 350°F (175°C) and cook the veal, uncovered for another 30 minutes, or until the meat is very tender and the prosciutto is crisp. Transfer the veal to a warmed serving platter and let it rest, loosely covered with aluminum foil, for 15 minutes.

6. Meanwhile, strain the braising liquid through a sieve into a large glass measuring cup; transfer the vegetables to a bowl. You will have about 1½ cups (375 ml) cooking liquid. Stir the arugula into the warm vegetables until it wilts. Transfer the vegetables to the serving platter with the veal.

7. Skim the fat from the cooking liquid, and pour it back into the roasting pan. Grate 1 teaspoon zest from the lemon, then cut it in half and squeeze 2 tablespoons juice from it. Add the zest to the cooking liquid. Mix the lemon juice with the cornstarch and whisk into the liquid. Bring to a boil, whisking until the sauce thickens. Strain, and check the seasoning.

8. Carve the breast between the bones and serve with the vegetables and sauce.

Why Parchment Paper?

I'm no stranger to parchment paper; I use it for baking and I love cooking en papillote and make parchment paper circles to protect sauces, but, until I began working on Bones, I never used it for braising. I discovered the technique in Thomas Keller's French Laundry Cookbook. Keller uses parchment paper circles instead of lids. However, I use them with lids to protect the meat and keep the moisture in the dish. I wet the paper first so it softens and sits down on the meat. This also means I can just tear off a piece and not have to cut it precisely to fit my pot. When the dish is cooked, I leave the parchment on top of the cooling meat to prevent its surface from drying out.

Four Bones in One Pot

Sometimes we forget how good food can be. This recipe has vegetables and three different cuts of meat all in one pot, plus there is the added bonus of the creamy rich marrow bones. Delicious. Perfect. All you need is a bottle of good wine and some bread to sop up the sauce. Plan ahead because the meat is marinated overnight before it is cooked, then the dish is refrigerated overnight so all the fat can be removed and the flavors can blend.

1 bottle (750 ml) Shiraz or other hearty dry red wine
1 large beef cross-cut shank piece, 1½ to 1¾ pounds (675 to 800 g)
1 slab short ribs, 1½ to 1¾ pounds (675 to 800 g)
4 large pieces oxtail, trimmed
5 medium onions, sliced
5 carrots, peeled and cut into ¼-inch (5-mm) slices
1 celery stalk, sliced
2 garlic cloves, halved
3 thyme sprigs
2 bay leaves
½ teaspoon freshly grated nutmeg
Kosher salt and freshly ground black pepper
2 tablespoons vegetable oil
4 marrow bones
1 cup (250 ml) Brown Stock (page 12)
2 tablespoons tomato paste
4 whole medium portobello mushrooms
Fleur de sel

1. Pour the wine into a large saucepan and bring it to a boil, then reduce the heat so the wine bubbles gently. Tip the saucepan slightly away from you, and using a long match, *carefully* light the wine. Let the wine bubble and burn, then, once the flames die out, light the wine again. Continue lighting the wine until it no longer burns. (This method burns off the alcohol in the wine.) Pour the wine into a large glass measuring cup or a bowl, and leave it to cool; there will be about 2½ cups (625 ml).

2. Using kitchen scissors, make a cut through the membrane that surrounds the shank to prevent the meat from curling as it cooks. Tie a piece of string around the shank to keep the meat in place. Cut the slab of short ribs in half. Place the shank, short ribs, and oxtails in a large shallow dish. Add one of the sliced onions, one of the sliced carrots, the celery, garlic, thyme, and bay leaves. When the wine has cooled to room temperature, add ¼ teaspoon of the nutmeg to it and pour over the meat and vegetables. Turn the meat and vegetables to coat, then cover and refrigerate overnight, turning once or twice.

3. One hour before cooking, remove the meat from the refrigerator. Preheat the oven to 300°F (150°C). Remove the meat from the marinade and drain on paper towels. Strain the marinade through a sieve into a measuring cup; reserve the garlic, thyme, and bay leaves and discard the vegetables.

4. Pat the meat dry and season with salt and pepper. In a large Dutch oven or flameproof casserole, heat the oil over medium heat. Brown the meat in batches, transferring it to a plate as it browns.

5. Add the remaining onions to the pot and cook for 5 minutes, stirring. Pour in the strained marinade, and bring to a boil, deglazing the pot by scraping up the browned bits from the bottom. Add the stock, tomato paste, and the remaining ¼ teaspoon of grated nutmeg to the pan along with the reserved garlic, thyme, and bay leaves, and stir well.

6. Add the shank, the oxtail pieces, and then the rib pieces on top, bone side up. Cover with a damp piece of parchment paper and then the lid and transfer to the oven. Cook for 1 hour.

7. Meanwhile place the marrow bones in a bowl of ice water to cover and add 2 tablespoons salt. Refrigerate them for 12 to 24 hours, changing the water 4 to 6 times and adding 2 tablespoons salt to the water each time.

8. Add the remaining carrots and the whole mushrooms to the pot and continue to cook, covered, for 2 hours or until all the meat is tender. With a slotted spoon, transfer the meat to a dish. Strain the liquid through a sieve into a bowl, and add the carrots, onions, and mushrooms to the meat; set the cooking liquid aside. Allow to cool, cover, then refrigerate the meat and the liquid separately overnight.

9. Preheat the oven to 300°F (150°C). Remove the meat and the cooking liquid from the refrigerator. Discard the layer of fat from the sauce. Slice each rib piece in two. Remove the string from the shank and cut the meat into 4 pieces, reserving the bone.

10. Place all the meats and the bone from the shank in a Dutch oven or flameproof casserole. Pour the cooking liquid into a saucepan, bring to a boil, and add about ½ teaspoon salt. Pour over the meat and vegetables, cover, and place in the oven for 1 hour, or until heated through.

11. Meanwhile, drain the marrow bones. Bring a large saucepan of salted water to the boil. Add the marrow bones and poach gently for 10 to 15 minutes, or until the marrow is hot in the center when tested with a metal skewer and there is no resistance. Drain them on paper towels, then add them to the Dutch oven.

12. Using tongs or a slotted spoon, divide the meat and vegetables among four shallow soup bowls, giving each diner a piece of oxtail, shank, rib, and a marrow bone. Ladle over the cooking liquid, and serve with fleur de sel.

Braised Beef Shanks with Grape Sauce

Beef shanks are big, and while the front shank is a little smaller than the hind shank, it is still too big to consider cooking whole. I ask my butcher to cut the shank into thick pieces. You may be able to find four smaller pieces for this recipe, but most often, I use two big ones. Once cooked, the meat can be divided and so there is only the argument over the marrow bones to deal with. But after the long, slow cooking, the marrow will slip out of the bones, so it too is easily shared.

I wanted a sauce to complement the rich, pleasantly chewy, shanks. The grapes add a slight sweetness, which mellows out the shank's beefy flavor. It doesn't matter if you use white, red, or black grapes, but their juiciness will affect how much sauce you end up with, and their sweetness will dictate how much vinegar to add to it. This would also make a fine sauce for oxtails.

3 pounds (1.35 kg) beef shank, cut into 1½-inch (4-cm)-thick pieces
3 tablespoons flour
Kosher salt and freshly ground black pepper
2 to 3 tablespoons vegetable oil
2 onions, diced
2 carrots, peeled and diced
1 celery stalk, diced
1 cup (250 ml) Brown Stock (page 12)
4 garlic cloves, peeled
1 thyme sprig
1 bay leaf
2 pounds (900 g) seedless grapes, stemmed
2 to 3 tablespoons white or red wine vinegar

1. Preheat the oven to 300°F (150°C). Pat the beef shanks dry. Using kitchen scissors, make a cut through the membrane that surrounds each shank piece to prevent the meat from curling as it cooks, tie a piece of string around each shank to keep the meat in place. Season the flour with salt and pepper, then dredge the shank pieces in the flour, shaking off the excess.

2. In a Dutch oven or flameproof casserole large enough to hold the meat in one layer, heat the oil over medium heat. Add the beef shanks and brown on both sides, then transfer to a plate. Add the onions, carrots, and celery to the pot and cook for 5 minutes, scraping the bottom of the pan. Pour in the stock and bring to a boil, deglazing the pot by scraping up the browned bits from the bottom. Boil until the stock has reduced to ¼ cup (60 ml). Add the garlic, thyme, bay leaf, and 1 teaspoon salt to the pot. Place the shank pieces on top in a single layer and add the grapes. Transfer to the oven and cook, uncovered, for 2 to 2½ hours, or until the shanks are very tender.

3. Transfer the shanks to an ovenproof serving dish, remove the string, and keep warm, loosely covered with aluminum foil. (Leave the oven on.) Discard the thyme and bay leaf. Transfer the cooking liquid, grapes, and vegetables to a blender in batches, and puree, then strain through a sieve into a large glass measuring cup or a bowl. Let the fat rise to the top of the sauce, then skim it off.

4. Pour the sauce into a saucepan and bring to a boil. Boil until reduced to 2 cups (500 ml), skimming any foam that comes to the top; this can take up to 15 minutes. Taste the sauce. It will be sweet from the grapes, but you want just a touch of sweetness. Adjust the sweetness by adding the vinegar. Pour the sauce over the shanks, and place in the oven, uncovered, until heated through.

5. Check the sauce before serving to see if it needs additional seasoning or a splash more vinegar.

NOTE: You can prepare the dish ahead. Cool the sauce and meat separately, then cover and refrigerate overnight. Reheat the sauce, add the vinegar, pour over the shanks, and reheat in a 300° (150°C) oven uncovered for 1 hour or until heated through.

DREAMING OF BONES

ºººººººººººººººººººººººººººººººººººººº

Dreaming of bones is not the portent of doom you might expect. According to books on the interpretation of dreams, bones represent hidden secrets. Dreaming of whole bones is said to mean you possess a hidden strength. Broken bones, though, may indicate an underlying weakness in your thinking or plans. While I was writing this book, my dreams were always about bones cooking in pots. No interpretation necessary.

Osso Buco with Fennel and Blood Orange Sauce

Osso means bone and *buco* means hole in Italian. This term *osso buco* is usually applied to pieces of veal shank, but osso buco can come from many animals. Although literally translated the name means hollow bone, these bones are full of marrow.

Veal shanks have more flavor and texture than a veal chop, plus there is the luscious marrow bone. The blood oranges add great color and berry-like depth of flavor to the sauce. Their season is short, though, so don't hesitate to make this dish with regular oranges instead. In the traditional Italian kitchen, osso buco is served with gremolata, a mixture of chopped parsley, garlic, and lemon zest, but I've replaced the lemon zest with blood orange zest and used fennel leaves instead of parsley. If you don't own a Dutch oven large enough to hold the veal in a single layer, with space for the vegetables, brown the veal in a frying pan, then transfer it to a large baking dish.

Four 1½- to 2-inch (4- to 5-cm)-thick pieces veal shank, about 12 ounces (350 g) each
2 tablespoons flour
Kosher salt and freshly ground black pepper
3 tablespoons olive oil
3 tablespoons red wine vinegar
1 cup (250 ml) White Veal Stock (page 13)
2 blood oranges
1 large fennel bulb with leaves
2 medium carrots, peeled and cut in 2 × ¾-inch (5 × 2-cm) batons
1 cup (250 ml) blood orange juice (from about 3 oranges)
1 teaspoon fennel seeds, crushed
2 garlic cloves, finely chopped

1. Preheat the oven to 325°F (160°C). Pat the veal dry. With kitchen scissors, cut completely through the membrane surrounding each veal shank piece in two places to prevent the meat from curling as it cooks. Tie a piece of string around each shank to hold the meat in place while it is cooking. Season the flour with salt and pepper. Dredge the veal shanks in the flour, shaking off the excess.

2. In a large Dutch oven or flameproof casserole, heat the oil over medium heat. Add the veal and brown on both sides, then transfer to a plate. Discard the fat from the pot, and pour in the vinegar and stock. Bring to a boil, deglazing the pot by scraping up the browned bits from the bottom. Remove the pot from the heat.

3. Using a vegetable peeler, remove the zest in long strips from 1 orange and add to the pot; reserve the orange. Return the veal shanks to the pot, with the wider end of the bone facing up (this helps keep the marrow from escaping). Cover with a damp piece of parchment paper, then the lid, and braise in the oven for 45 minutes.

4. Meanwhile, remove the feathery leaves from the fennel—you should have ⅓ cup (75 ml); set aside. Trim any coarse stalks or outside layers. Cut the fennel lengthwise in half, then cut into ¼-inch (5-mm) slices.

5. After the veal has cooked for 45 minutes, add the fennel, carrots, orange juice, and 1 teaspoon salt. Cook, covered with the paper and lid, for another 45 to 55 minutes, or until the veal is very tender and the vegetables are cooked. Transfer the veal, fennel, and carrots to a serving platter. Remove the strings from the veal and keep warm, loosely covered with aluminum foil.

6. Discard the orange peel and bring the cooking juices to a boil; boil hard for 5 minutes to reduce the sauce. Meanwhile, grate the zest of the remaining orange and place it in a small bowl, with the fennel seeds. Remove the pith from the 2 zested oranges and cut them into segments (see page 191). Add the segments to the sauce and check the seasoning. Keep warm.

7. Finely chop the reserved fennel leaves. Add the fennel leaves and garlic to the zest and fennel seeds and mix. Serve the veal and vegetables with the sauce spooned over and pass the orange gremolata separately.

Variations

∘ Replace the orange juice with dry white wine, and use lemon zest instead of orange zest.

∘ Replace the fennel with 12 ounces (350 g), about 4, skinned, seeded, and diced plum tomatoes, and use the chopped parsley, garlic, and orange zest in the gremolata, omitting the fennel seeds.

Veal Shank with Sage and Mustard

The popularity of osso buco means that we usually see our veal shanks cut into thick slices. Here the shank is cooked whole. I know the measurements of my Dutch oven, and I take my tape measure to the store. There my butcher saws off a piece of the bone (from the end where there is less meat) so the shank fits my Dutch oven, and this also enables me to get at the marrow inside the bone. Ask the butcher to cut the tendons free from this end of the bone too. This will allow the meat to shrink away from the bone as it cooks. When it is cooked, the meat will have gathered at one end of the bone.

1 veal shank, trimmed as described above, about 3 pounds (1.35 kg)
2 tablespoons flour
Kosher salt and freshly ground black pepper
1 tablespoon olive oil
1 cup (250 ml) dry white wine
4 garlic cloves, peeled
1 tablespoon finely diced shallot
12 sage leaves
½ cup (125 ml) White Veal Stock (page 13)
2 teaspoons grainy mustard
1 tablespoon heavy (35%) whipping cream

1. One hour before cooking, remove the shank from the refrigerator and pat dry. Preheat the oven to 300°F (150°C). Season the flour with salt and pepper, then dredge the shank in the flour, shaking off any excess.

2. In a large Dutch oven or flameproof casserole, heat the olive oil over medium heat. Brown the shank on all sides. Transfer to a plate, and discard the fat from the pot. Pour the wine into the pot and bring to a boil, deglazing the pot by scraping up the browned bits from the bottom. Add the garlic, shallot, and 6 of the sage leaves. Return the shank to the pot, and cover with a damp piece of parchment paper and then the lid. Braise in the oven for 1 hour.

3. Turn the shank, add the veal stock, and cook for another 1½ to 2 hours, or until the meat is very tender, almost falling off the bone. Carefully lift the shank out of the pot, transfer it to a platter, and keep warm, loosely covered with aluminum foil.

4. Place the pot over medium-high heat and bring the cooking liquid to a boil, scraping the sides of the pot. Boil until the liquid is reduced to ½ cup (125 ml). Meanwhile, cut the remaining 6 sage leaves into julienne.

5. Stir the mustard and cream into the sauce, add the sage, and check the seasonings. Pour the sauce over the veal. To serve, cut off big chunks of meat—you will be able to do this with a spoon. The marrow will slide out of the bone; don't forget to serve it.

Roasted Marrow Bones

This is the dish that started me on my bones journey. Scooping out the soft, warm marrow and spreading it on crisp toast is a sensual delight. A touch of salt, and all is right with the world. I suggest two marrow bones per person, since it is a very rich dish—but I could easily eat all eight. Marrow bones are cut from the shank bones of beef and veal; ask your butcher for bones cut from the center of the shank so the portion of marrow to bone will be higher and the marrow easier to extract.

Serve the bones French style, with only fleur de sel, or English style, with the parsley salad. Use good rustic bread for the toast. And plan ahead, as the bones must be soaked for 12 to 24 hours to remove any traces of blood.

8 veal or beef marrow bones, about 3 inches (7.5 cm) long (see the headnote)
Kosher salt
Vegetable oil
Parsley salad (recipe follows), optional
8 slices rustic bread
Fleur de sel

1. Place the bones in a bowl of ice water to cover, add 2 tablespoons salt, and refrigerate for 12 to 24 hours, changing the water 4 to 6 times and adding 2 more tablespoons salt to the water each time.

2. Preheat the oven to 450°F (230°C). Drain the bones and pat dry. Stand them up in a lightly oiled roasting pan, and roast for 15 to 25 minutes, or until the marrow has puffed slightly and is warm in the center. To test, insert a metal skewer into the center of marrow, then touch it to your wrist to see if it is warm. There should be no resistance when the skewer is inserted, and a little of the marrow should have melted and started to leak from the bones.

3. While the bones are roasting, prepare the parsley salad, if serving it, and toast the bread.

4. Divide the bones among four plates and serve hot, with the optional salad, toast, and fleur de sel. Each diner scoops out the marrow and spreads it on the toast, sprinkling it with the salt.

○ Parsley Salad

I first ate this salad with roasted marrow bones at London's St. John restaurant. My version is adapted from chef-owner Fergus Henderson's recipe in his book *The Whole Beast: Nose to Tail Eating*. Parsley mixed with the pale green leaves from celery hearts and peppery wild arugula cuts through the richness of the marrow. Be sure to use flat-leaf parsley. If the leaves are big, tear them into smaller pieces. Dress the salad just before serving, and be sparing with the salt because of the fleur de sel that will top the marrow.

3 cups (750 ml) mixed flat-leaf parsley, celery (pale green), and arugula leaves
1 tablespoon finely diced shallot
2 teaspoons capers, preferably salt-packed, rinsed and chopped
2 tablespoons extra virgin olive oil
2 teaspoons freshly squeezed lemon juice
Kosher salt and freshly ground black pepper

1. Place the leaves, shallot, and capers in a medium bowl. Whisk together the oil and lemon juice in a glass measuring cup or a small bowl, then season very lightly with salt and generously with pepper. Toss the salad with the dressing and serve.

Poached Marrow Bones

○ You can poach marrow bones in simmering salted water instead of roasting them, but they must still be soaked in advance. Poach them for 15 minutes or so, depending on the thickness of the bones; drain well before serving.

Fleur de Sel

This is the French name for the first harvest of salt produced in the coastal regions of France by evaporating seawater in a series of ponds. Harvested by hand, fleur de sel is prized for its crunchy texture and delicate taste. Full of minerals, this expensive salt is used only as a condiment, not for cooking. The most famous fleur de sel comes from the salt marshes of Guérande and the islands of Noirmoutier and Ré. While the salt is traditional with marrow bones in France, any good sea salt can accompany them. Maldon salt, a flaky-textured English salt, also goes well with the roasted bones and parsley salad.

Marrow Toppings

○○

○ Gremolata

The traditional accompaniment to the classic Italian dish osso buco is gremolata, a garnish of chopped parsley, garlic, and lemon zest. The gremolatas in this book (pages 42 and 237) also go well with roasted marrow bones.

○ Ginger and Salt

At Michel Bras' eponymous restaurant outside Laiguiole in central France, a blend of finely chopped fresh ginger and fleur de sel is served as accompaniment to marrow bones. It's perfect: the heat of the ginger cuts the marrow's richness.

○ Mustard-Lemon Bread Crumbs

The bread crumbs soak up the fat that escapes from the marrow bones as they roast.

Stir together ½ cup (40 g) fresh bread crumbs, 1 tablespoon chopped flat-leaf parsley, 1 teaspoon dry mustard, 1 tablespoon freshly squeezed lemon juice, and freshly ground black pepper to taste in a small bowl. The crumbs should just hold together when squeezed; if not, add a little more lemon juice. Top each of the marrow bones with some of this mixture after the first 10 minutes of roasting.

MARROW SPOONS

○○○○○○○○○○○○○○○○○○○○○○○○○○○○○○

Eating marrow has helped man survive harsh climatic conditions. It's easy to imagine early man just smashing open bones and sucking out their marrow. The Copper Inuit of Northern Canada, dependent on marrow for survival, carved marrow spoons from wood, with a two-pointed fork at one end to spear the meat in the cooking pot and a channeled spatula at the other to extract the marrow.

In the late seventeenth through the eighteenth century, eating marrow became very popular among the upper classes, and special silver marrow scoops were all the rage. Some of these had a regular spoon-shaped bowl and a handle that was a long scoop. Others were composed of two scoops, one a shorter, wider channel to scoop the marrow from larger bones, one long and narrow, for smaller bones. These fine silver spoons are highly collectible today and, in their time, were a common target of thieves. The proceedings of the Old Bailey Courts in London reveal that, in May 1771, a certain Robert Roberts was found guilty of stealing sixteen silver marrow spoons; his punishment was transportation to Australia.

Marrow spoons are coming back into fashion. For those who can't find or afford antique silver ones, horn and metal marrow spoons are readily available. These spoons are not essential to enjoy marrow; a table knife or an espresso spoon will easily extract the marrow. A lobster pick is also effective. And of course you can always just suck out the marrow. There's no need to smash your bones.

Braised Oxtail with Root Vegetables

The secret to preparing oxtail is to cook it a day or two before serving to allow all the fat to rise to the top of the dish, making it easy to remove. Should you be so lucky, any leftover meat, taken off the bone, makes a hearty pasta sauce or ragu. Oxtail can be substituted in almost any beef stew recipe. It takes a little longer to become meltingly tender, but its rich flavor and unctuous texture make it worthwhile. The English food writer Arabella Boxer inspired this recipe.

5 pounds (2.25 kg) oxtail, cut into pieces
¼ cup (30 g) flour
Kosher salt and freshly ground black pepper
3 tablespoons vegetable oil
4 carrots, peeled, 2 cut into chunks, 2 cut into batons
4 celery stalks, 2 cut into chunks, 2 cut into batons
1 large onion, cut into wedges
4 garlic cloves, peeled
1 bottle (750 ml) hearty dry red wine
2 cups (500 ml) Brown Stock (page 12)
2 tablespoons tomato paste
2 bay leaves
5 parsley stems
2 turnips, peeled and cut into batons
2 parsnips, peeled and cut into batons

1. Preheat the oven to 300°F (150°C). Trim the excess fat off the oxtail and pat dry. Season the flour with salt and pepper, then dredge the oxtail in the flour, shaking off any excess. In a Dutch oven or flame-proof casserole, heat the oil over medium-high heat. Brown the oxtail in batches; as they brown, transfer them to a plate.

2. Discard any fat from the pot, then add the chunks of carrot and celery, the onion, and garlic. Pour in 2 cups (500 ml) of the red wine and bring to a boil, deglazing the pot by scraping up the browned bits from the bottom. Stir in the stock and tomato paste, then add the bay leaves and parsley.

3. Return the oxtail to the pot, and cover with a damp piece of parchment paper and then the lid. Braise in the oven for 3 to 4 hours (timing will depend on the size of the pieces). The meat should be tender but not falling off the bone. Transfer the oxtail to a platter, and strain the liquid into a large glass measuring cup or a bowl. Leave to cool, then cover both and refrigerate overnight. The next day, remove all the fat from the top of the jellied liquid and any from the oxtail pieces. Preheat the oven to 350°F (175°C).

4. Put the liquid in a saucepan with the remaining wine, and bring to a boil. Reduce the heat and simmer for 10 minutes. Place the oxtail in a baking dish and pour the sauce over it. Set aside.

5. Bring a saucepan of salted water to a boil, and blanch the turnips, parsnips, and the remaining carrots and celery for 2 minutes. Drain and refresh under cold water. Scatter the vegetables over the oxtail. Transfer to the oven and cook, uncovered, for 1 hour, or until the oxtail is almost falling from the bone.

Oxtail Dividends

○ Oxtail makes an excellent pasta sauce. Take the cooked meat off the bones and add to your homemade sauce. Or use the meat to make a filling for wontons (page 18) to add to soup or consommé.

BIZARRE BONES

The bones in the famed Paris catacombs come from old graveyards that were built on as the city expanded. There is something both disconcerting and somehow oddly calming about the piles and piles of bones and skulls. The catacombs were not at all frightening, as I had expected.

In the Czech Republic, some 44 miles (70 kilometers) from Prague, is a town called Kutna Hora, another "bizarre bones" site. Architecturally rich, it appears on the UNESCO world cultural heritage list. The town boasts many beautiful churches, but a small chapel on the outskirts of town is the most fascinating. It stands on a graveyard originally attached to a Cistercian monastery. According to legend, sometime in the late thirteenth century the abbot of the monastery sprinkled the graveyard with soil from the Holy Land. This act turned it into a revered place that became famous throughout Central Europe. The graveyard was considered the best place to be buried, and tens of thousands of people were buried there. Its popularity meant that over time, bones had to be moved to make room for "new customers"; these bones were stored in what was called an ossuary, a common practice.

In the nineteenth century, woodcarver Frantisek Rint was hired to decorate the chapel's interior. But rather than using wood as his medium, he turned to the bones stored in the ossuary. It is estimated that the bones of more than forty thousand people now decorate the chapel. Some of the more impressive elements include large bells suspended in each corner of the chapel, a huge chandelier, a chalice, and two monstrances. When Rint signed his work, it was, of course, with bones. Today, the All Saints Chapel is a popular tourist stop.

Chinese-Style Oxtail

Oxtail is popular in Chinese cuisine, where sticky gelatinous textures are very much appreciated. I have two friends of Chinese origin who happily ate my braised oxtail (page 47) once a week, the night their cook was off, for over a month. Even though they love oxtail, I thought they must be tired of eating the same dish, so I developed a Chinese-inspired version. The morning after I delivered the first recipe trial, they called for the recipe. Coated in a rich anise-and-soy-flavored sauce, even the small pieces with little meat are irresistible. As with all oxtail dishes, make this at least a day in advance so you can chill it and remove the layer of fat.

5 pounds (2.25 kg) oxtail, cut into pieces
Kosher salt and freshly ground black pepper
2 to 4 tablespoons vegetable oil
½ cup (125 ml) Chinese wine (Shao Xing) or dry sherry
½ cup (125 ml) dark soy sauce
1½ tablespoons brown sugar
1 star anise, broken apart
3 green onions, trimmed and cut into 2-inch (5-cm) pieces
4 slices fresh ginger
2 garlic cloves, peeled
1 orange

1. Preheat the oven to 300°F (150°C). Trim any excess fat off the oxtail, then pat dry. Season lightly with salt, and generously with freshly ground black pepper. In a Dutch oven or flameproof casserole, heat 2 tablespoons oil over medium-high heat. Brown the oxtail in batches, adding more oil if necessary. As they brown, transfer the oxtail pieces to a plate.

2. Discard any fat from the pot, then pour in the wine and bring to a boil, deglazing the pot by scraping up the browned bits from the bottom. Mix the soy sauce and sugar with 2 cups (500 ml) water and pour into the pot. Add the star anise, green onions, ginger, and garlic and bring to a boil, then remove from the heat.

3. Using a vegetable peeler, remove 4 large strips of zest from the orange; reserve the orange. Add the zest and oxtail to the pot, cover with a damp piece of parchment paper and then the lid, and transfer to the oven. Cook for 1½ hours.

4. Turn the pieces of oxtail, cover again with parchment and the lid, and cook for another 1½ hours, or until the oxtail is very tender. Transfer the oxtail to a dish and strain the sauce through a sieve into a glass measuring cup or a bowl; discard the debris in the sieve. Cool, then cover the sauce and oxtail and refrigerate overnight.

5. The next day, preheat the oven to 300°F (150°C). Remove all the fat from the top of the jellied liquid and any from the oxtail pieces. Place the oxtail pieces in a single layer in a baking dish.

6. Heat the sauce in a small saucepan until liquid, then pour over oxtail. Cover, transfer to the oven, and cook for 30 minutes.

7. Uncover the baking dish and stir the oxtail. Increase the oven temperature to 400°F (200°C) and cook for 15 minutes. Turn the pieces of oxtail to coat with the sauce and cook for another 15 minutes, or until hot and glazed.

8. Meanwhile, squeeze ¼ cup (60 ml) juice from the orange.

9. Remove the glazed oxtail from the oven and pour in the orange juice. Stir the juice into the sauce, and serve.

Spiced Roasted Rack of Ribs
(page 30)

Osso Buco with Fennel and Blood Orange Sauce
(page 41)

Roasted Marrow Bones
(page 44)

Chinese-Style Oxtail
(page 49)

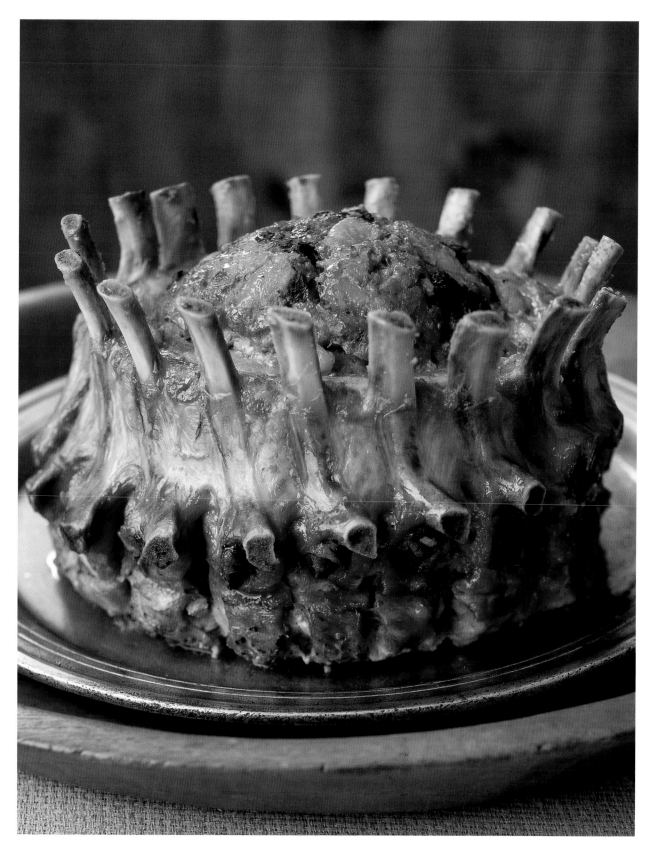

Crown Roast of Pork
(page 70)

Roast Leg of Pork with Crackling
(page 74)

Braised Hock with Fennel Three Ways
(page 80)

BONE MARROW

ooooooooooooooooooooooooo

Marrow is the soft, creamy, highly caloric substance found in the center of the bones. According to Waverley Root, in his reference work *Food,* bone marrow is "the rather mucilaginous matter which fills bones and is considered a particular delicacy by cannibals." Root was obviously not a fan, but cooked bone marrow has a mild taste and the consistency of soft butter; gourmands compare it to foie gras.

The most popular marrow is veal or beef, from the animals' leg bones. Don't neglect what you find in lamb and pork shanks, hams, and game bones. Even if you don't eat the marrow straight from the bone, remember to add those bones to your stockpot to enrich the final broth.

Since man began hunting, marrow has been an important food source. It provides fat, iron, phosphorous, and vitamin A, with trace amounts of thiamin and niacin. For people living at subsistence levels or in marginal areas, it could mean the difference between life and death. All mammals have marrow in their bones, as do birds—though to a lesser extent, because many bird bones are hollow, which helps them fly.

During the Middle Ages marrow, like suet (the fat from around the kidneys), was used in place of butter as an ingredient in pastries, sweet puddings, and desserts. In Victorian times, marrow was a popular dish at English high teas and in men's clubs, and it was often served, instead of pudding, at the end of the meal. Queen Victoria was a devotee, who it was said, ate marrow and toast every day. That may not have improved her figure, but it didn't shorten her life.

Although rich, beef marrow is easily digested. Because it is one of the richest foods there is, in the past it was the nutritional choice for anyone with a poor appetite or who needed building up. It was regarded as a health food, perfect for invalids and children. In one English recipe, the marrow is colored yellow with saffron and then whipped until it resembles butter. It was recommended for sickly children.

Fortunately, we don't need the excuse of feeling undernourished to eat marrow; we can eat it because we like it. However, because many of us pay attention to the amount of saturated fat in our diets, marrow is usually a special treat.

Knowing where your meat comes from, and how it has been raised, is especially important when it concerns bone marrow. Spinal marrow is found in the bones of chops and ribs, the neck, and tail. The safest bone marrow is that from the leg bones, because it has had no contact with brain tissues.

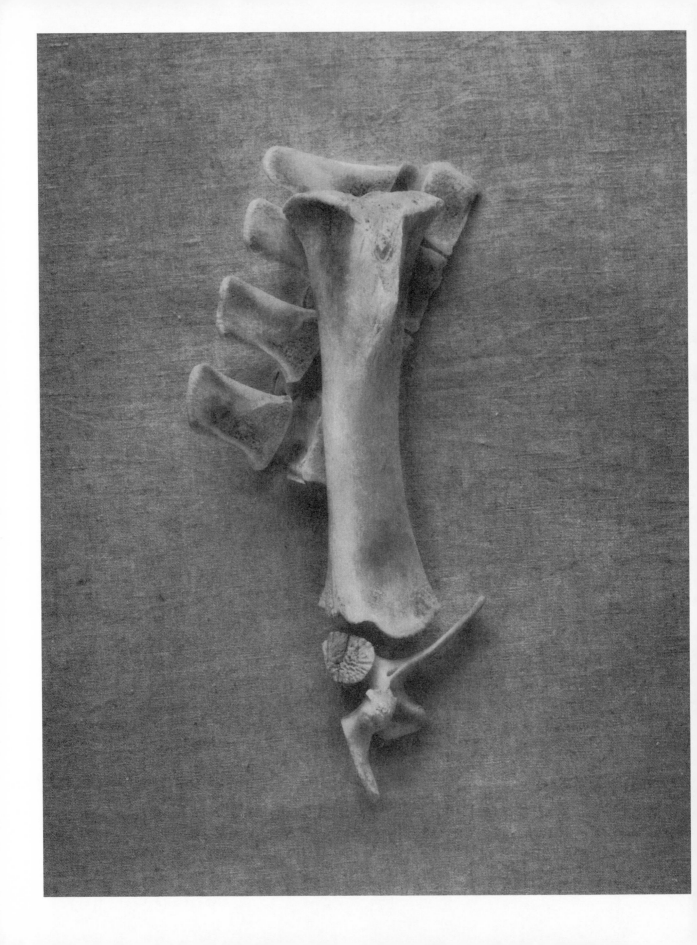

Pork

Pork bones are familiar friends, the reason why pork ribs are such a favorite. The best part of eating ribs is picking up the bones and chewing the sweet juicy meat still clinging to them; they satisfy a deep primal urge to eat with our fingers. Yet we often ignore pork's other bones and bone-in cuts, seduced by speed and convenience over flavor.

Pigs are important to bone lovers and today, more than ever, their bones are essential to cooks. Once prized for its fat, pork is now leaner than ever. Although heritage breeds are making a comeback, with pigs reared the old-fashioned way to give them a good layer of fat and lots of flavor, most of our pork is lean. That may be good for our waistlines but it does nothing for pork's taste. Cooking pork on the bone is one way of keeping its lean meat juicy, as the bones hold in the moisture. Pork, like any meat, is more flavorful when cooked on the bone, and the bones enrich the cooking juices or sauce. (The pig is especially lucky, because it has a second set of bones. Pork also gives us cured bones.)

Bones are just as important with hams or any cured meat as they are with the fresh. Meat cured on the bone has much more flavor. The finest hams always still have their bones—some even have even the foot attached. The bones keep the ham moist and flavorful as it ages. So always choose a bone-in ham. Sliced ham should be cut to order from a ham on the bone. And a ham bone can have a second life. Use it to flavor soups or to add a creamy richness and depth to dried beans and lentils.

When you are buying pork or ham, a knowledgeable butcher is essential. Cuts on the bone will be expertly prepared, with the chine or pelvic bones removed where necessary to make carving them easier. A good butcher can also provide less common cuts such as pig's feet and tails. Carefully prepared and cooked, these neglected bony extremities make succulent eating for the adventurous. Pig's feet can be added in place of calves' feet to any stock; a rich source of gelatin, they will add body and substance.

The pig is a unique animal in that we can eat it all—as the old expression says, "Everything but the oink." For the bone lover, the first step in enjoying both fresh and cured bone-in cuts is understanding the animal's skeleton. How you cook all these cuts depends on which part of the animal they are from.

The Front End

When a hog is butchered, the foot is often removed (see "The Extremities") from the front leg, which is then divided into two cuts. Closest to the shoulder is the Boston shoulder roast, also called the blade roast or pork butt. This meaty cut consists of several muscles and is marbled with fat. It is sold whole, cut in half, or sliced into blade chops or steaks. Country-style ribs are cut from the shoulder. These meaty ribs are actually butterflied blade chops and are sold individually. Despite its name, this cut, and its chops, are better braised than roasted.

The lower section of the front leg is oddly named the picnic shoulder. It should be braised or barbecued.

The Middle

The muscles in this part of the pig do the least work and, as a result, the meat here is the most tender. This is where the rack of pork, or pork rib roast, sold with up to eight ribs, lies. Your butcher can prepare an impressive crown roast with two complete racks cut from the same animal. The roast can also be cut into individual rib chops.

Closer to the back leg is the center loin roast. Here the bone divides the meat into the loin and the tenderloin. The chops cut from this roast resemble small T-bone steaks, with a piece of loin meat on one side of the bone and a small piece of tenderloin on the other. Cuts from the loin can be roasted, and the chops sautéed or grilled.

This ham bone, far from being a melancholy reminder, is still a treasure . . .
—EDOUARD DE POMIANE

The free maides that weave their thread with bones.
—WILLIAM SHAKESPEARE,
Twelfth Night, Act 2, Scene IV

It is unforgivable to take anything out of your mouth that has been put in it except dry bones . . .
—EMILY POST

I have a reasonable good ear in music; let us have the tongs and the bones.
—BOTTOM IN SHAKESPEARE'S
A Midsummer Night's Dream,
Act 4, Scene 1

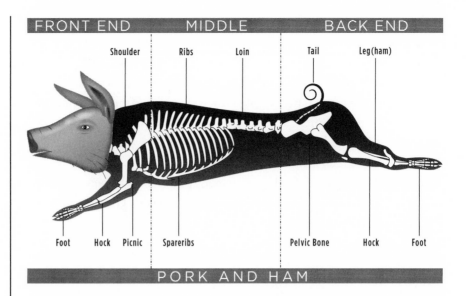

Shoulder   Ribs   Loin   Tail   Leg (ham)

Foot   Hock   Picnic   Spareribs   Pelvic Bone   Hock   Foot

PORK AND HAM

Bare bones are the framework or the essential part of something such as a book.

There is nothing finer than having a bone to gnaw on at the end of a meal; meat will cook better on the bone; and your stockpot appreciates the contribution of plenty of bones.
—FERGUS HENDERSON, *The Whole Beast: Nose to Tail Eating*

Whether in English or French the tastiest meat is close to the bone: The nearer the bone the sweeter the meat. *La chair la plus près des os est la plus tender.*

A Chinese expression laments that you can't get fat from a dry bone.

The ribs that bend around to form the pig's chest become spareribs. In a rack with up to thirteen ribs, the spareribs that come from the front of the animal are longer than those toward the back. What are called back ribs, with from eleven to thirteen bones, are cut higher on the animal, closer to the backbone. They are leaner than spareribs and more uniform in size. All ribs can be barbecued or braised.

The Back End

The leg, with the feet and tail removed (see "The Extremities") is one of the best pork cuts, and is sold either fresh or cured as ham (see page 77). Sometimes confusingly called a fresh ham, the leg often includes the pelvic bone, which should be removed before cooking. You can ask the butcher to do this. If the skin is left on the leg, it will turn into crisp crackling when it is roasted.

Because it is a very large cut, the leg is commonly divided in two. The sirloin or butt half is the end closer to the middle of the animal, and it has a higher portion of meat to bone, but the shank end has is easier to carve.

The Extremities

There are some pieces of the pig that seemingly disappear without a trace. The truth is, they are quickly snapped up by those who appreciate them. Ask your butcher to order them for you, or look for them in ethnic markets.

The shank, often called a hock, is the section between the knee and the foot. The back hocks may be left attached to the legs, while the smaller front hocks are almost always removed. Fresh hocks can be braised or poached, and smoked ones flavor dishes from beans to sauerkraut.

Pig's feet, or trotters, come in two sizes: the larger back feet, often attached to the shank, and the smaller front feet. Both are commonly sold split. If you're not adventurous enough to eat them, at least add them to your stockpot. Old recipes often suggest adding a calf's foot to stock, but a pig's foot is easier to find. Like calves' feet, pig's trotters are full of collagen. Two of them are a good substitute for a calf's foot.

Pig's tails are not really curly—they merely have a slight bend. They are sold with the skin and a piece of the backbone attached. They add taste and texture to soups and stews.

Pork Cooking Temperatures

Today pork is carefully controlled and while the parasite that causes trichinosis has not been entirely eliminated, it is much less prevalent. In any case it is killed when the meat is cooked to a temperature of 137°F (59°C). With their low fat content, many pork cuts, especially the loin, need careful cooking to prevent them from drying out. The loin can safely be left slightly pink and cooked to 150°F (65°C). Other cuts are cooked to 155° to 160°F (68° to 71°C). For accurate results, use an instant-read thermometer. Remember that larger cuts of meat, which need to rest before carving, will continue to cook during this time from the residual heat, raising their temperature by about 5°F (2°C). Always remove larger roasts from the oven before they reach their optimal temperature.

A bone of contention and having a bone to pick with someone refer to a dispute or disagreement.

A great bone of contention between Scindiah and Holkar.
—DUKE OF WELLINGTON, *Dispatches* 1,517 (1803)

There is a bone for gastronomers to pick
—WALTER SCOTT, *Lockhart, Life* VII, 215 (1830)

Brine for Pork

Although brining, soaking food in a heavily salted water, has been heralded as a new way to impart flavor to today's lean pork, it is really a very old method used for preserving foods. When the meat is submerged, for hours or as long as a day or two, depending on its weight, in a salt solution, osmosis takes place, which increases the amount of liquid inside the meat's cells. The result is a juicier, more flavorful piece of meat.

While a basic brine is simply a mixture of water and salt, most brines are balanced by the addition of sugar, and they can, like this one, be further enhanced with herbs and spices. Use a nonreactive container for brining, such as a glass or stainless steel bowl or even a plastic bucket, the container must be large enough to submerge the meat completely in the brining solution. This recipe makes enough brine for a crown roast of pork; it can easily be halved for brining a smaller piece of meat. Specific instructions are given with each recipe, as the brining time depends on the size and shape of the cut. Make sure the brining solution is cold before adding the meat.

1 cup (130 g) kosher salt
½ cup (100 g) sugar
1 tablespoon coriander seeds, crushed
1 tablespoon black peppercorns, crushed
8 allspice berries, crushed
6 juniper berries, crushed
4 garlic cloves, crushed
4 bay leaves, crushed
4 thyme sprigs

1. Put the salt, sugar, and 4 cups (1 l) water in a medium saucepan and bring to a boil, stirring to dissolve the salt and sugar. Boil for 1 minute, then remove from the heat and pour into the brining container. Add the coriander seeds, peppercorns, allspice and juniper berries, garlic, bay leaves, and thyme, and pour in 12 cups (3 l) cold water.

2. Once the brining solution is completely cool, add the meat. To submerge the meat, weight it down using a plate and a jar filled with water. (Do not use a metal weight or jar with a metal lid, as it would react with the brine.) Refrigerate the meat in the brine according to the individual recipe instructions.

Pork Stock

Admittedly not as useful as veal or chicken stock, pork stock nonetheless makes a good basis for certain soups and for sauces to accompany pork. Use only uncured pork bones to make it. The smoky flavor of ham bones or those from other cured cuts would overpower the stock; they are best added to lentils or beans. As with any bones, they can be saved in the freezer until you have enough, or ask your butcher to set them aside for you. Skin, feet, and ears are good additions to the stock because they increase the gelatin content. A small pig's foot (have your butcher cut it into pieces) or a piece of skin about 6 inches (16 cm) square, with the fat removed, will be enough for this stock. Add either one with the bones.

4½ pounds (2 kg) meaty pork bones, cut into 2- to 3-inch (5- to 7.5-cm) pieces
1 small pig's foot, cut into pieces, optional
2 medium carrots, sliced
2 celery stalks, sliced
1 large onion, unpeeled, cut into wedges
Green tops of 3 leeks, sliced
6 flat-leaf parsley stems
1 large thyme sprig
1 bay leaf
A large strip of lemon zest
3 garlic cloves
¼ teaspoon black peppercorns
Kosher salt, optional

1. Rinse the bones and foot, if using, under cold running water, then place in a large stockpot. Add the carrots, celery, onion, leeks, parsley, thyme, bay leaf, lemon zest, and garlic. Pour in enough cold water to cover the bones, about 12 cups (3 l), and bring slowly to a boil. As soon as the stock begins to boil, reduce the heat so that it simmers. Using a soup ladle, skim off any scum that has risen to the surface (rotate its bowl on the surface of the stock to make ripples: these will carry the scum to the edges of the pot, and you can then use the ladle to lift it off). Add the peppercorns and simmer, uncovered, for 5 hours, skimming from time to time.

2. Strain the stock through a sieve into a large bowl. Discard the debris left in the sieve, and cool the stock quickly by placing the bowl in a larger bowl or sink filled with ice water; stir occasionally as it cools. When you taste the stock, you will notice that something is missing—the salt. It was deliberately left out so that you can reduce the stock, if desired, without any fear that it will become too salty. If you will not be reducing the stock (see page 59), add about 1 teaspoon salt.

3. Refrigerate the stock for 6 hours, or overnight, to allow the fat to rise to the top and the debris to sink to the bottom. Remove the fat before using (and discard the debris at the bottom of the bowl). Divide into 1-cup (250-ml) quantities and refrigerate for up to 3 days or freeze for up to 6 months.

Concentrated Pork Stock

If your freezer space is tight, reduce your stock by following the method for Concentrated Brown Stock (page 14).

6 cups (1.5 l) unsalted Pork Stock (page 58)
Kosher salt

°°

The reduced stock will become syrupy and turn a deep golden color.

Court Bouillon

I use this flavored liquid to cook hocks (page 80), pig's feet (page 82), and tails (page 86). After you have cooked them, you will be left with a tasty liquid very high in gelatin—don't throw it away. Strain the court bouillon through a sieve and refrigerate it overnight so that you can lift off the chilled fat and discard it. I often use this instead of stock in soups and sauces for pork. It adds a velvety texture to sauce because of the gelatin, but it can be salty, so season carefully. The bouillon can also be clarified like stock (see page 61) and then used as a savory aspic.

¼ cup (60 ml) white wine vinegar
2 carrots, diced
2 onions, diced
2 leeks, trimmed and sliced
2 celery stalks, sliced
5 flat-leaf parsley stems
3 bay leaves
2 thyme sprigs
10 black peppercorns
6 allspice berries
2 cloves

1. Place the vinegar, carrots, onions, leeks, celery, parsley, bay leaves, and thyme sprigs in a large Dutch oven or deep saucepan, depending on what you will be cooking in it. Add 8 cups (2 l) water and bring to a boil. Skim off any scum, then add the peppercorns, allspice berries, and cloves. Reduce the heat and simmer for 10 minutes.

2. The court bouillon is now ready to use.

Clarified Bouillon

I don't like the idea of pork consommé. What I do is clarify court bouillon after cooking pig's feet; they add enough natural gelatin to set the liquid. I get a kick out of making aspic without any commercial gelatin, but I admit that the use for aspic in most home kitchens today is pretty well nonexistent. If, however, the urge strikes you to make an egg set in jelly or coat a pâté with a layer of aspic, you'll be ready.

6 cups (1.5 l) Court Bouillon, (page 60), used to cook pig's feet (page 82)
1 small leek, trimmed and diced
1 small carrot, peeled and diced
3 flat-leaf parsley stems
2 egg whites
Kosher salt

1. Place the bouillon in a large saucepan and heat it just until it liquefies. Remove the saucepan from the heat.

2. Place the leek, carrot, and parsley in a food processor and process until finely chopped. Add the egg whites and 2 tablespoons water and blend until well mixed. Stir this mixture into the bouillon and bring to a boil over medium-high heat, stirring constantly with a spatula or wooden spoon and scraping the bottom of the pan to prevent the egg white from sticking. As the liquid approaches the boil, it will appear to curdle; don't panic, this is what you want. As soon as the stock begins to boil, stop stirring, and remove the saucepan from the heat. The whites will form a congealed mass on the surface, which will puff up and then crack as the steam escapes.

3. Reduce the heat to very low and return the saucepan to the heat, making a larger hole in the egg white mass with the spoon to allow the steam to escape. Simmer very gently—you want to see the small bubbles of steam break through the hole in the egg white mass—for 45 minutes. Remove the saucepan from the heat and let it stand for 5 minutes.

4. Line a sieve with a double thickness of damp cheesecloth or a dampened thin cotton tea towel, and place over a bowl. Using a skimmer or large slotted spoon, carefully lift off as much of the egg white mass as you can and set aside in another bowl. Ladle the clarified liquid into the sieve and allow it to drip slowly through the cloth. As you get closer to the bottom of the saucepan, you might notice that the clear liquid is being muddied by bits of egg white. Don't worry, just add this to the sieve. Check the bowl with the egg white debris and pour any liquid that has escaped from it into the sieve. Allow all the liquid to drip slowly through the sieve; don't be tempted to press on the egg whites, as that would cloud the liquid. You will have about 5 cups (1.25 l) clear bouillon in the bowl and a mess of congealed egg white to discard. Season the bouillon with about ¼ teaspoon salt.

Mustard Sauce

Sauce Robert, a classic sauce for pork, is made from onion, wine, and mustard. With the addition of cornichons, it becomes sauce charcutière. With or without the cornichons, the sauce is a great match for pork chops, baked ham, or pig's feet and tails. If you can't find the small French cornichons, substitute diced sour gherkins.

3 tablespoons (45 g) unsalted butter
2 tablespoons flour
2 teaspoons dry mustard
1½ cups (325 ml) Pork Stock (page 58)
½ teaspoon kosher salt
1 shallot or small onion, finely diced
¼ cup (60 ml) dry white wine
2 tablespoons finely diced cornichons, optional
¼ cup chopped flat-leaf parsley, optional

1. Melt 2 tablespoons (30 g) of the butter in a small saucepan over medium heat. Add the flour and mustard and cook, stirring constantly, for about 3 minutes. Remove the saucepan from the heat and gradually whisk in the stock.

2. Return the pan to the heat and continue whisking until the mixture boils. Reduce the heat, add the salt, and simmer for 15 minutes, whisking occasionally.

3. While the sauce is simmering, melt the remaining 1 tablespoon (15 g) butter in a small frying pan. Add the shallot and cook until soft and just starting to color. Pour in the wine and boil until it has almost all evaporated.

4. Add the shallot mixture to the sauce, along with the cornichons and parsley, if using. Serve warm.

Split Pea Soup with Chestnuts

I grew up with the comfort and warmth of my mother's pea soup on cold days, so on one bone-chilling day, I ordered it for lunch in a Paris restaurant. It was delicious and restorative, and I felt better with each mouthful—but it wasn't anything like my mother's soup. What were those brown bits floating in it, mushrooms? No, they were sweet, floury chestnuts, an inspired addition.

This soup is delicious with or without chestnuts.

You can roast your own chestnuts for this soup, but cooked chestnuts are readily available vacuum-packed or canned in gourmet shops and grocery stores. If you buy the canned ones, be sure they are unsweetened.

10 ounces (350 g) split peas
1 large ham bone, with some meat left on it
1 large onion, diced
2 large carrots, peeled and diced
3 celery stalks, sliced
3 garlic cloves, halved
2 bay leaves
1 large thyme sprig
Kosher salt and freshly ground black pepper
12 cooked chestnuts, diced, optional

1. Put the peas in a colander and rinse well under cold running water. Place the peas, ham bone, onion, carrots, celery, garlic, bay leaves, and thyme in a large stockpot. Add 10 cups (2.5 l) water and bring slowly to a boil. Skim off the foam that has risen to the top, reduce the heat, partially cover, and simmer for 1½ to 2 hours, or until the meat is falling off the bone and the split peas are very soft. Remove from the heat.

2. Carefully remove the ham bone, bay leaves, and thyme from the soup, making sure you don't leave the knuckle or any bone splinters behind. Let the bone cool, then remove any remaining meat and dice or shred it.

3. Puree the soup using an immersion blender or in batches in a regular blender or food processor. Pour into a clean saucepan, stir in the meat, and season with salt and pepper. Add the chestnuts, if using. Reheat gently and check the seasoning.

TIP No ham bone? Use a small smoked ham hock. Add an extra 2 cups (500 ml) water, because the collagen in hock will make the soup thicker. Use only ½ cup (125 ml) of the meat from the hock for the soup, and keep the rest of it for a dish of lentils or beans.

Spicy Korean Pork Soup

When my husband and I went to our neighborhood Korean restaurant to try pork bone soup, the specialty, it was so spicy that after the first two mouthfuls, I couldn't taste a thing. And the soup, true to its name, was full of big bones. I make a slightly tamer version at home, and don't serve the bones in the finished soup. You can adjust the heat of the soup by adding more or less chili powder and/or kimchee. Kimchee is a spicy fermented cabbage condiment found in Asian markets; it keeps well in the refrigerator, and once you have it on hand, this soup is quick to prepare.

2 tablespoons vegetable oil
½ teaspoon chili powder
1 large carrot, peeled and sliced
1 large onion, sliced
2 garlic cloves, finely diced
4 cups (1 l) Pork Stock (page 58)
1 large potato, peeled and diced
1 teaspoon kosher salt
1 cup (250 ml) kimchee, chopped

1. Heat the oil in a large saucepan over medium heat. Add the chili powder and stir for 30 seconds. Add the carrot and onion and cook for 5 minutes, or until the vegetables start to stick to the pan and color. Add the garlic, stock, potato, and salt and bring to a boil. Skim off any foam, reduce the heat, and simmer, uncovered, for 10 to 12 minutes, or until the potato is cooked.

2. Stir in the kimchee and check the seasoning. Ladle the soup into bowls and serve.

Pork with Caramelized Milk Sauce

I've always associated this dish with northern Italian cooking, so I was interested to learn from one of Paula Wolfert's cookbooks that it is also a popular way of cooking in the Basque country. This dish is best cooked on top of the stove so you can keep your eye on it. It is important to use whole milk and to scrape the bottom of the pan every so often so that you can incorporate the caramelized bits into the sauce. By the time the pork is cooked, your sauce will resemble curdled *dulce de leche*. Don't despair—that is exactly how it should look. The taste will win you over. If by chance you have any left over, it is delicious cold.

Depending on your casserole the sauce will reduce by various amounts. Add the extra 1 cup (250 ml) milk only if necessary. (The bottom of the pot must always be covered with milk. If the milk evaporates too quickly add extra.)

1 bone-in pork shoulder roast, about 4½ pounds (2 kg)
Kosher salt and freshly ground black pepper
2 tablespoons vegetable oil
2 ounces (60 g) pancetta, finely diced
1 red onion, diced
6 bay leaves
4 garlic cloves, halved
3 to 4 cups (750 ml to 1 l) whole milk

1. Pat the pork dry and season with salt and pepper. In a large Dutch oven or flameproof casserole, heat the oil over medium heat. Brown the pork on all sides, starting with fat side. Transfer the shoulder to a plate, lower the heat, and add the pancetta. Cook, stirring, for 2 minutes, or until crispy. Add the onion and cook for another 3 minutes, or until the onion softens.

2. Add the bay leaves and garlic, then pour in 1 cup (250 ml) of the milk. Bring to a boil, deglazing the pot by scraping up the browned bits from the bottom. Add the pork fat side down to the pot along with any juices. Adjust the heat so that the milk is bubbling gently, partially cover, and cook for 30 minutes.

3. Turn the pork and scrape the bottom of the pot, then add another 1 cup (250 ml) milk. Return the liquid to a gentle boil and cook, partially covered, for 30 minutes.

4. Stir the sauce, and baste the meat with it. Cook, partially covered, for another hour, turning the pork after 30 minutes.

5. Add the final 1 cup (250 ml) milk. Cook, uncovered, at a gentle boil, for another hour, or until the pork is very tender; baste the pork 2 or 3 times. (The pork is cooked when the internal temperature registers 160°F [71°C] on an instant-read thermometer, but I like this cut almost falling off the bone, so I cook it until very tender.) During this final cooking, pay attention that the milk doesn't burn and that the meat doesn't stick. Move the meat in the pot when you baste it, and scrape the sides and bottom of the pot to incorporate all the caramelized bits into the sauce. Transfer the cooked shoulder to a platter and let rest, loosely covered with aluminum foil, for at least 15 minutes before slicing.

6. Tip the pot and skim off any fat from the sauce; discard the bay leaves. Bring the sauce to a boil, stirring constantly, and cook, stirring, for 5 minutes, or until the reduced to about 1½ cups (375 ml). Stir any juices from the resting pork into the sauce, and then check the seasoning.

7. Slice the pork and serve with the sauce.

LACE BONES

ooooooooooooooooooooo

The discovery of bone drop spindles and whorls dating from 5000 B.C. revealed that bones played an important role in early textile production. Early pin-beaters—the tool that separates the weave when making cloth—were also made of bone.

Somewhat more recently, bones were employed to make type of a lace. Called bone lace, it probably originated in sixteenth-century Flanders. Made by hand, it is crafted from numerous linen threads tied to bone bobbins.

Orange-Campari–Braised Pork Shoulder

Campari mixed with orange juice is one of my favorite drinks, so when I was looking for another flavor to add with the orange juice to this pork shoulder recipe, Campari was the natural choice. With its slight bitterness, herbal overtones, and bright red color, it enhances both the taste and color of the sauce.

Pork shoulders come in different shapes and sizes. Make sure the one you buy will fit into your pot with enough room for the celeriac.

1 bone-in pork shoulder roast, about 4½ pounds (2 kg), skin removed
Kosher salt and freshly ground black pepper
2 tablespoons olive oil
3 oranges
½ cup (125 ml) Campari
3 thyme sprigs
2 garlic cloves
1 celeriac (celery root)
2 teaspoons arrowroot

1. Preheat the oven to 325°F (160°C). Pat the pork dry and season well with salt and pepper. In a large Dutch oven or flameproof casserole, heat the olive oil. Brown the pork on all sides, starting with the fat side. Transfer the pork to a plate and discard the fat from the pot; set the pot aside.

2. Using a vegetable peeler, remove the zest in long strips from 1 orange. Halve the oranges and squeeze 1 cup (250 ml) juice from them. (You should have 1 orange half left; keep it so you can add its juice at the end of cooking.) Pour the juice into the pot and add the Campari, then add the zest, thyme, and garlic. Bring to a boil, deglazing the pot by scraping up the browned bits from the bottom.

3. Add the pork to the pot and cover with a damp piece of parchment paper and then the lid. Braise in the oven for 1 hour. Turn the pork over and braise for another 30 minutes.

4. Meanwhile, peel the celeriac and cut it into 2-inch (5-cm) chunks; keeping them in acidulated (lemon) water until ready to use.

5. Add the celeriac to the pork and cook for 30 minutes. Turn the pork and celeriac and braise for another hour, or until both the pork and celeriac are cooked. The pork should register 160°F (71°C) on an instant-read thermometer inserted into the center of the roast.

6. Transfer the meat and celeriac to a warmed serving platter and let the pork rest, loosely covered with aluminum foil, for 15 minutes.

7. Meanwhile, strain the sauce (set the pot aside), through a sieve into a glass measuring cup and let stand, briefly, then skim off the fat. Pour the sauce back into the pot, bring to a boil, and boil hard until it

is reduced to about ¾ cup (175 ml). Squeeze 2 tablespoons juice from the reserved the orange half, and mix the arrowroot with the orange juice.

8. Stir any juices from the pork into the sauce, then whisk in the arrowroot mixture and bring to a boil. Remove from the heat and check the seasoning. Carve the pork and serve with sauce.

Other Names for Pork Shoulder

The name Boston butt comes from the city of Boston, where this was a common cut. The term butt refers to the barrels or casks in which the pork was shipped. Picnic shoulder is a reference to the popularity of this cut when smoked. It made a small, cheaper ham that was easily transported and popular with picnickers early in the twentieth century.

Rack of Pork with Coffee Sauce

Rack of pork (also called a bone-in loin of pork) can simply be roasted with a rub of herbs and a coating of mustard, but it also benefits from brining it beforehand. I had seen several recipes for veal with coffee sauce and thought that it would complement pork even better. The coffee gives a subtle undertone to the meat and depth and edge to the sauce. Use a full-flavored coffee, but not espresso, which is too strong and can be bitter. The sauce could also be served with panfried pork chops or pot-roasted pork shoulder.

One 6-rib rack of pork about 3¼ pounds (1.5 kg)
Brine for pork (page 57)
Freshly ground black pepper
2 tablespoons Dijon mustard
1 tablespoon chopped rosemary
1 cup (250 ml) brewed coffee
1 tablespoon dark rum
½ cup (125 ml) Pork Stock (page 58) or Poultry Stock (page 130)
¼ cup (60 ml) heavy (35%) whipping cream
1 tablespoon brown sugar
Kosher salt
1 teaspoon cornstarch, optional

1. In a large container, submerge the pork bone ends up in the brine (don't worry if the bones are not completely covered) and refrigerate for 2 days.

2. One hour before cooking, remove the meat from the brine, and pat dry, brushing off any herbs or spices. Preheat the oven to 400° F (200° C).

3. Season the pork with pepper, then spread the fat side of the meat with the mustard and sprinkle on the chopped rosemary. Put the pork bone side down in a roasting pan. Roast for 15 minutes, then reduce the oven temperature to 325°F (160°C). Roast for another 1½ to 2 hours, or until an instant-read thermometer inserted in the center of the roast, away from the bone, registers 150°F (65°C). Transfer the roast to warm platter and let sit, loosely covered with aluminum foil, for 10 minutes.

4. Pour off any fat in the roasting pan, add the coffee, and bring to a boil, deglazing the pan by scraping up the browned bits from the bottom. Boil to reduce by one-quarter, then strain through a fine sieve into a saucepan.

5. Add the rum, stock, cream, and sugar and boil until slightly thickened. Check the seasoning, adding salt and pepper if necessary. If you want a thicker sauce, mix the cornstarch with 1 tablespoon cold water, whisk into hot sauce, bring to a boil, and simmer for 2 minutes.

6. Slice the rack between the bones into chops and serve with the sauce.

Crown Roast of Pork

A crown roast of pork is the perfect centerpiece for a special occasion. It always elicits oohs and aahs when presented at the table, and it is an ideal roast to serve that way because it is so easy to carve. You do have to invite a good crowd, because the smallest crown roast has 14 ribs; smaller pork racks can't be shaped into a crown. If there is any left over, though, both the pork and stuffing are delicious cold the next day. Start this recipe three days in advance so that you can brine the roast, which will then be much juicer. After the advance preparation, the roast essentially cooks itself, leaving the cook free to enjoy the celebration.

1 crown roast of pork (14 to 16 ribs), 7 to 8½ pounds (3.15 to 3.8 kg)
Brine for Pork (page 57)
16 pitted prunes, diced
16 dried apricots, quartered
2 cups (500 ml) freshly squeezed orange juice
2 tablespoons (30 g) unsalted butter
1 onion, finely diced
2 celery stalks, thinly sliced
1 tablespoon finely grated fresh ginger
3 garlic cloves, finely diced
1½ pounds (675 g) ground pork
1 cup (120 g) pecans, toasted and chopped
1 cup (80 g) fresh bread crumbs
1 tablespoon kosher salt
Freshly ground black pepper
1 cup (250 ml) Pork Stock (page 58) or strained Court Bouillon (page 60)
1 tablespoon honey
1 tablespoon cornstarch

1. Submerge the pork roast in the brine in a very large nonreactive container. (With a crown roast, all the weight is at the bottom, so it doesn't usually need to be weighted down; don't worry if the bones rise up out of the liquid.) Cover and refrigerate for 3 days. Eight hours before you will roast the pork, mix the prunes and apricots in 1 cup (250 ml) of the orange juice and set aside to soak.

2. One hour before cooking the pork, remove it from the brine and pat dry, brushing off any herbs or spices. Set aside on a platter. Preheat the oven to 400°F (200°C).

3. Melt the butter in a large frying pan over medium heat. Add the onion and celery and cook until soft, 5 to 6 minutes. Add the ginger and garlic and cook for 2 minutes, stirring occasionally. Transfer to a large bowl and allow to cool.

4. Add the ground pork, pecans, bread crumbs, and soaked fruit with liquid to the onion mixture. Add 2 teaspoons of the salt and season with pepper, then mix well. Test the seasoning of the stuffing by frying a spoonful of it in a small frying pan. Correct the seasoning if necessary.

5. Season the pork roast with the remaining salt and pepper. Place a rack in a large roasting pan, then put a square of aluminum foil in the center of the rack. Place the roast on top of the foil (the foil will prevent the stuffing from falling out). Pack the stuffing into the center of the roast, mounding it slightly. You will have some extra stuffing, to be cooked in a separate dish during the last hour with the roast; keep the remaining stuffing refrigerated until then. Cover the tips of the bones with a band of aluminum foil to prevent them from burning and place a piece of aluminum foil over the stuffing. Pour about 1 cup (250 ml) water, or enough to cover the bottom of the pan, into the roasting pan.

6. Roast the pork for 15 minutes, then reduce the oven temperature to 325°F (160°C). Continue to roast for 3½ to 3¾ hours (depending on the size of the roast), or until the internal temperature of the pork reaches 150°F (65°C) on an instant-read thermometer. Check the roast every so often to make sure there is still some water covering the bottom of the pan, and add more if necessary.

7. An hour before you estimate that the pork will be ready, put the remaining stuffing in a shallow baking dish, cover with aluminum foil, and place in the oven.

8. When the pork and the stuffing are cooked, remove them from the oven. Transfer the roast to a warm platter and let it to rest for 15 minutes, loosely covered with aluminum foil. During this time, the internal temperature of the pork should rise to 155°F (68°C). Keep the extra stuffing warm.

9. Pour the liquid from the roasting pan into a glass measuring cup (set the pan aside). Let stand briefly, and skim off the fat. You should have about 1 cup (250 ml) liquid; if necessary, make up the difference with additional stock, orange juice, or water. Add this liquid to the roasting pan, along with with the pork stock and the remaining 1 cup (250 ml) orange juice. Bring to a boil, deglazing the pan by scraping up the browned bits from the bottom. Whisk in the honey, then lower the heat. Mix the cornstarch with 1 tablespoon cold water and whisk into the sauce. Return to a boil, whisking, until the sauce thickens slightly. Season with salt and pepper, then strain through a sieve and keep warm.

10. Remove the foil and string from the pork. Carve the roast into individual chops, and serve with the stuffing and sauce.

Carving Pork Loin and Crown Roasts

As your butcher will have removed the chine, or backbone, bone-in loin roasts

and crown roasts simply need to be sliced down between the bones.

Chinese-Style Spareribs

My childhood friend Melinda and I attended the same school as our mothers had. I remember going to the restaurant her mother owned, one of the finest Chinese restaurants in Melbourne, complete with chefs from Hong Kong. There I learned about shark's fin soup, jellyfish, and other delights. When I asked Melinda for a sparerib recipe, she suggested this one. Now living in Frankfurt, Germany, she likes to return to her roots by preparing a Chinese dinner for friends. Melinda makes this dish ahead of time so she can remove the fat and have one dish already prepared; it reheats beautifully. I couldn't resist adding the sliced green onions. Have the butcher cut the ribs for you.

1 rack spareribs, about 2¼ pounds (1 kg), cut crosswise in half through the bones and papery membrane removed (see page 73)

2 tablespoons vegetable oil

6 garlic cloves, sliced

¼ cup (60 ml) fermented black beans, coarsely chopped

⅓ cup (75 ml) julienned fresh ginger

1 chile pepper, such as Serrano, seeded and finely chopped

1½ cups (375 ml) Pork Stock (page 58)

2 tablespoons light soy sauce

2 teaspoons sugar

4 green onions, sliced in ½-inch (1-cm) lengths

1. Cut the racks into individual ribs. In a Dutch oven or flameproof casserole, heat the oil over medium heat. Add the ribs, in batches, and brown well. Remove the ribs as they brown and drain on paper towels.

2. Discard the fat from the pot, add the garlic, beans, ginger, and chile, and cook, stirring, until fragrant, about 30 seconds. Stir in the stock, soy sauce, and sugar and bring to a boil, scraping up the browned bits from the bottom of the pot. Add the ribs, and reduce the heat to a simmer. Cover and cook for 1½ hours, or until the ribs are tender, turning them from time to time.

3. Transfer the ribs to a plate, and strain the sauce through a sieve into a glass measuring cup; reserve the garlic and other flavorings in the sieve. Let the sauce stand so the fat can rise to the top of the liquid. (At this point, the ribs, the flavorings in the sieve, and the sauce can be cooled, covered, and refrigerated, separately, overnight. Remove the fat from the chilled sauce before proceeding.)

4. Return the garlic, beans, ginger, and chile to the pot. Remove the fat from the sauce, then pour the sauce into the pot and bring to a boil. Add the ribs and cook, turning the ribs until the sauce reduces and glazes the ribs. Stir in the green onions and serve.

Maple Tomato Glazed Ribs

Everybody has a favorite glaze for ribs. Some like it sweet and sticky, others like hot and spicy. I like both, and this recipe mixes sweet and hot. Increase the spiciness by adding more chipotle pepper and adobo sauce, if you wish. I've used back ribs but you could use spareribs or country style if you prefer.

3 racks of pork back ribs, about 3 pounds (1.35 kg)
Kosher salt and freshly ground black pepper
2 tablespoons vegetable oil
2 medium onions, diced
3 garlic cloves, finely diced
One 28-ounce (796 ml) can whole tomatoes
1 chipotle pepper, packed in adobo, seeded and finely diced, plus 2 teaspoons adobo sauce
2 teaspoons tomato paste
½ cup (125 ml) maple syrup

1. Preheat the oven to 325°F (160°C). Remove the papery membrane from the bone side of the ribs (see below). Place the ribs in a single layer bone side down, on a rack in a roasting pan (use two pans if necessary). Season the meat side with salt and pepper, then add 2 cups (500 ml) water to the pan and cover with aluminum foil. Cook for 45 minutes to 1 hour, or until the ribs are tender.

2. Meanwhile heat the oil in a large saucepan over medium heat. Add the onions and cook over medium heat until they begin to color, about 5 minutes. Add the garlic, tomatoes with their juice, chipotle pepper and sauce, and tomato paste and bring to a boil, stirring to scrape the bottom of the pan. Reduce the heat so the sauce bubbles gently and cook, uncovered, for 30 minutes.

3. Remove the sauce from the heat and stir in the maple syrup. Puree in a blender until smooth.

4. Remove the ribs from the oven. Increase the oven temperature to 400°F (200°C). Transfer the ribs to one or two baking sheets lined with aluminum foil and brush with the glaze. Bake for another 10 to 15 minutes, brushing with the glaze. You could also glaze the ribs on a hot grill.

Variation

○ Try the Mustard Oregano Glaze (page 111) on your pork ribs. Or use this glaze on lamb ribs (page 110).

TIP There is a papery membrane on the bone side of pork ribs that should be removed before cooking. Using a small sharp knife, detach the membrane from the bone at one end of the rack. Grab the loose piece of membrane with a dish cloth and pull it off.

Roast Leg of Pork with Crackling

When I was growing up, after church on Sunday, we always had a roast of some sort with all the trimmings, presented and carved at the table. My favorite was roast leg of pork with crackling. This is my Aunty Pat's specialty, and she still makes it every Christmas, though she serves it at room temperature, more appropriate for the weather at that time of year in Australia. It is good hot or cold, but keeping the crackling crisp is more of a challenge when serving it cold.

Order the pork in advance, and ask the butcher to leave the skin on the rounded (top) side of the leg. The skin wraps right around the leg, but the underside will never crisp; have him remove that piece, or do it yourself—it's not difficult. For the skin to crisp, it must be scored. Your butcher will no doubt do this, but I find that I need to go over it again. I use a small very sharp knife (a scalpel is great) sharp enough to pierce the tough skin and small enough not to pierce the meat under the skin and fat. After the skin has been scored, let the roast sit, uncovered, skin side up in the refrigerator for a day before you roast it. Letting the skin dry out will help it to crisp up.

½ leg of pork, 8 to 10 pounds (3.6 to 4.5 kg) (see headnote)
Fine sea salt and freshly ground black pepper
Olive oil
2 Golden Delicious apples, peeled, cored, and thinly sliced
1 tablespoon brandy or Calvados
2 cups (500 ml) apple cider
1 cup (250 ml) Pork Stock (page 58)
1 tablespoon cornstarch

1. One hour before cooking, remove the pork from the refrigerator.

2. Preheat the oven to 450°F (220°C).

3. Season the meat side of the pork with sea salt and pepper. Dry the skin with a paper towel, then rub it with the oil and sprinkle generously with sea salt. Place the pork on a rack in a roasting pan. Add enough water to the pan to come almost to the bottom of the pork. Roast for 45 minutes.

4. Reduce the oven temperature to 325°F (160°C) and continue to roast for 3½ to 4 hours, or until the internal temperature reaches 155°F (68°C) on an instant-read thermometer. As the water in the pan evaporates, replace it with hot water, making sure that there is always enough to cover the bottom of the pan.

5. Meanwhile, place the apple slices and brandy in a small saucepan, add 2 tablespoons water, cover, and cook over low heat, stirring from time to time, until the apples are very soft. Remove from the heat and season with salt and pepper. Transfer to a serving dish, cover, and set aside. (This can be done up to a day ahead.)

6. Remove the roast from the oven and transfer it to a large warmed platter. Remove the cracking from the roast and set aside. Cover the roast loosely within aluminum foil and allow it to rest for 15 minutes; during this time, the internal temperature will rise to 160°F (71°C). Pour the pan juices into a glass measuring cup or small bowl and allow to settle, then skim off the fat (set the pan aside).

7. Sometimes the crackling is just not crispy enough. If that is the case, don't worry: Turn up the oven to 450°F (220°C) and cut the skin into 2 to 3 pieces. Place the pieces on a baking sheet and put them in the oven to crisp up while you make the sauce and carve the roast. You can also place them under the broiler to crisp. With this method, the skin puffs and curls, but you must watch carefully so it doesn't burn.

8. Return the roasting pan to the heat, add the cider, and bring to a boil, deglazing the pan by scraping up the browned bits from the bottom. Boil until the cider is reduced by half, then pour in the skimmed pan juices and the stock. Mix the cornstarch with 1 tablespoon cold water and whisk into the sauce. Return to a boil and boil, stirring, until the sauce thickens slightly. Remove from the heat.

9. Carve the leg, cut up the crackling, and serve with the apple puree. Pass the gravy separately.

TIPS You can also use this method to roast a bone-in pork loin with skin. It will cook faster and you'll need less of a crowd.

If you want to eat the crackling cold and crunchy, do not cover it as it cools.

Carving a Leg of Pork or a Whole Ham

To carve a cooked ham or pork leg: *First remove the skin if necessary. Cut off several slices from the less meaty underside of the ham to provide a flat base. Set the ham on this base, with the bone facing away from you. Make a vertical cut at the shank end straight to the bone. Then make a second cut behind this one on an angle and remove the wedge of meat.*

Now cut thin slices, on the angle, away from the shank, down through to the bone.

Run the knife along the bone to free the slices.

If you have half a leg the carving depends on which half it is.

For the shank end: *Remove the meatier side whole by cutting parallel to the bone. Place it skin or fat side up and cut into slices. Remove the bone from the remaining roast, turn rounded side up, and slice.*

The butt end is more complex: *Place it flat side down and cut down the length of the bone to remove the meatiest section. Then slice this section across the grain into slices. Stand the remaining piece bone away from you and, keeping the knife parallel to the board, cut slices across the meat down to the bone.*

Glazed Ham

Because a glazed baked ham is best served at room temperature, it is the perfect do-ahead dish for a large crowd. A whole ham can weigh from 10 to 20 pounds (4.5 to 9 kg) and so will feed twenty with plenty of leftovers. For most families, half a bone-in ham will do. The shank end will be easier to carve, but the sirloin end is meatier. The ham may be partially or fully cooked. Consult with your butcher to see if it should be soaked to remove excess salt before cooking.

Bake both partially and fully cooked hams at 325°F (160°C). Remove the skin from the ham and place the ham on a rack in a large roasting pan. Pour in enough Pork Stock (page 58), Court Bouillon (page 60), or water to cover the bottom of the pan. Baste the ham with this liquid every 30 minutes, and add more liquid as necessary, making sure the bottom of the pan is always covered.

A partially cooked ham will take 15 to 20 minutes per pound (450 g); a fully cooked ham needs 10 to 15 minutes per pound (450 g). The larger the ham, the less time needed per pound (450 g). An instant-read thermometer is a necessity, as cooking time also varies with the shape and thickness of the ham. The internal temperature should reach 155°F (68°C) for a partially cooked ham, 140°F (60°C) for a fully cooked ham. Once the ham reaches the proper temperature, remove it and increase the oven temperature to 425°F (220°C).

Classically the fat on a ham is scored in a crisscross pattern and a whole clove inserted in each diamond. The crisscross is not necessary, but it makes a nice presentation, with or without the cloves. A simpler method is to cut parallel diagonal lines in one direction only and forget about the cloves. Cutting the fat gives it interest, or more definition, and allows the glaze to penetrate to the meat, but you can leave it uncut.

Spoon or brush the ham with some of the glaze, then bake for 20 to 30 minutes, basting it with the glaze every 10 minutes. Watch closely to make sure the glaze doesn't burn. Once the ham is nicely glazed, remove it from the oven and leave to cool to room temperature before serving.

The glaze can be as simple as a dusting of confectioner's (icing) sugar or sifted brown sugar. Or try one of the following recipes, which make about ¾ cup (175 ml) glaze, enough for ½ a ham. The recipes can be doubled easily.

PORT GLAZE
¾ cup (175 ml) port
¼ cup (60 ml) honey
¼ packed cup (50 g) dark brown sugar
1 tablespoon freshly squeezed lemon juice
Pinch of ground cloves

ORANGE DIJON GLAZE
½ cup (125 ml) marmalade
3 tablespoons Dijon mustard
Grated zest of 1 orange
¼ cup (60 ml) freshly squeezed orange juice

APRICOT-MANGO GLAZE
½ cup (125 ml) apricot jam
¼ cup (60 ml) mango nectar
¼ cup (60 ml) freshly squeezed lime juice
2 tablespoons finely diced fresh ginger
1 teaspoon ground coriander

°°

1. To make any of the glazes, simply mix all the ingredients together in a small saucepan and bring to a boil, stirring constantly. Boil for 2 to 3 minutes, stirring. Cool slightly before using.

HAM

°°°°°°°

A ham is the cured back leg of a pig. The leg is first salted, with a dry rub or by brining, or both. Mass-produced hams are injected with a brining solution, because that works faster. Then the ham is air-dried or smoked and aged. The breed of the pig, its diet, the method of curing, the wood used for smoking, and the length of aging all influence the flavor of a ham.

Unsmoked hams are increasingly popular, especially the famous San Daniele ham from Parma, commonly called prosciutto. Another acclaimed ham hails from Spain—*Jamón Iberico*, or *pata negra*. This artisanal ham is produced in very small quantities from the Spanish Iberian black pig. The hoof is left on the ham during the curing, hence the name *pata negra*, which means black foot.

Many countries have their own famous hams. The English have York, the Chinese Yunnan, the Germans Westphalian, and the French Bayonne. In the United States, Virginia is renowned for its hams, especially Smithfield ham. These hams come from pigs fed on a diet of acorns. The hams are then cured over hickory and apple wood and aged for at least a year.

Some hams must be cooked before serving. Partially cooked and fully cooked hams need different handling—read the label carefully or check with your supplier. Very salty hams should be soaked before cooking.

Many hams need no further preparation and are eaten thinly sliced, accompanied by fresh fruit, like melon and figs, which complements their saltiness.

Pork Hock Cooked with Spiced Honey

ooooooooooooooooooooooooooooooooooooooooooooooooooooooooooooooooooooooooooooo { SERVES 2 } ooooooooooo

I shared this dish with my husband in a small Paris restaurant located in the fifteenth arrondissement. Admittedly, I was unenthusiastic at first. There were other dishes on the menu I would rather have eaten, but the pork hock and red cabbage was for two and my husband was keen to try it. So I conceded. When it arrived at the table complete with a large sprig of burning rosemary jutting out of it, I was convinced it was a bad choice. I was wrong. Both the succulent meat of the hock and the glaze were infused with star anise, coriander, and cinnamon. I ate with gusto and the flaming rosemary branch was quickly forgotten.

This recipe has several stages, so you do need to start a day or two in advance.

1 fresh pork hock, skin on, about 2¼ pounds (1 kg)
Spiced Salt (page 84)
Court Bouillon (page 60)
5 star anise, broken into pieces
7 green cardamom pods
4 teaspoons coriander seeds
1 long cinnamon stick, broken in half
½ cup (125 ml) acacia honey
2 teaspoons white wine vinegar

1. A day or two before you cook the hock, coat it in the spiced salt. Cover and refrigerate, turning it 2 or 3 times.

2. Preheat the oven to 275°F (135°C). Place the hock in a large pan and add the court bouillon, 3 of the star anise, 4 of the cardamom pods, 1 teaspoon of the coriander seeds, and half of the cinnamon stick. Bring to a boil, then remove from the heat.

3. Cover the hock with a damp piece of parchment paper and then the lid. Braise in the oven for 2 to 2 ½ hours, or until the meat is very tender. Remove the hock, drain it well, place on a plate. Keep the cooking liquid. (This can be done up to 2 days ahead. Refrigerate the hock and liquid separately.)

4. Toast the remaining 2 star anise, 3 cardamom pods, 1 tablespoon coriander seeds, and the cinnamon stick half in a heavy frying pan until aromatic, about 30 seconds. Crush them slightly using a mortar and pestle, then put them in a small saucepan, add the honey, and bring to a boil. Boil hard for 3 to 5 minutes, or until the froth turns dark and the honey begins to caramelize. Remove from the heat and *carefully* pour in 1 cup (250 ml) of the reserved cooking liquid. The honey will spit and sputter. Stir to mix, then reheat gently, stirring to dissolve the honey, and simmer for 10 minutes. Strain through a sieve; discard the spices. (The glaze can be made 2 days ahead.)

5. Preheat the oven to 350°F (175°C). Place the hock in a small roasting pan and add ½ cup (125 ml) of the cooking liquid. Cook for 15 minutes.

6. Increase the oven temperature to 400°F (200°C), pour half the strained honey mixture over the hock, and cook for 15 minutes, basting 2 or 3 times. Pour the remaining honey mixture over the hock and cook for another 15 minutes, basting every 5 minutes. Watch the glaze carefully, and add a little more cooking liquid to the roasting pan if it begins to burn.

7. Transfer the glazed hock to a serving dish and keep warm, loosely covered with aluminum foil. Add ½ cup (125 ml) more cooking liquid to the roasting pan (discard any remaining liquid) and bring to a boil, deglazing the pan and scraping up the browned bits from the bottom. Boil until reduced to ½ cup (125 ml), then add the vinegar.

8. Serve the hock with the sauce. The addition of a flaming rosemary branch is optional.

GREASY BONES

Early man didn't waste his bones. He extracted the fat left in bones to use for lighting and water-proofing. He also realized that where the carcass of a dead animal had rotted plants flourished. We are still using these bones by-products today. Blood and bone makes a popular and effective fertilizer, also called bone dust, and the fat rendered from bones is found in candles, cheap soap, and lubricating grease.

From the late seventeenth century on, the town of Cork in Ireland was an important center for the export of salted meats, especially pork and bacon. As a result, pork offal was readily available, cheap, and a local favorite. Children ate cooked pig's tails from newspaper cones while they played, and babies were calmed with pacifiers made from washed pig's knuckles. *Crubeens*, or *cruibins*, were a popular Saturday night pub food. *Crubeen* is the Irish term for pig's trotters, and the cooked feet, liberally sprinkled with salt, were the perfect accompaniment to a glass or two of stout. In Ireland, as elsewhere, though, increasing prosperity and fascination with new exotic foods led to the decline of local specialties. The popularity of pig's extremities has waned, benefiting only the publicans who now have fewer greasy beer glasses to wash.

Braised Hock with Fennel Three Ways

I've always liked licorice. A similar flavor is found in aniseed and fennel, and that flavor matches very well with pork. Here I have used it three times to layer the taste, first with fresh fennel, then with the aniseed-flavored pastis, and finally with fennel seeds. If your fennel bulb has fresh, leafy fronds keep them: Chop them and add to the sauce just before serving.

This sauce is also excellent with veal osso buco; replace the pork hock with pieces of veal shank and use veal instead of pork stock.

1 fresh pork hock, about 2¼ pounds (1 kg)
Kosher salt and freshly ground black pepper
2 tablespoons vegetable oil
1 small onion, diced
1 inner celery stalk with leaves, sliced
1 carrot, peeled and sliced
1 small leek, trimmed and sliced
½ small fennel bulb, diced
3 garlic cloves, minced
¼ cup (60 ml) pastis or Pernod
One 14-ounce (398-ml) can whole tomatoes
1 teaspoon fennel seeds, crushed
1 cup (250 ml) Pork Stock (page 58) or Court Bouillon (page 60)

1. Preheat the oven to 300°F (150°C). If the skin is still on the hock, remove it and keep it for stock. Pat the hock dry and season it with salt and pepper. In a Dutch oven or flameproof casserole, heat the oil over medium heat. Brown the hock on all sides, then transfer it to a plate. Add the onion, celery, carrot, leek, and fennel to the pot and cook, stirring, for 5 minutes or until the vegetables begin to brown.

2. Add the garlic and pastis and bring to a boil, deglazing the pot by scraping up the browned bits from the bottom. Add the tomatoes, with their juice, the fennel seeds, pork stock, and 1 teaspoon salt and bring to a boil. Remove from the heat and add the hock, along with any juices. Spoon some of the liquid over the top of the hock. Cover with a damp piece of parchment paper and then the lid and place in the oven. Cook for 2 to 2½ hours, turning the hock after 1½ hours, until the meat is very tender, almost falling off the bone.

3. Serve the hock with the braising liquid.

Smoked Hock with Black-Eyed Peas

Smoked hocks make great soups and are the perfect match with dried beans. One of the best known such dishes is Boston baked beans, with its sweet molasses-and-pork-flavored sauce. This recipe has its origins farther south in the United States. I like the way black-eyed peas look here, but any whole dried pea or bean will do. Collard greens may be more authentic, but I prefer the taste and texture of kale.

Smoked hocks vary in size and larger ones will need longer cooking before the peas are added. By the time the beans are cooked, the meat should be almost falling off the bone.

2 tablespoons vegetable oil
1 red onion, sliced
2 celery stalks, sliced
3 garlic cloves, halved
1 chile pepper, halved
1 bay leaf
3 large thyme sprigs
6 allspice berries, crushed
¼ teaspoon black peppercorns
1 small smoked ham hock, about 1½ pounds (675 g)
12 ounces (350 g) black-eyed peas, rinsed, soaked overnight in cold water, and drained
16 cups (4 l) loosely packed kale leaves, shredded (1 bunch; 1 pound 10 oz [750 g])
2 tomatoes, diced
2 tablespoons white wine vinegar
1½ teaspoons kosher salt

1. Preheat the oven to 350°F (175°C). In a Dutch oven or flameproof casserole, heat the oil over medium heat. Add the onion and cook for 5 minutes, or until it starts to soften. Add the celery and garlic and cook for 3 minutes. Stir in the chile pepper, bay leaf, thyme, allspice berries, and peppercorns.

2. Add the hock, then pour in 8 cups (2 l) water, bring to a boil, and skim off the foam. Cover the hock with a damp piece of parchment paper, then transfer to the oven and cook (without a lid) for 1 hour.

3. Add the peas and continue to cook, still covered only with the parchment paper, for 1½ hours, or until the peas are soft and the meat is tender. Using a slotted spoon or skimmer, transfer the hock and peas to a warm platter (discard the bay leaf and thyme stems) and keep warm, loosely covered with aluminum foil.

4. Bring the cooking liquid to a boil and boil to reduce slightly. Add the shredded kale and tomatoes and cook until the kale wilts. Add the vinegar and salt. Meanwhile, cut the meat off the hock in chunks.

5. Stir the meat and peas into the kale mixture, and check the seasoning. Serve in shallow soup bowls.

Pig's Feet

Pig's feet are cheap and delicious. I have to admit, though, that pig's feet are really my husband's dish. He eats them every time we are in Paris. I find them very rich and gelatinous. But this recipe, which began as an attempt to make the classic French dish of cooked, crumbed whole pig's feet for him, developed into a delicious variation that I really enjoy. It is less intimidating than the original and a great dish for those who are prepared to use their fingers to pick around the many small bones to find the meat. Various arguments and prejudices are aired about whether you should use front or back feet. The only difference I can really attest to is size, the back ones being bigger. Some proponents believe that there is more to eat on them, but others argue that the proportion of meat to bones is higher on the front feet. I prefer the front feet just because they aren't so big. They won't overwhelm novice feet eaters.

Wrapping the feet before cooking may seem a lot of work but it helps them keep their shape as they cook, and that makes them easier to coat with the bread crumbs.

4 pig's feet, split and cleaned
Spiced Salt (page 84)
Court Bouillon (page 60)
1 egg white
¼ teaspoon kosher salt
2 tablespoons Dijon mustard
1¼ cups (100 g) dry bread crumbs
4 cups (1 l) mixed bitter lettuces, such as curly endive, radicchio, Belgian endive, and arugula
Orange Mustard Dressing (recipe follows)

1. A day or two before you are going to cook the pig's feet, coat them in the spiced salt. Cover and refrigerate, turning them once or twice.

2. Preheat the oven to 275°F (135°C). Rinse the pig's feet under cold running water. Tie each of the two halves together by wrapping long strips of cheesecloth or cotton sheet around them.

3. Place the feet in a large deep Dutch oven or flameproof casserole and pour over the court bouillon. If there is not enough liquid to cover the feet, add up to 2 cups (500 ml) water. Place a piece of damp parchment paper over the top, then cover with the lid, transfer to the oven, and cook for 3 hours. At 1½ hours, check to make sure that the feet are still submerged; if not, add a little more water. After 3 hours, test the feet by inserting a skewer through the cloth into the meat. The feet are cooked when the skewer slides easily through and they feel very soft and tender. Remove them from the oven, uncover, and allow them to cool slightly in the cooking liquid. (If you leave the feet in the cooking liquid until they are completely cool, they will set in the resulting jelly.)

4. When they are cool enough to handle, remove the feet from the liquid and carefully unwrap them. Place them, skin side up in a shallow dish, removing the largest bone at the shank end—it will probably

just fall out. Cover with a piece of parchment paper, then a cutting board or stiff cardboard. Place a weight on top (two cans or a jar of pickles, for example) and refrigerate overnight. This helps compact the flesh. Be sure to strain the cooking liquid through a sieve, discarding the solids, and keep it for sauces, soup, or aspic.

5. The next day, carefully remove the feet from the dish and put on a plate. Owing to their gelatinous nature, they will be stuck to the dish; discard any excess jelly.

6. Preheat the oven to 450°F (230°C). Line a baking sheet with parchment paper and brush it lightly with vegetable oil. Whisk the egg white with the salt in a small bowl, then whisk in the Dijon mustard.

7. Using a pastry brush, coat the the feet with the mustard mixture, then dip them in the bread crumbs.

8. Place the feet skin side up on the baking sheet. Bake for 20 to 25 minutes, or until golden brown and heated through. You will need a spatula to remove the feet, which despite the oil and paper will probably still stick.

9. Toss the lettuces leaves with just enough dressing to coat. Serve with the pig's feet, using the remaining dressing as a sauce for them.

Variation

○ Replace the feet with cooked pig's tails (see page 86). The coated tails will take up to 35 minutes in the oven and must be turned halfway through cooking.

○ Orange Mustard Dressing

{MAKES 1 CUP (250 ML)} This dressing is good with the pig's feet, as the mustard and orange juice cut through their richness. There is enough to dress the salad and use as a sauce for the pig's feet. Of course you can also use it just as a salad dressing, on spicy greens.

1 heaping tablespoon Dijon mustard
2 tablespoons finely chopped shallots
Grated zest of 1 orange
⅓ cup (75 ml) freshly squeezed orange juice
½ cup (125 ml) extra virgin olive oil
2 tablespoons chopped flat-leaf parsley
Kosher salt and freshly ground black pepper

1. Place the mustard in a small bowl and add the shallots and zest. Whisk in the orange juice, then the oil. Stir in the parsley and season with salt and pepper.

◦ Spiced Salt

{ MAKES ¼ CUP (35 G) } I use this mixture to season pig's feet and tails. You can brine them as well, but these cuts of pork have their own special unctuous quality and lots of fat so are never dry. Store the salt mixture in a glass jar and use it also as a rub on pork roasts or in place of kosher salt in pork recipes.

Quartre-épices is a French seasoning mix that varies according to the whim of the producer. Commonly it is a mix of white pepper, nutmeg, cloves, and ginger, but cinnamon and allspice may be included. While it does not have the same flavor, ground allspice can be substituted.

¼ cup (35 g) kosher salt
1 teaspoon *quatre-épices* or ground allspice

Mix the salt and spices well. Store in a tightly sealed jar.

BONES, BUTTONS AND BEADS

°°°

The word *fibula* means pin in Latin and it's easy to see why. The pig's fibula is an ideal shape for a pin, with its natural head and tapering form. Before buttons became commonplace in medieval times, pins were one of the principal ways of securing clothing. Most were just simple straight pins, but some had a hole cut into the head of the pin through which a tie could be looped. Archaeologists have unearthed numerous early Christian and Viking pins. A select few are intricately carved or covered in gold leaf. These pins were not mere clothing fasteners but were worn as jewelry for special occasions.

Different bones are easily fashioned into useful items without much work. Smaller animal scapulas, or shoulder blades, made good utensils for scooping flour or grain. Long thin scoops, rather like a very large marrow spoon, could be made from the metacarpals of sheep, and perhaps these scoops were used to core apples or to sample cheese to test its ripeness. Hollow bones can be cut into lengths and threaded together. The American Indians made necklaces by stringing together small pieces of bird leg bones or individual salmon vertebrae.

More complex exploitations of bone developed and flourished later. A beautiful early example, dating from 700 A.D., is the Franks Casket, a whalebone box that is a masterpiece of bone carving. (It is named after the man who presented it to the British Museum, not the unknown artist who carved it.) Bone is durable and readily available. It can be carved by anyone, from skilled Italian craftsmen to prisoners of war. The Embriachi family was famous during the Italian renaissance for their exquisitely carved and inlaid bone jewelry boxes. Prisoners of the Revolutionary and Napoleonic Wars, held by the British, whiled away their incarceration by carving bone. Many of these soldiers had learned their skills as comb makers in Europe or as scrimshanders on whaling ships. With bones scrounged from the prison kitchens, they made toys, boxes, trinkets, and intricately detailed model ships, which they could sell or trade.

To return to more practical purposes, more than three hundred thousand perforated bone strips were found in the German town of Constance, dating from the late thirteenth to the early sixteenth centuries, remnants from bone button and bead manufacture. Along with pins, clothes were fastened with leather knots and loops, and these knots were often reinforced with bone disks. Eventually bone buttons replaced the disks and knots. However, the most important boost to the bone manufacturing industry was the expansion of the Holy Roman Empire, which resulted in increased demand for rosaries. Traditional rosaries were made from glass, amber, precious stones, or metal, but these were expensive and out of reach of the general population. Bone rosaries provided an affordable alternative.

The working of bone was an important industry during the Renaissance, and bones were crafted into everyday items from combs to spoons, spectacle frames, tweezers, and toothpicks. Military applications were not overlooked, with scabbards, bow splints, and hilts or handles for knives and swords all made from bone.

While other materials, especially plastic, have mostly supplanted bone today, it is still carved and is a common replacement for ivory.

Pig's Tails Two Ways

Pig's tails are a different challenge from feet. I actually like them better, as there is more meat and they are less gelatinous. There is a good amount of fat where the tail joins the spine and this should be trimmed. Pig's tails come in various lengths (and they are not curly). Unlike the feet, tails don't need any wrapping before cooking or pressing, as they hold their shape well.

4 pig's tails, 8 to 10 ounces each (250 to 300 g)
Spiced Salt (page 84)
Court Bouillon (page 60)

ooooooooooooooooooooooooooooooooooooooooooooooooooooooooooooooooooooooooooooooooooooooooooooooooooo

1. A day or two before you will cook the tails, coat them in the spiced salt. Cover and refrigerate, turning once or twice.

2. Preheat the oven to 275°F (135°C). Rinse the pig's tails under cold running water and place them in a large deep pan or Dutch oven. Pour over the court bouillon; if there is not enough liquid to cover the tails, add up to 2 cups (500 ml) water.

3. Cover with a piece of damp parchment paper, then the lid, and transfer to the oven. Cook for 2 to 2½ hours, or until the tails can be easily pierced with a skewer. Leave them in the stock until cool enough to handle.

4. If not using right away, carefully transfer the tails to a dish. Cover and refrigerate for up to 2 days. Be sure to strain the cooking liquid through a sieve, discarding the solids, and keep it for sauces or soup.

○ Pig's Tails with Ginger, Soy, and Garlic

{ S E R V E S 4 A S A N A P P E T I Z E R } Before you embark on this recipe, you really should buy a metal splatter screen if you don't have one. Make sure it is all metal, so it can go in the oven. It's not essential, but it will protect you and your oven from exploding pig's tails. As there is always some moisture left in the tails, they like to splutter and burst in the hot oven. This possibility is greatly reduced by leaving them whole and covering them with the screen. Place the screen over the fat end of the tails. (Remember that the handle of the screen *will be very hot*, so use an oven mitt to take it off the pan— and put it out of reach once you have cooked the tails.)

The ginger helps cut the richness of the pig's tails. Even so, one per person is enough.

4 cooked pig's tails
2 tablespoons vegetable oil
4 large garlic cloves, thinly sliced
⅔ cup (150 ml) julienned fresh ginger
¼ cup (60 ml) rice wine vinegar
½ cup (125 ml) light soy sauce

2 tablespoons sugar
1 teaspoon cornstarch
8 green onions, trimmed and sliced

1. Preheat the oven to 425°F (220°C). Lightly brush a baking dish with oil and add the pig's tails. If they are long cut them into two and position the thick fat sections together in the dish. If your tails have a lot of fat, trim some of it off.

2. Cover the tails with a splatter screen, if you have one, and bake for 15 minutes.

3. While the tails are cooking, heat the oil in a large frying pan over medium heat. Add the garlic and ginger and cook until they begin to stick to the pan. Pour in the vinegar and 1 cup (250 ml) water and bring to a boil, stirring to deglaze the pan by scraping the browned bits from the bottom. Add the soy sauce and sugar, cover, and simmer for 3 to 4 minutes, or until the garlic softens. Remove from the heat, uncover, and set aside.

4. After 15 minutes, *carefully* turn the pig's tails and cook for another 10 to 15 minutes. They should be crispy, dark, but not burnt. When the tails are cooked, drain them on paper towels, then chop into small pieces.

5. Add the tails to the sauce and reheat. Mix the cornstarch with 2 teaspoons cold water, stir into the sauce, and bring to a boil, stirring to thicken it slightly. Add the green onions, and serve very hot.

○ Pig's Tails with Lentils

{ SERVES 4 TO 6 AS AN APPETIZER } In this recipe, the lentils absorb fat and flavor from the tails. The cooking time will vary depending on the type of lentils. You want them cooked but not mushy.

4 cooked pig's tails (page 86)
1 to 2 tablespoons vegetable oil
1 small onion, diced
1 small carrot, peeled and diced
12 ounces (350 g) lentils, preferably French le Puy, rinsed
2 to 2½ cups (500 to 625 ml) reserved cooking liquid from the tails
1 bay leaf
Kosher salt and freshly ground black pepper

1. Cut the fat and skin from the back end of the tails and dice it. Cut the rest of the tails into 1-inch (2.5 cm) pieces.

2. Mix 1 tablespoon of the oil and the diced skin and fat in a medium saucepan, covered with a splatter screen, and cook over low heat until the pieces begin to pop; add the extra oil only if necessary, there should enough fat in the tails. Add the onion and carrot and cook for 5 minutes, again covered with the screen. Add the lentils and 2 cups (500 ml) of the cooking liquid and bring to a boil, then lower the heat and add the bay leaf and the pig's tails. Cover with a lid and simmer until the lentils are tender, 20 to 30 minutes, depending on the lentils.

3. Check the lentils regularly after 20 minutes, so as not to overcook them, and add the extra liquid only if necessary. The liquid should all be absorbed by the time the lentils are cooked.

4. Season the cooked lentils and tail with salt and pepper.

TIPS Tails and feet need special attention when it comes to cleaning. I have been lucky the ones I have bought have had very little hair. I removed any remaining bristles by singing them over a gas flame. Fergus Henderson, an authority on extremities, recommends using a disposable razor in his book, *The Whole Beast: Nose to Tail Eating*.

MUSICAL BONES

∞∞∞∞∞∞∞∞∞∞∞∞∞∞∞∞∞∞∞∞∞∞∞∞

The Latin word *tibia* means both shinbone and flute. Archaeologists have found many Roman flutes made from the tibias of sheep or large birds like cranes or geese. Although the tibia is ideal for making a flute, any long, straight hollow bone will work. American Indians made their flutes using both the long wing bones of birds and their leg bones. Others turned bones into into whistles and tuning pegs for lyres and harps. With little work, they could become percussion instruments. Simply struck, rattled together, or placed between the fingers and knocked against each other, like spoons, they were used to keep rhythm.

Metacarpal bones of pig and sheep with a hole drilled in the center have been recovered from many archaeological sites but their use is not as clear-cut. Some speculated that these bones were used as toggles to fasten clothing, but more recent research has convinced many scholars that they were "buzz bones": the bone was attached to a twisted cord and spun, causing it to make a humming or buzzing noise.

Bones don't just make music or other sounds, they are celebrated in many songs. The most famous bone song is the African American spiritual "Dem Bones, Dem Bones, Dem Dry Bones." With its origins in the book of Ezekiel, the song is about resurrection; it tells of the power of God and teaches basic human anatomy at the same time. Then there is the jazz classic "Saving the Bones for Henry Jones." Written by Danny Baker and Vernon Lee, it was recorded by Nat King Cole and Johnny Mercer. Henry Jones doesn't eat meat, but he's no vegetarian. The clever Mr. Jones prefers bones: "We'll save the bones for Henry Jones 'cause Henry don't eat no meat."

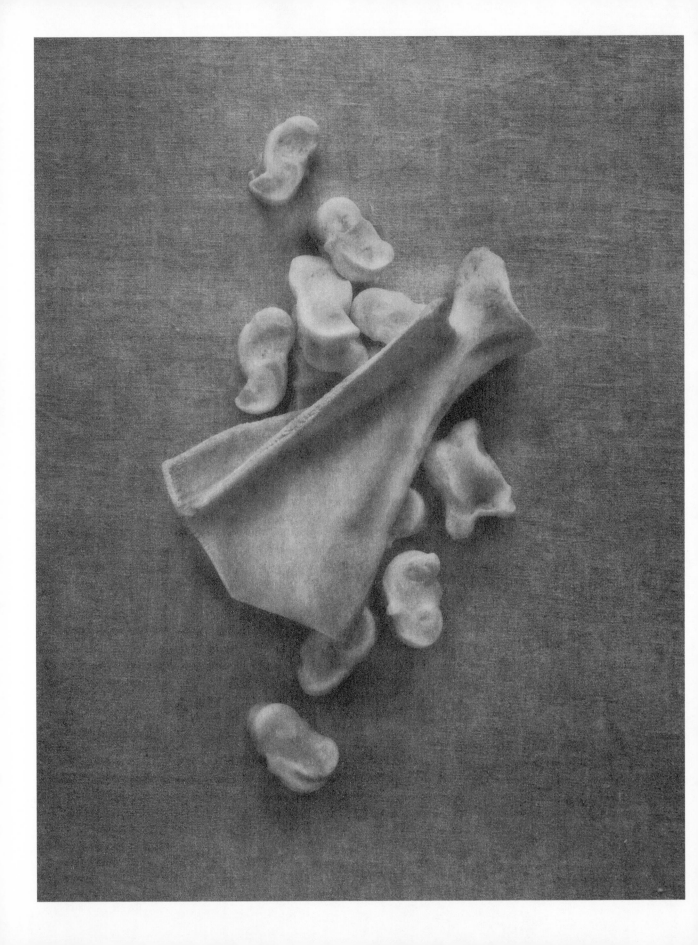

Lamb

Bones have never deterred lamb lovers, and rack and leg of lamb are perennial favorites. The problem is that lamb lovers are the minority in North America. Many people are scared away from lamb by misconceptions about its taste and smell. Why is this meat so popular worldwide but unloved in North America?

Generally, lambs are between three months and a year old (to be called lamb, the animal must be slaughtered before its first birthday). In North America, the lamb is often at the older end of this range. As lamb ages, its meat becomes more robust in taste, and it develops a distinctive smell. The most assertively flavored meat is mutton, which comes from animals over a year old, but it is not readily available. The best lamb is under six months old because its meat is tender and mild.

The animal's diet is also a major influence on its flavor. Lambs that graze on herbs or salt grasses produce a delicious meat infused with the aromas of these herbs. The mildest of all lamb is less than three months old and has been fed entirely on milk. The other main factor affecting lamb is its source. While smaller lambs are usually younger, and therefore milder, that is not always the case with imported lamb, which can be small but more highly flavored.

As there is such a wide choice in the lamb available, the best place to buy it is at a good butcher's, where he will know the age, source, and origin of the meat and be able to advise you. Whatever the lamb's provenance, you should look for finely grained meat that is pale to dark pink in color. The layer of fat should be smooth and white. Unlike other animal fats, lamb fat is not very tasty and can be quite unpleasant cold, so buy well-trimmed cuts. Lamb racks and chops do not need marbling to be tender—just a feathering of fat through the meat is sufficient. Braising cuts, such as shoulder chops and shanks, consist of several muscles and have seams of fat running through them that keep the meat moist and succulent during cooking.

The best news for the cook is that because lamb is a small animal, it often arrives whole at the butcher, which means there is a wide choice of cuts on the bone and that less-common cuts are easier to obtain. Be adventurous and think beyond legs, racks, and chops. Lamb shoulder can be tender enough to roast, making a great alternative to leg. Lamb shanks are more familiar, owing to their popularity on restaurant menus, but what about the breast ribs and neck? These cuts are full of flavor and simple to cook. Then there are the bones themselves. Lamb stock makes great soups and will add depth and flavor to any lamb dish or sauce.

Looking at the lamb's skeleton and familiarizing yourself with where the various cuts lie, will help you understand how to cook them.

The Front End

The front leg, with or without the shank (see "The Extremities"), is sold as the shoulder. It can be roasted or braised, depending on the age of the animal. Ask your butcher to remove the blade bone, which will make it easier to carve. Often the shank is removed, as well as several shoulder chops, reducing the size of this cut and making it square in shape. Chops cut from the shoulder are meaty but because they consist of several muscles, they vary in tenderness and are best braised.

The Middle

The leanest, most tender part of the animal, this is the source of the popular rack of lamb. Usually seven or eight ribs in size, the rack has the backbone or chine bone removed to make carving it easier. The ends of the rib bones are usually frenched (see page 108) for presentation. Two complete racks, preferably from the same animal, can be used to create either a guard of honor or a crown roast (see page 108). The rack can also be cut into individual rib chops.

As the ribs wrap around the animal to form its chest, they have more fat

To make no bones about it is to openly admit something without hesitation.

Boneset is a plant with white flowers that is used medicinally while a bone setter is someone who, while not qualified as a doctor, nonetheless mends broken bones.

Bones is a nickname often given to doctors of medicine. One of the most famous is the fictional Bones of the *Starship Enterprise,* Dr. Leonard McCoy.

In all cultures, bones and hard work are linked, especially when that work goes unrewarded, as in "to work one's fingers to the bones."

My German friend Frerk says "that's bone work," when describing washing pots and pans.

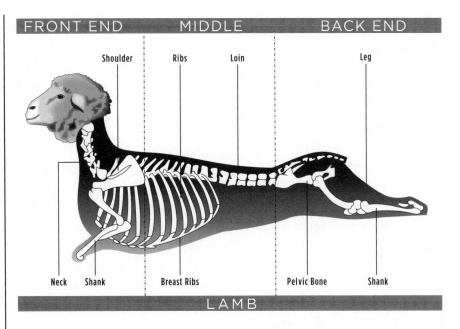

Shoulder   Ribs   Loin   Leg

Neck   Shank   Breast Ribs   Pelvic Bone   Shank

LAMB

There is a Tamil expression, "working until my bones were wasted."

The French say, "*tu vas y laisser tes os,*" meaning that you are taking a great physical risk doing something or you will work yourself to death.

The Japanese expression is "to work so hard you break your bones, but in vain."

However, as all our parents said, "Hard work breaks no bones."

and less meat. A rack of breast ribs has a tapering shape, as the ribs shorten toward the back legs. You can cook these like a rack of pork ribs or cut them into individual ribs to braise.

Toward the back leg, close to the backbone, is the loin. Here the bone divides the meat into two pieces—the loin and the tenderloin. Loin chops resemble very small T-bone steaks, with meat on both sides of the bone. If this section is butchered without splitting the backbone, the two joined loins are called the saddle. It can be roasted whole or cut into double lamb loin or English-cut chops. Ideally, any chops from the rib or loin should be at least 1 inch (2.5 cm) thick. They can be sautéed or grilled.

The Back End

After the feet and tail of the lamb are removed (see "The Extremities"), before the pelvic bone is removed from the leg, it may then be sold as a whole long leg. The whole leg can be divided into two cuts, the sirloin, or butt end, and the shank end. If the sirloin end is removed from the leg, the remaining cut is called a short leg. The sirloin end has a higher portion of meat to bone, but the shank end is leaner and easier to carve.

Bone-in steaks or chops cut from the leg are distinguished by the small round bone they contain. They should be at least 1 inch (2.5 cm) thick, and they are delicious grilled.

The Extremities

The most popular lamb extremities are the shanks. They are cut from the lower portion of the leg, most commonly the front leg. This is a tough part of the lamb, but when slowly braised, it becomes very tender and its abundant collagen yields a rich sauce. You can ask the butcher to cut the shanks into thick pieces to make lamb osso buco.

Often overlooked, lamb neck is also rich in collagen. It is sold whole or cut into pieces. Pieces are more practical and they can be cooked like shanks or used in stews.

There are many recipes for lamb's tails and feet in older cookery books. However, today most lambs have their tails docked and what's left is removed at the abattoir. At a good butcher's you can find lamb's ankles, which contain the metatarsal bones. (These are left on after slaughter to prevent the meat from shrinking up the leg and are used to suspend the carcass.) Add them to your stock—they will increase its gelatin content and give it a velvety texture. These are the bones are used for the game knucklebones (see page 117).

Lamb Cooking Temperatures

Use an instant-read thermometer to check for doneness. And remember that when the meat is resting, the temperature will continue to rise by up to 5°F (2°C). Lamb is juicier and more flavorful roasted rare or medium-rare. When braising, cook lamb until fork tender and almost falling off the bone.

Rare	135°F (57°C)
Medium-rare	140°F (60°C)
Medium	150°F (65°C)
Medium-well	155°F (68°C)

Portion Size

Imported lamb can be smaller than domestic, so they yield smaller cuts. About 12 ounces (350 g) of meat on the bone per person is a good guide. With fattier cuts like shoulder, though, you should increase the amounts per person.

Mutton and Goat

If you do come across mutton, try it in the more highly flavored braised dishes. Goat is becoming more available in our markets, and young goat makes an excellent substitute for lamb in any recipe. It is butchered like lamb so the cuts are identical but are leaner and smaller.

A bone ace is either a card game or the ace of diamonds.

Roll the bones, or to throw dice, especially in the game of craps.

Thou wons't my money too, with a pair of base bones.
—JOHN FLETCHER, *Rule of a Wife* (1624)

Bone turquoise or odontolite is a bright blue mineral formed from a fossil bone or tooth.

Bonewood, also called cheese wood, is a yellowish white wood from Australasia.

Lamb Stock

There is a widespread perception that lamb stock is greasy and strong, but while lamb stock may not be as versatile as veal or chicken, a good one makes great soups and adds depth to slow-cooked lamb dishes.

As with any other stock, the fat will rise to the surface as the stock cools. But lamb fat can remain quite soft, making it more difficult to remove. Leave the skin on the onion; it adds color to the stock.

4½ pounds (2 kg) lamb bones and trimmings, cut into 2- to 3-inch (5- to 7.5-cm) pieces
1 large onion, unpeeled, cut into wedges
1 large carrot, sliced
2 celery stalks, sliced
1 leek, trimmed and quartered lengthwise
1 garlic head, separated into cloves
3 flat-leaf parsley stems
1 bay leaf
1 large thyme sprig
1 rosemary sprig
¼ teaspoon black peppercorns
Kosher salt, optional

1. Rinse the bones well under cold running water and place them in a large stockpot, along with the onion, carrot, celery, leek, garlic, parsley, bay leaf, thyme, and rosemary. Pour in enough cold water to cover the bones, about 12 cups (3 l), and bring slowly to a boil. As soon as the stock begins to boil reduce the heat so that it simmers. Using a soup ladle, skim off any scum that has risen to the surface (rotate its bowl on the surface of the stock to make ripples: these will carry the scum to the edges of the pot and you can then use the ladle to lift it off). Add the peppercorns and simmer, uncovered, for 5 hours, skimming from time to time.

2. Strain the stock through a sieve into a large bowl. Discard the debris left in the sieve, and cool the stock quickly by placing the bowl in a larger bowl or sink filled with ice water; stir occasionally as it cools. When you taste this stock, you will notice that something is missing—the salt. Once you add it, the flavor will sparkle. But it was deliberately left out so that you can reduce the stock, if desired, without any fear that it will become too salty. If you are not reducing the stock (see page 96), add about 1 teaspoon salt.

3. Refrigerate the stock for 6 hours, or overnight, to allow the fat to rise to the top of the stock and the debris to sink to the bottom. Remove the fat before using (and discard the debris at the bottom of the bowl). Divide into 1-cup (250-ml) quantities and refrigerate for up to 3 days or freeze for up to 6 months.

Concentrated Lamb Stock

If your freezer space is tight, reduce your stock following the method for Concentrated Brown Stock (page 14).

6 cups (1.5 l) unsalted Lamb Stock (page 95)
Kosher salt

The reduced stock will become syrupy and turn the color of freshly pressed apple cider.

Lamb and Barley Soup

This soup started as a Scotch broth, an homage to my roots, but then it took on a life of its own. Once you have the lamb stock and barley, the choice of vegetables is up to you and the time of year. Carrots, rutabaga, and spinach are good in the winter, while green peas, favas, and asparagus tips are perfect in the spring. Cooking the barley separately means it doesn't drink up all your stock.

¼ cup (45 g) pearl barley
Kosher salt
3 cups (750 ml) Lamb Stock (page 95)
1 medium turnip, peeled and diced
1 leek, trimmed and sliced
1 cup (250 ml) finely shredded Savoy cabbage
1 medium tomato, diced
1 teaspoon kosher salt
1 tablespoon thyme leaves
1 teaspoon freshly squeezed lemon juice
Freshly ground black pepper

1. Rinse the barley, then place it in a small saucepan with 1 cup (250 ml) water and a pinch of salt. Bring to a boil, reduce the heat, and simmer, covered, for 30 to 35 minutes, until the barley is tender but firm. Remove the saucepan from heat and set aside, covered. As it stands, the barley will absorb the remaining water.

2. Pour the lamb stock into a large saucepan, add the turnip and leek, and bring to a simmer. Reduce the heat slightly and simmer gently, covered, until the turnip is cooked, about 10 minutes.

3. Stir in the cooked barley, cabbage, tomato, and salt and return to a boil; remove from the heat. Add the thyme, lemon juice, and black pepper to taste and serve.

Lamb and Jerusalem Artichoke Soup

Jerusalem artichokes may taste like artichoke, but they are really a relative of the sunflower. The explorer Samuel de Champlain ate them during his travels in Canada, and wrote home about their artichoke-like flavor, beginning the confusion. Why they were linked to Jerusalem is less clear. One suggestion is that it is an English corruption of the Italian word for sunflower, *girasole*. Today they are often called sunchokes and their earthy flavor matches well with lamb stock. Once you have the stock on hand in the freezer, soup is easy to make and you can often create something out of almost nothing: diced vegetables, some cooked rice or pasta. Fresh herbs are always a good addition, along with a little lemon juice, to highlight all the flavors.

2 tablespoons olive oil
1 cup (250 ml) diced fennel
1 cup (250 ml) peeled, diced Jerusalem artichokes
3 cups (750 ml) Lamb Stock (page 95)
1 cup (250 ml) fresh or frozen peas
2 teaspoons freshly squeezed lemon juice
A little freshly grated nutmeg
Kosher salt and freshly ground black pepper
¼ cup (60 ml) chopped chives

1. Heat the oil in a large saucepan over medium heat. Add the fennel and artichokes, and cook for about 5 minutes, or until lightly colored. Pour in the stock and bring to a boil, then reduce the heat and simmer, covered, for 5 minutes, or until the artichokes are tender.

2. Add the peas and simmer for 2 to 3 minutes longer, or until they are tender. Add the lemon juice, nutmeg, and salt and pepper to taste, then stir in the chives and serve.

Lamb Shoulder with Preserved Lemon and Dates

Preserved lemons are a staple in North African cuisines. Cured with salt, they develop a distinctive pickled taste and soft texture that is quite unlike fresh lemons. You can buy them in gourmet stores or Middle Eastern groceries. The lemon's acidity cuts the lamb's richness, while the dates add sweetness—and the whole dish has a beautiful golden hue from the saffron. Fresh dates are found in specialty markets, and are generally available all year, with the peak season being November to March.

1 lamb shoulder, square cut or with the shank (see "The Front End," page 92),
    about 4½ pounds (2 kg)
Kosher salt and freshly ground black pepper
2 tablespoons olive oil
2 medium onions, diced
3 garlic cloves, finely diced
1½ teaspoons paprika
1½ teaspoons ground ginger
½ teaspoon saffron threads
1 cinnamon stick
¼ cup (60 ml) chopped flat-leaf parsley
¼ cup (60 ml) chopped mint
1 preserved lemon
12 fresh dates, halved and pitted
½ cup (80 g) whole blanched almonds, lightly toasted
½ cup (125 ml) freshly squeezed lemon juice

1. If the shank is still attached to shoulder, make a cut around the end of the bone to release the tendons (or have the butcher do it).

2. Preheat the oven to 300°F (150°C). Pat the lamb dry and season with salt and pepper. In a large heavy roasting pan, heat the oil over medium-high heat. Add the lamb and brown on the fat side. (If the shank is still attached, there may be patches that won't brown; don't worry.) Turn the lamb and brown as well as you can on the bone side. Transfer the lamb to a platter and discard all but 1 tablespoon fat from the pan.

3. Add the onions and garlic to the pan and cook for 2 minutes. Blend the paprika, ginger, and saffron with 2 cups (500 ml) water, pour into the pan, and bring to a boil, deglazing the pan by scraping up the browned bits from the bottom. Remove from the heat and return the lamb, with any juices, to the pan, fat side down. Add the cinnamon stick and half the chopped parsley and mint.

4. Cover the lamb with a damp piece of parchment paper, and then aluminum foil, and transfer to the oven. Braise the lamb for 2½ hours, turning it halfway through. (The dish can be made ahead to this point. Refrigerate overnight, and remove the fat in the morning. You may need more than 30 to 45 minutes to fully cook the lamb.)

5. While the lamb is cooking, cut the preserved lemon into quarters. Remove the pulp and discard. Cut the peel into matchstick-sized pieces.

6. After the lamb has cooked for 2½ hours, add the lemon, dates, almonds, and lemon juice. Stir to mix, cover again with parchment paper and foil, and cook for another 30 to 45 minutes, or until the lamb is very tender.

7. Sprinkle the lamb with the remaining chopped herbs and check the seasoning, as preserved lemons vary in saltiness. Transfer the lamb to a warmed platter and carve into thick pieces. If you'd like, you can boil the sauce for 5 minutes to thicken it slightly.

SHOULDER POWER

ooooooooooooooooooooooooooooooo

Knucklebones were used for more than just games. It was believed that these bones had magical powers, and they were tossed to foretell the future or carried to prevent sciatica or cramp.

Lamb bones were also popular for divination and talismans, especially in Britain. A woman could rekindle the affection of an unfaithful husband or lover, it was said, with a knife and a sheep's shoulder bone. No, it didn't require a direct threat. She had only to repeat a certain verse and stab her knife into the sheep's scapula. The guilty party would be compelled, even against his will, to return to her.

Lamb Shoulder Ratatouille-Style

Lamb and ratatouille are often paired in the south of France. In this recipe, the shoulder is cooked to the halfway point before the vegetables are added. Cutting the vegetables into big chunks ensures that they won't disintegrate as they cook. The vegetables, especially the eggplant, soak up the flavors of the lamb, and the acid from the tomatoes tames the richness of the meat. There is a good amount of sauce for the vegetables and the meat. So serve with bread to get every last drop of it.

1 lamb shoulder, square cut or with the shank (see "The Front End," page 92),
   about 4½ pounds (2 kg)
6 Roma (plum) tomatoes
Kosher salt and freshly ground black pepper
2 tablespoons olive oil
2 onions, sliced
1 to 2 cups (250 to 500 ml) dry white wine
1 cup (250 m) Lamb Stock (page 95)
6 garlic cloves, peeled
3 large basil sprigs
4 red bell peppers
4 small eggplants, about 1 pound (450 g)
3 zucchini
1 cup (250 ml) packed basil leaves, shredded

1. If the shank is still attached to the shoulder, make a cut around the end of the shank bone to release the tendons (or have the butcher do it).

2. Core the tomatoes, then drop them into a saucepan of boiling water for 2 minutes. Transfer them to a bowl of ice water to cool, then peel the tomatoes and cut lengthwise in half. Remove the seeds, working over a sieve set over a bowl to catch the juices. Discard the seeds but keep the juice. Cut each tomato half into 4 equal pieces; set aside.

3. Preheat the oven to 300°F (150°C). Pat the lamb dry and season with salt and pepper. In a large heavy roasting pan, heat the oil over medium-high heat. Add the lamb and brown on the fat side. (If the shank is still attached, there may be patches that won't brown; don't worry.) Turn the lamb and brown as well as you can on the bone side. Transfer the lamb to a plate. Add the onions to the pan and cook, stirring, until they begin to brown, 5 to 7 minutes. Add enough wine to the strained tomato juice to make 2 cups (500 ml), then pour into the pan. Bring to a boil, deglazing the pan by scraping up the browned bits from the bottom.

4. Add the stock, garlic cloves, and basil sprigs, then return the lamb to the pan and bring to a simmer. Cover the lamb with a damp piece of parchment paper and then aluminum foil, and braise in the oven for 1½ hours.

5. While the lamb is cooking, broil or grill the peppers, turning frequently, until their skins are well blackened. Place them in a large bowl, cover with plastic wrap, and leave until they are cool enough to handle.

6. Cut the eggplants into large chunks, about 1 × 1½ inches (2.5 × 4 cm) and place in a colander. Sprinkle generously with salt, toss to coat, and let stand for 20 minutes.

7. Peel and seed the cooled peppers, working over a bowl to catch any juices. Cut them into large chunks about the same size as the tomatoes. Strain the liquid from the peppers through a sieve and reserve. Rinse the eggplant and pat dry.

8. After 1½ hours, remove the lamb from the oven and baste with the cooking liquid. Add the tomatoes, peppers, and eggplant, cover, and cook for another 1 hour, stirring halfway through.

9. Cut the zucchini into ½-inch (1-cm) slices. Increase the oven temperature to 400°F (200°C) and add the zucchini slices to the pan, stirring them into the vegetables. Cook, uncovered for 30 to 45 minutes, or until the lamb is golden brown and the lamb and vegetables are tender.

10. Transfer the lamb to a warmed serving platter. Skim off any fat from the sauce and vegetables and check the seasoning and stir in the basil leaves. Carve the lamb into thick slices, and serve accompanied by the vegetables and sauce.

Lancashire Hot Pot Revisited

When I saw the photograph of this recipe in a cookbook, I knew I just had to try it. There was a deep dish covered with a crust of golden potatoes. Piercing the crunchy topping were long, thin bones reaching skyward. As I researched the recipe, I discovered that the original dish used chops from Pennine sheep, a British breed known for its long rib bones. Older recipes for the dish often include oysters, then plentiful and cheap. I've omitted the oysters, as I don't like the idea of cooking oysters for two hours.

After several attempts, though, I gave up the idea of bones bursting through the potatoes. It didn't work with bones of regular length. I also switched to shoulder chops, which have more fat and flavor and are better suited to slow cooking. The French have a version of this recipe called Champvallon. It is named after a mistress of Louis XIV who won his favor by cooking him this dish.

4 medium turnips, peeled and sliced
5 to 6 tablespoons vegetable oil
3 onions, diced
4 medium carrots, peeled and diced
1 celery stalk with leaves, diced
1¼ cups (310 ml) Lamb Stock (page 95)
2 garlic cloves, finely diced
1 tablespoon rosemary leaves, chopped
1 bay leaf
Kosher salt and freshly ground black pepper
¼ cup (30 g) flour
8 lamb shoulder chops
1 tablespoon sweet vermouth
4 potatoes, peeled and sliced
1 tablespoon (15 g) unsalted butter for the foil

1. Arrange the turnips in the bottom of a baking dish large enough to hold the lamb chops in a single layer, overlapping them slightly. Set aside.

2. Heat 2 tablespoons of the oil in a large frying pan over medium heat. Add the onions and cook for 7 to 10 minutes, or until they soften and just begin to color. Add the carrots and celery, stir well and add ¼ cup (60 ml) of the stock. Cover the pan and cook for 5 minutes. Add the garlic, rosemary, and bay leaf, and season well with salt and pepper. Cover and cook for 5 minutes to soften the carrots slightly. Spoon the mixture over the sliced turnips. Wipe out the frying pan.

3. Preheat the oven to 325°F (160°C). Season the flour with salt and pepper. Pat the chops dry, then dredge them in the flour, shaking off any excess; keep the leftover flour. Heat another 2 tablespoons of the oil in the frying pan over medium-high heat, and brown the chops in batches quickly on each side, adding more oil as necessary. Place the chops on the bed of onions and carrots.

4. Add the reserved flour from the chops to the frying pan, off the heat, and whisk it into the fat. You will probably need to add more oil. There should be enough residual heat in the pan to cook the flour: continue to whisk until the flour and oil mixture becomes tan colored. If it does not, return the pan to low heat and whisk until the flour colors. Gradually whisk in the remaining 1 cup (250 ml) of stock, bring to a boil, and boil for 2 minutes. Season well with salt and pepper, and stir in the vermouth.

5. Pour the sauce over the chops. Top with the sliced potatoes, overlapping them slightly. Cover with buttered aluminum foil, butter side down. Place the dish on a baking sheet and bake for 1½ hours.

6. Remove the aluminum foil, increase the oven temperature to 400°F (200°C), and bake for 30 minutes longer, or until the potatoes are browned. Serve, making sure everyone gets 2 chops and vegetables.

ICE BONES

One of the more curious uses of bones was as ice skates. From the Bronze Age, bone skates were common throughout the world's colder regions. Crafted from the metacarpal and metatarsal bones of cattle, these bones were drilled at one or both ends so that they could be attached to a shoe or the skater's ankle. The skater did not skate as we do today. Rather, he balanced on his skates, keeping the thin edge of the bone flat against the ice, and he carried a pole clad in iron at one end to strengthen it. To move, he dug the pole into the ice and pushed to propel himself across a frozen lake. While not very graceful, it was a practical way to travel through a frozen landscape. Larger bones, like whale jawbones, served as sled runners so that goods could be transported across ice.

Lamb Roasted over Potatoes

For me, roast lamb is always meant leg of lamb, but shoulder is equally succulent, if a little fatty—don't overlook it. You can use either leg or a shoulder here. A shoulder will probably only feed four people because of the bones and fat, whereas a leg will feed six people. A long leg (see page 93) will have had the pelvic bone removed by the butcher, so make sure that he secures the meat with string to make a compact shape. It will take 20 to 30 minutes longer to roast.

This recipe takes advantage of the tasty lamb drippings to flavor a bed of potatoes.

1 bone-in shoulder or leg of lamb, 4 ½ to 5 pounds (2 to 2.5 kg)
3 large garlic cloves, cut into slivers
2 tablespoons olive oil
2 teaspoons dried oregano, preferably Greek oregano (see page 111)
6 large potatoes, peeled
Kosher salt and freshly ground black pepper

1. Trim any excess fat from the lamb; be sure to check the underside, especially if using shoulder. Leave a thin covering of fat. Using a small knife, make ½-inch (1-cm)-deep slits, at an angle, through the fat into the meat and insert a garlic sliver into each one. Drizzle the lamb with 1 tablespoon of the olive oil, then sprinkle with the dried oregano. Set on a platter and let stand at room temperature for 1 hour before roasting.

2. Preheat the oven to 450°F (230°C). Slice the potatoes ⅛ inch (3 mm) thick. Drizzle the remaining 1 tablespoon olive oil over the bottom of a roasting pan. Place the potatoes in the pan, overlapping slices if necessary, and season with salt and pepper.

3. Season the lamb with salt and pepper and place rounded or fat side down on top of the potatoes. Roast for 15 minutes, then lower the oven temperature to 350°F (175°C) and cook for 1 to 1¼ hours longer, or until the internal temperature registers 135°F (57°C) on an instant-read thermometer.

4. Transfer the roast to a warm platter and let it rest, loosely covered with aluminum foil, for 15 minutes; the temperature will rise to 140°F (60°C), or medium-rare. Increase the oven temperature to 450°F (230°C) and continue cooking the potatoes until they turn brown and crispy. Slice the lamb and serve with pan juices.

Variations

◦ Simply roast the lamb without the potatoes, and then make a sauce with the drippings. Discard the fat and add about 1 cup (250 ml) red wine, lamb stock, or a combination to the pan. Bring to a boil, deglazing the pan by scraping up the browned bits from the bottom, then strain and season with salt and pepper. Add fresh herbs or some pomegranate juice to the sauce to highlight the flavor, if desired.

∘ Serve the lamb with the anchovy-vinegar sauce (page 122). While the roast is resting, discard the fat from the pan, add the wine, and bring to a boil, deglazing the pan by scraping up the browned bits from the bottom. Add the anchovy-vinegar mixture and boil to reduce to a sauce. For anchovy lovers, add some chopped anchovies to the olive oil before roasting.

∘ Brush the lamb with the Mustard-Oregano Glaze (page 111) an hour before roasting. Then roast or use one of the lamb rack toppings (see variations, pages 107–108) on the roast.

Carving Lamb Leg or Shoulder

A leg of lamb can be carved like a ham (see page 75), but I prefer to carve it the following way: Turn the leg, rounded side up. Hold it firmly with a carving fork inserted into the shank end of the leg, and cut slices from the rounded side, parallel to bone. Once you reach the bone, turn the leg over and carve more slices parallel to the bone. Finally, carve slices from the shank end, again parallel to the bone.

The shoulder has part of the spine running down one side of it. From this, there are several rib bones on one side and small flat feather bones on the other. These are really not a problem, as the meat sits on top of them. The problem is the hidden blade bone. If you are going to roast the shoulder, ask your butcher to remove the blade bone. This will allow you to slice the meat from the fat side down to the ribs and spine, then you can free the slices by cutting along the bone. If the blade bone has not been removed, just slice the meat until you strike the bone, then free the slices by cutting them away from the bone. Once the blade bone is exposed, twist it out, and continue slicing to the ribs; you may also have to cut out pieces of fat as you carve. If the shoulder is braised, the blade bone is not a problem: the meat will lift easily from the bone and most of the fat will have melted away.

Olive-Crusted Lamb Racks

A rack of lamb is one of the easiest cuts to prepare. Low in fat and high in flavor, it is quick to cook. Perfect for an intimate dinner for two, and impressive enough for a fancy dinner party. (You can double or triple this recipe with no problem.) Buy good-quality olives for this recipe—that will probably mean they have pits. Pitting them is simple, just smash each one with the flat side of a knife, like a garlic clove, to loosen the pit, then remove it.

One 8-rib lamb rack, about 1½ pounds (625 g), well trimmed and frenched
⅓ cup (60 g) black olives, pitted
1 tablespoon rosemary leaves, chopped
2 garlic cloves
1 tablespoon Dijon mustard
Grated zest and juice of 1 lemon
Kosher salt and freshly ground black pepper
1 tablespoon olive oil
½ cup (125 ml) dry red wine
½ cup (125 ml) Lamb Stock (page 95)

1. Remove the lamb rack from the refrigerator 30 minutes before cooking and allow it to come to room temperature. Preheat the oven to 450°F (230°C).

2. Place the olives, rosemary, garlic, and mustard in a food processor, add the lemon zest and juice, and blend until the olives are finely chopped.

3. Pat the lamb rack dry and season with salt and pepper. In a large ovenproof frying pan, heat the oil over high heat and brown the lamb on both sides. Remove from the pan and spread the meat/fat side with the olive paste.

4. Return the rack bone side down to the pan and roast for 15 to 20 minutes, or until the internal temperature registers 135°F (57°C) on an instant-read thermometer. Let the rack rest, loosely covered with aluminum foil, for 10 minutes; the temperature will rise to 140°F (60°C) for medium-rare.

5. While the rack is resting and *remembering that the handle will be very hot,* discard the fat from the pan. Add the wine and bring to a boil, deglazing the pan by scraping up the browned bits from the bottom. Add the stock and boil for 3 to 4 minutes, until the sauce is reduced and syrupy.

6. Carve the rack into individual or double chops to serve with the sauce.

Variations

○ There are endless variations to this recipe. Always begin by browning the rack, or racks, in a pan. You can then simply roast them plain, or with various coatings. If roasting several racks and they won't fit in your frying pan, transfer them to a roasting pan.

○ Brush the lamb with Dijon mustard and sprinkle with chopped herbs such as rosemary, thyme, or parsley, or a mixture. You can also mix the herbs with fresh bread crumbs and minced garlic, and moisten with olive oil, then pat the mixture onto the mustard-brushed racks.

Carving Rack of Lamb

Lamb racks are usually carved down between the bones to serve, a simple task if the chine bone has been removed by the butcher.

Frenching

The term frenching refers to the technique of removing the meat and fat from the bones of a cut of meat, usually rib bones. The cleaner the bones, the more impressive the cooked rack or chop will look. Your butcher will do this for you.

GUARD OF HONOR OR CROWN ROAST

For serious lamb lovers, there are two special-occasion roasts that your butcher can prepare for you. They are best made with two racks from the same animal, so give him plenty of notice.

A guard of honor roast is two racks placed together so their bones interlock, fat side out. The alternating crossed bones resemble the crossed swords of a military guard of honor. The racks are then tied together with string so that they maintain their shape during cooking.

For a crown roast, the two racks are stitched together at one end, then curved, bone side out and fat into the center, to form a crown or circle shape; they are sewn at the other end to secure them. Unlike a pork crown roast (page 70) the center of the lamb is not filled with a stuffing, because it would not have enough time to cook. Rather, a piece of crumpled aluminum foil should be placed in the center before roasting so that the roast holds its shape. Once it is cooked, though, the center of the crown roast can be filled with cooked vegetables. Before cooking, protect the tips of the bones of either of these roasts by covering them with strips of aluminum foil.

Season the roast with salt and pepper, olive oil, and fresh herbs. Roast at 450°F (230°C) for 15 minutes, then reduce the oven temperature to 350°F (175°C). Cook for 30 to 45 minutes longer, or until the internal temperature registers 135°F (57°C) on an instant-read thermometer. Allow the roast to rest for 10 minutes, loosely covered with aluminum foil, before carving. The temperature will rise to 140°F (60°C), or medium-rare.

Make a simple sauce by discarding the fat from the roasting pan and adding 1 cup (250 ml) dry red wine. Bring to a boil, deglazing the pan by scraping up the browned bits from the bottom. Continue to boil until the wine reduces by half, then add 1 cup (250 ml) Lamb Stock (page 95) and continue to boil until the sauce thickens slightly. Season with salt and pepper, strain, and serve. Remove string from roast and carve between the bones like a rack.

Lamb Chops with Caramelized Leeks

When dinning with friends in a trendy Melbourne restaurant, I was surprised to see crumbed lamb chops on the menu. Not very hip, I thought, recalling how often I ate them as a child—crumbed cutlets, my mother called them. But they were delicious. I make this for two, but if you are prepared to deal with two frying pans at once, you can easily double the recipe.

3 leeks, trimmed
Kosher salt
6 lamb rib chops, 1 inch (2.5 cm) thick, frenched and trimmed
¼ cup (30 g) flour
Freshly ground black pepper
1 egg
1 tablespoon milk
2 lemons
1 tablespoon thyme leaves, chopped
½ cup (40 g) fresh bread crumbs
2 tablespoons olive oil
2 tablespoons (30 g) unsalted butter
1 teaspoon sugar

1. Split the leeks lengthwise in half and rinse well. Tie the leek halves together with string. Cook them in simmering salted water for 8 to 10 minutes, or until tender. Remove the leeks and drain on paper towels. When they are cool, remove the string.

2. Preheat oven to 300°F (150°C). Season the flour with salt and pepper. Whisk the egg with the milk in a shallow bowl. Grate the zest from 1 lemon (keep the lemon for juice) and stir the zest and thyme leaves into the bread crumbs. Dredge the chops in the seasoned flour, shaking off the excess, then dip them in the egg mixture, and, finally, coat them in the seasoned bread crumbs.

3. Place a large frying pan over medium-high heat. Add 1 tablespoon of the oil and 1 tablespoon (15 g) of the butter. When the butter begins to foam, add the chops and cook for 2 minutes on each side. Lower the heat and cook for another 2 minutes on each side or until medium rare. Transfer the chops to a oven-proof plate, loosely cover with aluminum foil, and then place in the oven.

4. Wipe out the frying pan and add the remaining 1 tablespoon oil and 1 tablespoon (15 g) butter. Sprinkle in the sugar, then add the leeks cut side down. Cook over medium heat until the leeks caramelize slightly and are heated through. Halve the zested lemon, and add a squeeze of juice to the pan. Remove from the heat.

5. Cut the remaining lemon into wedges. Place 3 leek halves on each plate, top with the chops, and serve with lemon wedges.

Lamb Ribs

Lamb ribs are delicious but, a word of warning—no matter how much you trim them, there will always be fat. As well as the coating fat, there is a layer of fat between the meat and the bone. The amount of fat varies with the animal and your butcher. Eat these ribs hot out of the oven or straight off the grill, and be prepared to eat around the fat. Don't be tempted to cook them ahead. It is better to glaze the hot ribs straight out of the oven, to keep the lamb fat warm.

If the ribs you buy are not well trimmed, it's simple to do yourself. Start at the thick end of the ribs, and pull the skin and fat back as you use a sharp knife to separate the fat from the meat. At the wide end of the ribs, there will also be a wad of fat under the top layer of meat. Pull the meat back to expose this fat and cut out as much as you can. Turn the ribs over and trim off any visible fat, then pierce the thin opaque membrane covering the bones and pull it off.

4 racks lamb ribs, about 1 pound (450 g) each before trimming
Kosher salt and freshly ground black pepper
Mustard Oregano Glaze or Spiced Yogurt Glaze (recipes follow)

1. Preheat the oven to 325°F (160°C). Season the ribs with salt and pepper, then place them on racks in two large roasting pans. Add enough water to cover the bottom of each pan, then cover the pans with aluminum foil.

2. Cook the ribs for 1½ hours, checking 2 to 3 times to make sure there is always some water in the bottom of each pan. Remove the ribs from oven, and increase the temperature to 450°F (230°C). (You can also glaze them on a hot grill or under the broiler.)

3. Line a large baking sheet with aluminum foil and put the ribs on it, meat side up. Baste with some of the glaze and bake for 10 to 15 minutes, basting 3 to 4 times with the glaze, until the ribs are browned and glazed.

4. Using a chef's knife, cut the ribs into individual pieces. Serve with the remaining glaze for dipping.

◦ Mustard Oregano Glaze

{ MAKES 1 CUP (250 ML) } This is a recipe where dried herbs are actually preferable to fresh ones. Try to find dried Greek oregano, as it is more aromatic. It is harvested when it flowers and is dried in bunches. The sharpness of the mustard and lemon cuts through the fat of the lamb ribs.

Finely grated zest of 1 lemon
¼ cup (60 ml) freshly squeezed lemon juice
¼ cup (60 ml) Dijon mustard
½ cup (125 ml) honey
2 teaspoons dried oregano, preferably Greek oregano

Mix all the ingredients together. Refrigerate until ready to use.

◦ Spiced Yogurt Glaze

{ MAKES 1 CUP (250 ML) } This recipe has its origins in the Indian marinade used to tenderize meats before they are cooked in a tandoor oven. The meat develops a distinctive orange color from the food coloring that is traditionally used. I have substituted paprika, which gives the glazed meat a lighter reddish tinge.

1 tablespoon finely grated fresh ginger
2 garlic cloves, finely diced
1 tablespoon sweet paprika
1 tablespoon cumin seeds, toasted and ground
2 teaspoons garam masala
¼ teaspoon chili powder, or to taste
2 teaspoons freshly squeezed lime juice
½ teaspoon kosher salt
1 cup (250 ml) yogurt

Mix all the ingredients, except the yogurt, in a small bowl, then whisk in the yogurt. Refrigerate until ready to use.

Both these glazes can be made up to 3 days in advance.

Wasabi-Coated Lamb Chops

Anyone who has eaten sushi is familiar with wasabi, so-called Japanese horseradish. It is that green paste that packs a powerful, sinus-clearing punch. Wasabi is also used to make a great snack, available in Japanese food stores: peas coated in wasabi powder and roasted, perfect with drinks. Ground up, the peas make a great coating for lamb chops, replacing the traditional bread crumbs. They add texture and heat to the sweet meat.

These peas do vary in heat; I tested this recipe with two bags of the same brand, and one bag was significantly hotter than the other. Taste one or two before you begin, so you can adjust the heat by adding more or less wasabi powder to the egg white mixture.

1 cup (90 g) wasabi peas
1 egg white
1 teaspoon soy sauce
½ teaspoon wasabi powder
6 lamb rib chops, 1 inch (2.5 cm) thick, frenched
Kosher salt and freshly ground black pepper
2 to 3 tablespoons olive oil

1. Place the peas in a food processor and process until coarsely crushed. Turn out onto a plate.

2. Whisk the egg white with the soy sauce and wasabi powder in a bowl. Let stand for 5 minutes.

3. Trim any excess fat from the lamb chops, and season them with salt and pepper. Dip the chops into the egg white mixture, then coat them with the crushed peas.

4. Heat 2 tablespoons oil in a large frying pan over medium-high heat. Add the chops and cook for 2 minutes per side or until medium-rare. Lower the heat, add the 1 tablespoon remaining oil, if necessary, and cook the chops for another 2 minutes per side.

Lamb Ribs with Beans and Spinach

When cooking dried beans, fat is often added to improve their taste. Here lamb ribs provide both the flavor and fat. However, don't neglect to trim them (see Lamb Ribs, page 110) before cutting them into individual pieces. To cut the ribs into pieces, begin at the thick end and slice down between the bones with a heavy knife; some pressure is necessary to cut through the cartilage at the bottom of the ribs. Remember that the beans must be soaked for 8 hours before you begin the recipe.

2 cups (375 g) dried pea beans (small navy beans), rinsed and soaked overnight in water to cover
2 racks lamb ribs, about 1 pound (450 g) each before trimming
Kosher salt and freshly ground black pepper
2 tablespoons vegetable oil
2 cups (500 ml) Lamb Stock (page 95)
2 tomatoes, peeled and diced
1 onion, sliced
1 small carrot, peeled and diced
1 celery stalk, diced
3 thyme sprigs
1 garlic clove, crushed
1 bunch spinach, trimmed and shredded (about 8 cups [2 l])

1. Drain the beans, place them a saucepan, and cover with cold water. Bring slowly to a boil, skim off the foam, and strain, keeping the cooking water.

2. Preheat the oven to 325°F (160°C). Cut off as much fat as possible off the lamb ribs. Cut into individual pieces (see headnote) and season with salt and pepper. In a Dutch oven or flameproof casserole, heat the oil and brown the ribs in batches. Cook over medium heat, as you want the ribs to render some of their fat as they brown. As the ribs brown, transfer them to a plate.

3. Once all the ribs are browned, discard any fat from the pot then pour in the lamb stock. Bring to a boil, deglazing the pot by scraping up the browned bits from the bottom. Add the tomatoes, onion, carrot, celery, thyme, and garlic. Add the beans and browned ribs, with 1 teaspoon salt. The liquid should almost cover the beans; add a little of the bean cooking water if necessary (reserve the remaining cooking water).

4. Cover, transfer to the oven, and cook for 2 hours, or until the lamb and beans are tender. Check them after 1 hour, and stir the top layer of beans into the liquid. The liquid should be just below the level of the beans; if too much has evaporated, add a little more cooking water.

5. When the lamb and beans are cooked, remove the lid and tilt the pot slightly so that you can spoon off any surface fat. Gently stir in the shredded spinach, cover, and cook for another 10 minutes, or until the spinach wilts. Check the seasoning and serve.

Seven-Hour Leg of Lamb

Friends were invited for dinner and I wanted to spend time with them, not in the kitchen. Knowing that my friends would be late, I made this traditional French dish, which can happily spend an extra hour in the oven or sit, covered, for thirty minutes while you enjoy a predinner drink.

Despite the name, this lamb dish needs only about 5½ hours to cook. No carving is necessary—you can serve this dish with a spoon.

Just as my lamb was ready, one couple called to say they would be late. I left my lamb in the oven, turned it off, and enjoyed a drink.

1 leg of lamb, about 5 pounds (2.5 kg)
Kosher salt and freshly ground black pepper
3 tablespoons (45 g) unsalted butter
2 tablespoons vegetable oil
3 onions, halved and sliced
4 medium carrots, peeled and sliced into ½-inch (1-cm)-thick rounds
1 bottle (750 ml) dry white wine
4 garlic cloves, peeled
About 2 cups (500 ml) Lamb Stock (page 95)
3 bay leaves
1 large rosemary sprig

1. One hour before cooking, remove the lamb from the refrigerator. Preheat the oven to 350°F (175°C).

2. Pat the lamb dry and season with salt and pepper. In a large Dutch oven or flameproof casserole, melt half the butter with half the oil over medium heat. Add the lamb and brown on all sides. Transfer the lamb to a platter.

3. Discard any fat from the pot, and add the remaining butter and oil. Add the onions and cook until softened. Add the carrots and cook until the onions begin to brown. Pour in the wine, add the garlic, and bring to a boil, deglazing the pot by scraping up the browned bits from the bottom.

4. Place the lamb meatiest side up atop the vegetables, then add enough stock so that the leg is two-thirds submerged. Add the bay leaves and rosemary, season with salt and pepper, and bring to the boil. Cover the lamb with a piece of damp parchment paper and then the lid, transfer to the oven, and cook for 2½ hours.

5. Remove the lamb from the oven and baste it with the cooking juices. Lower the oven temperature to 300°F (150°C), and cook the lamb, uncovered, for 2½ to 3 hours, basting every 30 minutes. The lamb is cooked when the meat comes away from the bone; the meat will be a rich dark brown.

6. Discard the bay leaves and rosemary. Skim off the fat from the cooking liquid, but *don't* try to remove the lamb from the pot, as it would fall to pieces. Serve the lamb directly from the pot, with the carrots and cooking juices.

Lamb Shoulder with Preserved Lemon and Dates
(page 99)

Lamb Ribs with Beans and Spinach
(page 113)

Lamb Shanks Cooked in
Paper with Guinness
(page 118)

Lamb Neck with Lettuce and Dill

(page 120)

Poached Chicken with Seasonal Vegetables
(page 142)

Grilled Quail with Sage Butter
(page 148)

Chicken with Morel Cream Sauce
(page 154)

Duck Legs with Cumin, Turnips, and Green Olives
(page 157)

Lamb Shanks in Pomegranate Sauce

In this recipe, lamb shanks are braised slowly in their own juices, making a rich concentrated sauce that is offset by the acidity of the pomegranate juice. Bottled pomegranate juice is becoming more readily available, but it has a rather grapey taste, and I prefer fresh pomegranate juice; it is easy to make (see page 116). If pomegranates are not in season, try the recipe using the bottled juice, or instead substitute 1 cup (250 ml) orange juice and ½ cup (125 ml) lemon juice, both freshly squeezed, for the pomegranate juice.

4 lamb shanks, about 12 ounces (350 g) each
Kosher salt and freshly ground black pepper
2 tablespoons vegetable oil
12 garlic cloves, peeled
1 large rosemary sprig
1¼ cups (310 ml) pomegranate juice
⅓ to ½ cup (75 to 125 ml) pomegranate seeds for garnish

1. Preheat the oven to 300°F (150°C). Pat the lamb shanks dry and season them with salt and pepper. In a Dutch oven or flameproof casserole, heat the oil over medium-high heat and brown the shanks on all sides. Remove the pot from the heat and add the garlic cloves.

2. Cover the lamb with a damp piece of parchment paper and then the lid, place the pot in the oven, and braise for 1 hour, turning the shanks 2 or 3 times and checking to make sure that there is always a little liquid in the pot. There should be enough lamb juices to coat the bottom of the pot but, if necessary, add a couple of spoonfuls of water.

3. After 1 hour, add the rosemary, and check that there is still some liquid in the bottom of the pan, adding a little more water if necessary. Cook the shanks, covered, for another 1½ to 2 hours, or until the meat is very tender and almost falling off the bone.

4. Carefully transfer the shanks to a platter and keep them warm, loosely covered with aluminum foil. Discard the rosemary, and pour the juices and garlic into a glass measuring cup or small bowl; set the pot aside. Let the juices stand for a few minutes to allow the fat to rise to the top, then skim off the fat and discard.

5. Strain the liquid through a fine sieve back into the pot, pressing the cooked garlic through the sieve. Add 1 cup (250 ml) of the pomegranate juice to the pot, place over medium heat, and bring to a boil, deglazing the pot by scraping up the browned bits from the bottom. Continue to a boil until the sauce reduces and thickens. Check the seasoning.

6. Return the shanks to the pot and reheat gently, turning to with the sauce. Add enough of the remaining pomegranate juice to sharpen the flavor.

7. Serve the shanks coated with the sauce and sprinkled with pomegranate seeds.

Note: This recipe can be made up to 3 days ahead. Reheat the shanks in the sauce in a 300°F (150°C) oven for 35 to 45 minutes. Stir in the extra pomegranate juice and garnish with the seeds just before serving.

Pomegranate Tips

The pomegranate is a dangerous fruit—its juice escapes easily, and it stains everything it hits.
The best method for removing the seeds and risk of splattering juices is Paula Wolfert's.
Using a small knife, cut out the crown or (blossom end) from the pomegranate, leaving a small crater. Then score the fruit lengthwise into four sections, cutting through the skin but not into the seeds. Fill a large bowl with cold water. Hold the fruit underwater and break it into 4 sections by placing your thumbs in the crater and pulling hard. Hold each section underwater, with the skin facing toward you, and press hard, pushing the seeds out. Most of the seeds will fall out, and the others can be removed from the white membrane by rubbing it with your fingertips. When you think all the seeds are out, turn the section over and check—there are always a couple hidden away. The seeds will sink to the bottom of the bowl, while the membrane will float. (Any white membrane that sinks still has a seed attached.)
An average pomegranate yields about 1 cup (250 ml) seeds.
To juice a pomegranate, take the seeds you've just removed and put them in a blender. Blend until liquid, then strain through a fine sieve, pressing well to extract all the juice. A cup (250 ml) of seeds will yield about ½ cup (125 ml) juice.

BONE GAMES

∘∘∘∘∘∘∘∘∘∘∘∘∘∘∘∘∘∘∘∘∘∘∘

Although we grew up on opposite sides of the world, my husband and I both played jacks. His Canadian jacks were formed from thin metal strips fused together in the center, so when you tossed them, they landed on the spokes. My jacks would have been familiar to the ancient Greeks and early Romans; they were made from the knucklebones of sheep's ankles. One source I read while working on this book stated that the tradition of using real knucklebones survived only until the last days of the nineteenth century. Well, I can vouch that it lasted at least until the 1970s in Australia.

Plastic jacks were available, but my mother, ever frugal, boiled up the lower leg bones of sheep to extract the small knucklebones. If you want to try this at home, ask your butcher for lamb metatarsal bones. These are the bones between the hind leg shank and the foot, and they are usually left on the carcass and tied together to suspend it. Then most butchers toss them away with the string still wound around them. They come in pairs, so ask for three pairs, although you will only need five knuckles to play jacks. Mix them with some meatier lamb bones and make stock. Then, once the stock is strained, you can retrieve these leg bones and leave them to cool. Use a small knife, preferably a flexible boning knife, to cut into the ankle joint, where you will find the small knucklebone. (There is a bonus to all this: these metatarsal bones will have added extra gelatin to your stock, making it set like a jelly.) To clean and whiten the knucklebones, soak them in a sodium carbonate cleaner, such as a household carpet cleaner or spot remover.

Knucklebones is a very old game, and its origins are difficult to pin down. It may in fact have been one of the first games ever played. It is easy to imagine early man sitting around the fire and passing his time playing games with leftover bones.

In the British Museum, there is a small terracotta sculpture dating from third century B.C. that depicts two young girls playing with knucklebones. During the classical and Hellenistic periods of Greek art, numerous scenes of young women and goddesses playing this game were sculpted and painted. These girls would have played with either real bones or ones made from ivory, bronze, or terracotta. The game remained popular with children through the ages, as Brueghel's 1560 painting "Children's Games" reveals. It illustrates more than two hundred children playing different games, and in the bottom left-hand corner of the painting, you can see young girls playing knucklebones.

Astragali was the Greek name for knucklebones; the Romans called it *tali*. They both played several versions of the game ranging from a simple tossing and catching game to one that involved gambling. Knucklebones have an elongated S shape. There are four long sides, the front, the back, and the two sides of the S and when tossed, the bone can land on any of them. The other two "sides" are the top and bottom of the S; they don't come into play, as the bone cannot land on these curved sides. The four long sides were assigned the values 1, 3, 4, and 6, marked by dots or Roman numerals. Four bones were tossed together and a complicated scoring system was used.

All around the world dice games are played using bones. In India, there is one called *k'abatain*, its name coming from the Arabic word *k'ab*, meaning ankle bone. Even in English, dice are called bones. Ankle bones were probably the forerunners of the six-sided cubes we use today. A cube is the most practical to toss as all sides have an equal chance of coming up and so it became the most popular shape. The placement of the numbers on the dice varied, but the general convention became that the numbers on opposite faces of the die would total 7.

Other games like draughts, checkers, chess, and dominos all began with bone playing pieces.

Lamb Shanks Cooked in Paper with Guinness

I saw a beautiful photograph in a food magazine of lamb shanks cooked in parchment paper. It appealed to my food-styling genes, plus I love cooking *en papillote*. With this technique, the food is sealed in a paper package with flavorings and baked. I had only cooked food quickly using this method so I was curious about braising this way.

Ask the butcher to french the shanks for you, or do it yourself. You want to expose about 3 inches (7.5 cm) of the shank bone. This allows you to tie the parchment paper to the bone. These packages won't be airtight, so they don't puff up like the Whiting en Papillote (page 185), but the technique concentrates the flavors and makes a great presentation. If it's too fussy for you, just make the dish in a Dutch oven or flameproof casserole.

4 lamb shanks, about 12 ounces (350 g) each, frenched
Kosher salt and freshly ground black pepper
3 tablespoons vegetable oil
8 medium onions, sliced
1 large carrot, peeled and diced
1 celery stalk, diced
4 large rosemary sprigs
1 bottle (330 ml) Guinness beer
⅓ packed cup (70 g) brown sugar
1½ teaspoons dry mustard
4 garlic cloves, halved
1 orange

1. Pat the lamb shanks dry and season with salt and pepper. Heat the oil in a large frying pan over medium-high heat and brown the lamb shanks on all sides. Transfer them to a plate. Add the onions to the pan, stirring well to coat them in the fat, then cover and cook for 10 minutes, or until soft, stirring 2 or 3 times and scraping the bottom of the pan each time.

2. Add the carrot, celery, and rosemary and cook, uncovered, 2 to 3 minutes, scraping the bottom of the pan from time to time. Pour in the beer and bring to a boil, deglazing the pan by scraping up the browned bits from the bottom. Add the sugar, mustard, and garlic and continue to boil, stirring from time to time, for 10 minutes, or until the beer becomes thick and syrupy.

3. Meanwhile, remove 4 large strips of zest from the orange with a vegetable peeler, and squeeze ¼ cup (60 ml) juice from the orange. Add the zest and juice to the pan and continue to cook until the liquid just glazes the onions. Remove from the heat and let cool. You will have 3 to 4 cups (750 ml to 1 l) onion mixture.

4. Preheat the oven to 300°F (150°C). Cut four 15-inch (38-cm) squares of parchment paper. Divide the onion mixture among the squares of parchment paper, placing it in the middle of each one; make sure that each square has a rosemary sprig, an orange zest strip, and two garlic halves. Stand a lamb shank on top of each one—it will lean to one side—and pull up the corners of the parchment paper to form a package, tying it with string around the exposed bone.

5. Stand the packages in a Dutch oven or baking of dish and bake for 3 hours.

6. Remove from the oven and place the packages on warmed plates. Cut the strings, but allow each diner to open his or her own package.

Shanks, Necks, and Other Ideas

You can easily replace the lamb shanks in any of these recipes with pieces of neck. Just remember that the neck pieces will cook more quickly. Also think about substituting lamb shanks or neck in the game recipes. Try lamb shanks in place of venison in Venison Shank in Rosemary-Wine Sauce (page 234), for example, or lamb neck pieces in Venison Osso Buco (page 236). Again, the cooking time for neck will be shorter.

Lamb Neck with Lettuce and Dill

I began this recipe thinking of Irish stew, a dish I ate several times a month as a child, but I wanted to cook something lighter and fresher. In the end, the result bears no resemblance to my childhood original. Dill is an herb I tend to overlook and while it is not usually matched with lamb, it adds freshness, and with the lemon, cuts through the richness of the lamb neck. I love the French method of braising peas and lettuce together, and it brings a touch of spring to this recipe. If you can't get lamb neck (see Lamb Neck Tips, page 121), use shoulder chops. The dish has quite a bit of sauce, so serve it in large shallow soup bowls.

8 pieces trimmed lamb neck, 1 inch (2.5 cm) thick, about 3 pounds (1.35 kg)
Kosher salt and freshly ground black pepper
1 small onion, sliced
4 green onions, trimmed and cut into 1 inch (2 cm) lengths
2 garlic cloves
4 dill sprigs plus ¼ cup (60 ml) chopped dill
2 strips lemon zest
1 cup (250 ml) dry white wine
8 small red potatoes
1 head Boston lettuce, coarsely shredded
1 cup (250 ml) fresh or frozen peas

1. Make sure the lamb neck pieces are trimmed of all excess fat. If you can still see a band of sinew surrounding any of the pieces, make a few nicks in it to prevent the pieces from curling as they cook. Season the lamb with salt and pepper.

2. Scatter the onion, green onions, garlic, dill sprigs, and lemon zest over the bottom of a Dutch oven or a heavy, deep frying pan with a lid. Lay the lamb on top and pour in the wine and 1 cup (250 ml) water. Bring to a boil and skim off the foam, then lower the heat to a gentle simmer and simmer, partially covered, for 30 minutes.

3. Turn the lamb pieces and cook gently for another 30 minutes, still partially covered. Transfer the lamb to a dish, strain the cooking liquid into a glass measuring cup or a bowl and set aside to allow the fat to rise to the top; add the strained vegetables and herbs to the lamb.

4. Rinse out the Dutch oven or frying pan. Slice the potatoes and layer them in the clean pot. Place the neck pieces and vegetables on top. Skim the fat from the cooking liquid, add ½ teaspoon salt, and pour over the lamb. Bring to a boil, then lower the heat to a simmer, cover with a damp piece of parchment paper and the lid, and cook gently for 1 to ¼ hours, or until the lamb is tender and potatoes are almost cooked.

5. Add the lettuce, peas, and half of the chopped dill. Cover with the lid only and cook for 10 to 15 minutes, or until the lettuce is wilted and the peas cooked; stir to mix the lettuce into the cooking liquid. Check the seasoning, sprinkle with the remaining dill, and serve.

NOTE: You can cook this dish in two stages. Stop after you strain the liquid, and refrigerate it (separately) and the lamb with the vegetables overnight. The next day, remove any fat and continue with the recipe.

Lamb Neck Tips

Like ribs, lamb neck is a fatty cut and must be well trimmed. Lamb necks may be big or small, and the pieces vary in diameter. Ideally you need equal-sized pieces. I averaged about 6 pieces per neck but the 2 smallest pieces, which were mainly bone, I consigned to the stockpot, I needed 2 necks to serve 4. When my friend Miriam tested these recipes, her lamb necks were shorter and fatter than mine and so she served 1 piece of neck per person. Use your own judgment to determine how many pieces you will need, remembering the high bone to meat ratio.

Lamb Neck with Anchovies

This recipe came from Uta Taylor, a friend's mother who is Italian. She calls it *agnello all'acciuga*—it sounds so much better in Italian. Anchovies are often paired with lamb and they reveal one side of lamb's split personality. It takes well to the milder spring flavors of dill and peas (see page 120) but it can handle the punch of anchovies and red wine vinegar. Lamb neck is suggested, but pieces of shank or shoulder chops will work. As the lamb cooks, the liquid concentrates and all the ingredients meld into a thick powerful sauce that coats the meat.

8 pieces trimmed lamb neck, 1 inch (2.5 cm) thick, about 3 pounds (1.35 kg)
1 to 2 tablespoons olive oil
Kosher salt and freshly ground black pepper
1 cup (250 ml) Lamb Stock (page 95)
2 garlic cloves, sliced
6 anchovy fillets, rinsed
1 tablespoon rosemary leaves, chopped
½ cup (125 ml) red wine vinegar
½ cup (125 ml) dry red wine

1. Make sure the lamb neck pieces are trimmed of all excess fat. If you can still see a band of sinew surrounding any of the pieces, make a few nicks in it to prevent the pieces from curling as they cook.

2. Lightly coat the bottom of a large heavy frying pan with the olive oil and heat over medium-high heat. Season the lamb lightly with salt and generously with black pepper. Add the lamb to the pan, in two batches if necessary, and brown on both sides, about 3 minutes per side. Transfer the browned lamb to a plate and discard the fat from the frying pan.

3. Add half of the stock to the pan and bring to a boil, deglazing the pan by scraping up the browned bits from the bottom. Reduce the heat to a simmer, add the lamb neck, in a single layer if possible, and simmer, partially covered, for 30 minutes, turning the lamb once. Make sure there is always a little liquid covering the bottom of the pan.

4. While the lamb is cooking, put the garlic, anchovies, and rosemary in a food processor. Process until finely chopped, then add the wine and vinegar and process again.

5. After the lamb has simmered for 30 minutes, stir in the anchovy-vinegar mixture and bring back to a simmer. Cover tightly and braise for 1 to 1½ hours, or until the lamb is very tender. Turn the lamb pieces every 30 minutes, and make sure there is always liquid covering the bottom of the pan.

6. Transfer the lamb necks to a warmed platter and keep warm, loosely covered with aluminum foil. Place the pan over medium-high heat and bring to a boil. Cook, stirring occasionally, until the juices have reduced to about ¾ cup (175 ml) and are slightly thickened and glossy. Check the seasoning, and add salt if necessary. Pour the sauce over the lamb and serve.

BONE JEWELRY

ooooooooooooooooooooooooooo

In 2004, a discovery of beads in a cave at the southern tip of Africa revealed that man's love of adornment is very old. These beads were made from shells and dated at over seventy-five thousand years old. Bone tools were found alongside them. We view jewelry as purely ornamental, but for early man it had many meanings. While its intrinsic beauty counted, jewelry could also be an amulet or worn to denote the social status of its wearer. Early jewelry was fashioned from objects at hand like shells, seeds, and, of course, bones.

Bones were a powerful symbol. For early man the power and strength of an animal resided in its bones. By wearing the bones of a certain animal, he could assume its characteristics: skill at hunting, for example, or strength or speed. Bones from horned animals were especially valued. The horn was a phallic symbol, and the bones of these animals naturally bestowed sexually potency on their wearers.

Beginning with simple pendants made from hollow bones strung on plant fibers, bones were carved, polished, and pierced to create intricate jewelry—sometimes ceasing to look like a bone. Bone is slightly softer to carve than gold, so it was an ideal medium for practicing the art of engraving. Many early jewelers and metal workers refined their skills on bones before embarking upon precious metals. More recently, the ban on ivory revived the interest in bone jewelry and it is enjoying a renaissance.

Bone has one more connection to jewelry. Bone ash is an ingredient in jewelry cleaning and polishing compounds.

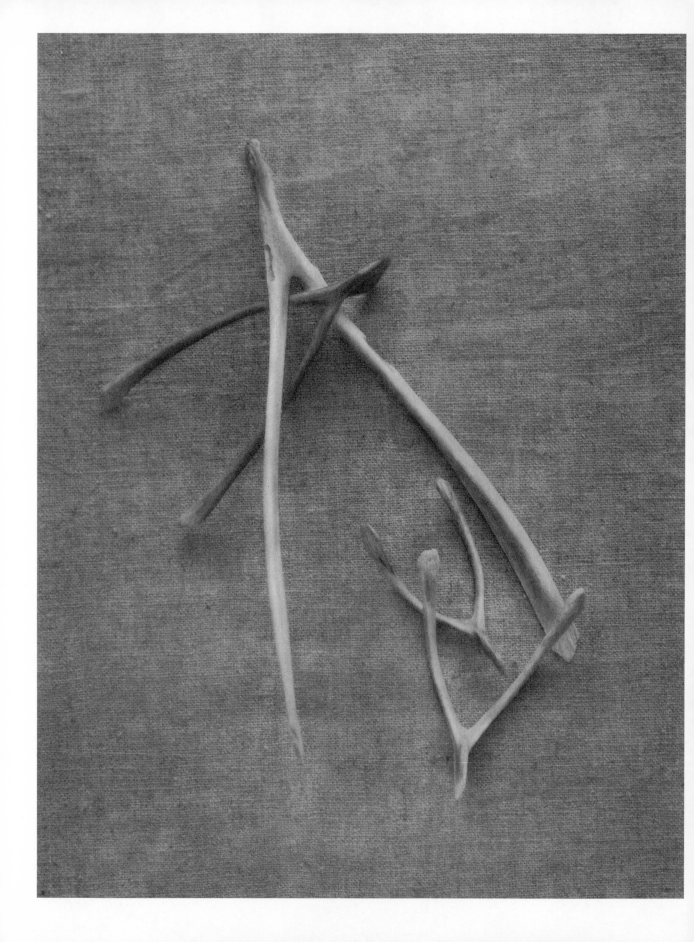

Poultry

When it comes to bones, chickens have fared the worst. If modern science could breed a bird with only wing bones, it would be a success. Wings bones, it seems, are the only chicken bones anyone wants to bother with. Those familiar with the well-known cartoonist Gary Larson will remember his cartoon "Boneless Chicken Ranch" depicting a ranch populated with hapless chickens who have no bones. As they can't stand, they lie in strangely contorted positions on the ground or draped over the fence. It's a visual joke that makes us laugh but, increasingly, the birds we eat are being separated from their bones and as a result, they are losing their flavor.

Why should we bother with whole chickens and bone-in pieces? Boneless pieces cook faster, but those few minutes gained do not outweigh the loss of taste. The first step toward tastier poultry is to reacquaint it with its bones. Bones prevent the bird's flesh from drying out, especially when cooking leaner breasts and small birds. More important, the bones add flavor.

The provenance of the poultry is also important. Birds fed a varied diet and allowed to exercise are the tastiest. These free-range birds can be identified by a thick layer of fat under their skin and their calloused feet. Today, however, except for some game birds, we rarely see whole birds with their feet still attached. The reality, in a world of endless recipes for boneless, skinless breasts, is that a lot of poultry is sold already portioned. We must rely on our producers and butchers to provide us with fresh tasty poultry.

Make friends with your butcher and you will discover that chicken bones, backs, and trimmings are readily available for stock. A couple of extra backs or necks tossed into the roasting pan with the whole bird will not only serve as a makeshift roasting rack, they'll greatly improve the taste of the finished sauce. Take advantage of the obsession with boneless breasts to snap up the less popular, more flavorful bone-in legs and thighs. Feet and necks, often tossed away, can be cooked and eaten or added to the stockpot. Even the leftover carcass from a roasted bird can add flavor as a base for soup.

The choice of poultry has increased with the growing availability of game birds. Today's farm-raised birds may not be as intensely livery as those shot in the wild, but they are of consistent quality, more tender, and free of buckshot—for cooks, they greatly simplify game bird cookery. Leaner than domesticated poultry, they rely on their bones to keep their meat juicy.

All birds, big or small, from the common chicken and its exotic cousin the guinea hen to the tiny quail and the large turkey, all have the same basic skeleton. Looking at the bird's skeleton and seeing where all those bones and the meat are attached will help you when cooking, carving, and eating any poultry from the smallest game bird to the largest turkey.

The Whole Bird

There is a tremendous choice of poultry ranging in size and taste from single serving to crowd satisfying, from mild flavored to rich and gamey.

Most whole birds are sold oven-ready. Simply put your hand inside and pull out the neck and the plastic bag of giblets (see "The Extremities and Odds and Ends") and the bird is ready to cook. Game birds, though, often need some preparation before cooking. If they are sold with the head and feet attached, ask your butcher to cut them off and take the trimmings with you.

The leanest and most tender poultry meat comes from the middle section of the bird, its breast. The breast is supported by the breastbone and the ribs. At the neck end of the breast is the furcula, or wishbone. It sits with its two forks attached to the collarbone and the tip joined by cartilage to the breastbone.

The wings consist of three sections. The first, closest to the body, has a single bone, the next section has two parallel bones, and the tip has several tiny bones. While chicken and turkey wings are quite meaty, the wings of ducks, geese, and birds that regularly fly have little meat and are very chewy.

For the cook to bone means to remove bones from meat or fish, but for a carpenter it means to look along the sight line of several objects to make sure they are in line or level. It comes from French word *bornoyer*, which means to look with one eye. It is also a British slang expression meaning to steal.

Boneless: means having no bones, or lacking character

POULTRY

Some people cut them off before the bird is roasted, but I often leave them to help truss the bird (see page 144).

The legs and thighs do the most work so they have firmer, darker, and more flavorful meat. There is one bone in the thigh and another in the leg. The legs or drumsticks of larger birds and some game birds also have what seem to be very thin bones attached to the leg bone, but they are actually tendons.

The Extremities and Odds and Ends

Except for some game birds, the head, neck, and feet are generally removed from birds before they are sold. The skinless neck is usually inside the bird, along with a separate bag containing the giblets (the heart, liver, and gizzard). Don't toss any of these away. The liver can be used in a filling for dumplings (see page 209). The gizzards can be prepared separately but, along with the neck, their most practical use is in the stockpot. Or, if the neck is large and meaty, add it to the pan when roasting the bird to improve the sauce. I used to throw the neck away after roasting, until my friend

Caroline revealed that she happily gnaws at it—extracting every morsel of meat as a cook's treat.

The two nuggets of juicy meat nestled against the bird's backbone, close to the hip joint are called the "oysters." The name comes from their shape, not their taste. Don't forget them when carving the bird.

The tail end of the bird also has a quaint name—the parson's or pope's nose. Not a flattering term, it was used colloquially by both Catholics and Protestants. It's this fatty morsel that holds the bird's tail feathers in place. When roasted and crispy, it is a favorite, especially with chicken skin lovers.

Feet, mostly chicken, can be bought separately at Asian or farmers' markets. Like chicken wings, only chewier, feet require advance preparation but they make a great snack for those who like gelatinous textures. Feet can also be added to the stockpot.

Common Poultry Weights

- Poussin—¾ to 1 pound (350 to 450 g)
- Cornish game hen—1 to 1 ¼ pounds (450 to 570 g)
- Chicken—3 to 7 pounds (1.35 to 3.15 kg)
- Capon—6 to 9 pounds (3 to 4 kg)
- Duck (duckling)—4 to 5 pounds (1.8 to 2.25 kg)
- Goose—6 to 14 pounds (2.7 to 6.3 kg)
- Turkey—10 to 25 pounds (4.5 to 11.25 kg)

Common Farm-Raised Game Bird Weights

- Quail—6 to 8 ounces (170 to 225 g)
- Squab—1 ¼ pounds (570 g)
- Partridge—1 pound (450 g)
- Guinea hen—2 to 3 pounds (900 g to 1.35 kg)
- Pheasant—3 pounds (1.35 kg)

How to Cut Up a Bird

Depending on the size of the bird, you can cut it into 2, 4, 6, or as many as 8 pieces.

To cut a bird into halves, place the bird breast side up on a cutting board. Slice from the top of the wishbone down the length of the chicken through the

> "I remember when I was a child, being taken to the celebrated Barnum's Circus, which contained an exhibition of freaks and monstrosities, but the exhibit on the program which I most desired to see was one described as 'The Boneless Wonder.' My parents judged that spectacle would be too revolting and demoralizing for my youthful eyes and I have waited 50 years to see the boneless wonder sitting on the Treasury Bench."
>
> —WINSTON CHURCHILL, *Hansard*, January 28, 1931, referring to the prime minister of the day, Ramsay Macdonald

skin and meat to the breastbone. Using a knife or poultry shears, cut through the breastbone to split it in half. Turn the bird over, then cut down along either side of the backbone to remove it.

To cut a bird into 4, 6, or 8 pieces, you follow the same general procedure. For 4 pieces, place the bird breast side up, pull one leg away from the body, and cut down through the skin. Using the tip of the knife, cut around the "oyster" of meat nestled in the backbone so that it remains attached to the thigh. Twist the leg firmly until the hip pops out of its socket, and cut between the ball and socket. Repeat with the other leg.

Next, cut from the top of the wishbone down the length of the chicken through the skin and meat to the breastbone. Using a knife or poultry shears, cut through the breastbone to split it in half. Now cut down the length of the chicken through the rib bones to remove the breast halves from the backbone. Cut the backbone, with ribs attached, into smaller pieces and reserve for the stockpot.

For 6 pieces, cut the leg pieces in half, then separating the thigh and the drumstick.

For 8 pieces, then cut the breasts in half on the diagonal, though the breastbone, so that one section still has the wing attached.

Poultry Cooking Temperatures

Use an instant-read thermometer, to determine if a bird is cooked: Insert the thermometer into the thickest part of the thigh without touching the bone.

Chicken	165°F (73°C)
Game birds	155°F (68°C) (juices will still be pink, not clear)
Duck	180°F (82°C)
Guinea hen	185°F (83°C)

Portion Size

As with most meat on the bone, about 12 ounces (350g) per person is a good amount. However, some birds, such as smaller turkeys, duck, and geese, have large carcasses, so there is a higher ration of bone to meat; duck and geese lose a lot of body weight in fat. So in these cases, 1 pound (450 g) per person is a better estimate.

Poultry Stock

This versatile stock can be used almost anywhere stock is required. Using just bones is fine, but many birds' bones are hollow (which enables them to fly). To make up for this lack of marrow, meaty pieces like wings, backs, and necks are usually added to poultry stock. You can mix and match the bones of different birds. The finished stock is the building block for hundreds of soups. For some suggestions, see the note at the end of the recipe.

4½ pounds (2 kg) poultry bones and backs, cut into 2- to 3-inch (5- to 7.5-cm) pieces
2 medium carrots, sliced
2 celery stalks, sliced
1 onion, unpeeled, cut into wedges
2 leeks, trimmed and quartered lengthwise
6 flat-leaf parsley stems
3 garlic cloves
1 large thyme sprig
1 bay leaf
1 large strip of lemon zest
¼ teaspoon black peppercorns
Kosher salt, optional

1. Rinse the bones and backs under cold running water, then place in a large stockpot, along with the carrots, celery, onion, leeks, parsley, garlic, thyme, and bay leaf. Pour in enough cold water to cover the bones, about 12 cups (3 l), and bring slowly to a boil. As soon as the stock begins to boil, reduce the heat so that it simmers. Using a soup ladle, skim off any scum that has risen to the surface (rotate the bowl of the ladle on the surface of the stock to make ripples: these will carry the scum to the edges of the pot, and you can then use the ladle to lift it off). Add the lemon zest and peppercorns, and simmer uncovered for 5 hours, skimming from time to time.

2. Strain the stock through a sieve into a large bowl. Discard the debris left in the sieve, and cool the stock quickly by placing the bowl in a larger bowl or sink filled with ice water; stir occasionally as it cools. When you taste this stock, you will notice that something is missing—the salt. Once you add it, the flavor will sparkle. But it was deliberately left out so that you can reduce the stock if desired without any fear that it will become too salty. If you will not be reducing the stock (see page 132), add about 1 teaspoon salt.

3. Refrigerate the stock for 6 hours, or overnight, to allow the fat to rise to the top and the debris to sink to the bottom. Remove the fat before using (and discard the debris at the bottom of the bowl). Divide it into 1-cup (250-ml) quantities and refrigerate for up to 3 days or freeze for up to 6 months.

Brown Poultry Stock

○ Roasting the bones first results in a darker, fuller-flavored stock and is a particularly good technique to use with game bird or duck bones, as it will give a richer base for the sauce. Toss the bones with a little vegetable oil, then spread them in a single layer in a roasting pan and roast in a 425°F (220°C) oven until browned, about 40 minutes.

Transfer the bones to a stockpot. Discard the fat from the roasting pan, then pour about 2 cups (500 ml) water into the pan and bring to a boil. Deglaze the pan by scraping up the browned bits from the bottom, then add this liquid to the stockpot and continue as for regular poultry stock, adding only about 10 cups (2.5 l) more water.

Chicken Soup Ideas

○ Fresh egg noodles and chopped herbs

○ Spinach, lemon, and rice

○ Pureed avocado, buttermilk, and lime juice; serve cold

STOCK TIP The exact amount of stock will probably vary each time you make it. If using bones that have been stored in the freezer and are not completely thawed and drained, you may find yourself with a greater quantity of liquid. Taste the strained stock, if it's too weak, it can be boiled down to concentrate the flavor.

Concentrated Poultry Stock

If your freezer space is tight, reduce your stock following the method for Concentrated Brown Stock (page 14).

6 cups (1.5 l) unsalted Poultry Stock (page 130)
Kosher salt

○○

The reduced stock will become syrupy and turn the color of tea.

Poultry Consommé

000000000000000000000000000000000000000000000000000000000000000000000000 { SERVES 6 } 0000000000

Poultry consommé is perfect without any additions, but if you wish to dress up this golden broth, there are several suggestions at the end of the recipe. Using this recipe, you can also make duck or a game bird consommé, which will be richer and darker. Make these consommés from Brown Poultry Stock (page 131). Poultry consommé is equally good served cold. When chilled it forms a light jelly, which is refreshing on a hot summer night.

6 cups (1.5 l) Poultry Stock (page 130)
1 small leek, trimmed and chopped
1 small carrot, chopped
3 flat-leaf parsley stems
6 ounces (175 g) diced or ground poultry meat
2 egg whites
Kosher salt

1. Place the cold stock in a large saucepan and heat it just until it liquefies. Remove the saucepan from the heat.

2. Place the leek, carrot, and parsley in a food processor and process until finely chopped. Add the meat, egg whites, and 2 tablespoons water and blend again until well mixed. Stir this mixture into the stock and bring to a boil over medium-high heat, stirring constantly with a spatula or wooden spoon, scraping the bottom of the saucepan to prevent the egg white from sticking. As the liquid approaches a boil, it will appear to curdle; don't panic, that is what you want. As soon as it begins to boil, stop stirring, and remove the saucepan from the heat. The whites will form a congealed mass, which will puff up and then crack as the steam escapes.

3. Reduce the heat to very low and return the saucepan to the heat, making a larger hole in the egg white mass with a spoon to allow the steam to escape. Simmer very gently—you want to see small bubbles of steam break the egg white mass—for 45 minutes. Remove the saucepan from the heat and let stand for 5 minutes.

4. Line a sieve with a double thickness of damp cheesecloth or a dampened thin cotton tea towel and place it over a bowl. Using a skimmer or large slotted spoon, carefully lift off as much of the egg white mass as you can and set aside in another bowl. Ladle the consommé into the sieve and allow it to drip slowly through the cloth. As you get closer to the bottom of the saucepan, you might notice that the clear consommé is being muddied by bits of egg white. Don't worry, just add it to the sieve. Check the bowl with the egg white debris and pour any liquid that has escaped from it into the sieve. Allow all the liquid to drip slowly through the sieve; don't be tempted to press on the egg whites, as that would cloud the consommé.

5. You will have about 5 cups (1.25 l) clear consommé in the bowl and a mess of congealed egg white to discard. Season the consommé with about ¼ teaspoon salt. Serve hot or allow it to cool, then chill and serve cold. If you serve the consommé cold, you will probably need to boost the seasoning, as cold dulls the flavor.

Consommé Garnishes

- Finely shredded savory crepes, chopped herbs, or finely diced cooked chicken

- Finely blanched and diced vegetables

- Wonton wrappers filled with chicken liver puree (page 209)

Roasted Bird Broth

This recipe is an excellent way to use that leftover turkey carcass that lurks menacingly in the back of your post-Thanksgiving refrigerator. You can, of course, use the carcass of any leftover roasted bird, but if it is chicken, use a couple or halve the recipe. You can combine the carcasses of different birds, but use only cooked poultry bones—*don't* mix fresh and cooked bones.

The result will be a light basic stock that can be used for Post-Thanksgiving Soup (page 136) or in any sauce or dish containing turkey or chicken. It freezes well.

Carcass from a 12- to 16-pound (5.4- to 7.2-kg) turkey
2 tablespoons vegetable oil
1 large onion, unpeeled, halved
1 large carrot, peeled and sliced
2 celery stalks, sliced
¼ cup (60 ml) brandy
A 1 × 1-inch (2.5 × 2.5-cm) piece of fresh ginger, peeled and sliced
1 bay leaf
1 thyme sprig
¼ teaspoon black peppercorns

1. Preheat the oven to 425°F (220°C). Break or chop the turkey carcass into 3 or 4 pieces. Pour the vegetable oil into a large roasting pan and add the chopped turkey carcass, onion, carrot, and celery (the onion's skin will help color the broth). Roast for 30 minutes, stirring 2 or 3 times.

2. Transfer the turkey and vegetables to a large stockpot. Pour off any fat from the roasting pan and discard, then place the pan over medium heat and add the brandy and 2 cups (500 ml) water. Bring to a boil, deglazing the pan by scraping up the browned bits from the bottom. Pour into the stockpot and add the ginger, bay leaf, and thyme.

3. Pour in about 10 cups (2.5 l) cold water, or enough to almost cover the turkey pieces. Bring slowly to a gentle boil, skim off any scum, and add the peppercorns. Reduce the heat and simmer, uncovered, for 2 hours.

4. Strain the broth through a sieve into a large bowl. Discard the debris left in the sieve and cool the broth quickly by placing the bowl in a larger bowl or sink filled with ice water; stir occasionally as it cools, then refrigerate overnight. Remove any fat from top of the broth before using and discard the debris at the bottom of the bowl.

Post-Thanksgiving Soup

Use the Roasted Bird Broth made from the carcass and any leftover turkey meat (remove the skin and any visible fat) in this soup or use just the vegetables here. The ginger, lemon, and mint combination gives this soup a light fresh taste.

4½ cups (1.25 l) Roasted Bird Broth (page 135)
2 carrots, peeled and thinly sliced
3 leeks, white part only, thinly sliced
2 tablespoons julienned fresh ginger
1 cup (250 ml) diced cooked turkey
2 tablespoons freshly squeezed lemon juice
½ teaspoon kosher salt
Freshly ground black pepper
¼ cup finely shredded mint leaves

1. Place the broth in a large saucepan, add the carrots, and bring to a boil. Cover, reduce the heat, and simmer for 5 minutes, then add the leeks and ginger. Cover and continue to cook until the vegetables are just tender, about another 5 minutes.

2. Add the turkey and lemon juice. Season with the salt and pepper, and simmer until the turkey is heated through, about 2 minutes. Add the mint and serve immediately.

WISHBONES

Our family collection of wishbones, mostly chicken and the occasional turkey one, hung in our kitchen. Turkey was a special-occasion bird, making its big, impressive wishbone rare and highly prized. Expertly removed from the bird when it was carved, the wishbones were cleaned, then suspended over the sink on the handle of a manual can opener. From this central spot, we would watch them dry while we washed and dried the dishes. The drying took forever, or so it seemed, but if not sufficiently dry, the wishbones would bend, not snapping cleanly. Once my mother deemed them ready, two in the family were chosen to try their luck. Little fingers curled tightly around the slender white brittle bones that formed the fork, we paused for a moment, eyes closed, to consider then silently utter our wishes, . . . 1, . . . 2, . . . 3, . . . snap.

In most families, so I later learned, it ends there—if you had the longer piece, your wish came true. In our family, life was not so simple. The winner held both pieces of the broken bone in his or her hand, with just the tips of the unbroken ends jutting out. The loser attempted to redeem his luck by choosing the longer bone. Naturally, careful observation of the tips of the bone before the initial snap paid off.

The furcula, or wishbone, is found in all birds and is the forked bone between the bird's neck and breast. Its older name, merrythought, dates from 1607. That name also referred to the custom of two people pulling on the bone until it broke. The person left with the longer piece would soon be married, a merrythought.

I mistakenly assumed everyone grew up with the tradition of carefully drying the wishbone. This custom, however, appears to be peculiarly Anglo-Saxon, with uncertain origins and many bizarre and contradictory explanations put forward. This is often a sign that the tradition derives from an ancient belief and in this case, the ritual of breaking wishbones may be linked to the prophetic power of the goose. Many religions and sacred ceremonies from Scandinavia and Europe to India and China depict the goose, often in the company of gods. Why the goose? Geese are migratory birds and early peoples observed that their reappearance each year signaled the return of the sun and the arrival of spring, and with it, fertility and prosperity. So, the goose was thought to have prophetic powers and these resided in its bones.

Before flying south for the winter, the geese grazed on the harvested fields to fatten up for the long flight. The fattened geese made excellent eating, and afterward, their bones, in particular the breastbone, were examined to predict the severity of the approaching winter. Goose feasts became an important pagan tradition. Like many pagan rituals, they were expropriated by Christianity and transformed into feasts for saints. In Britain, the goose feast was linked to the archangel Saint Michael, whose feast day is September 29, known as Michaelmas. In Europe, Saint Martin's day, or Martinmas, November 11, was the day to eat goose. Both occasions celebrated the magical prophetic powers of the goose. In 1455, a German physician, Dr. Hartleib, described how the goose's breastbone was dried overnight, then examined to predict the coming winter. The goose, like the groundhog, was an early weather forecaster, but unfortunately for the goose, it meant death. The doctor also noted that the Teutonic knights used a goose's wishbone to determine the most advantageous time to wage war.

In parts of Scotland, predicting with a wishbone was not so simple. First, a hole was drilled in the flat top of the bone, then it was balanced on the bridge of the nose, like spectacles. The wearers of the bone had to pass a piece of thread through the hole, and the number of times it took them to succeed at this task would be the number of years before they married.

Once Europeans discovered the turkey, in Mexico, the goose was replaced on festive tables by this exotic new bird. Within a hundred years of Dr. Hartleib's writings, turkey was common throughout Europe. Although goose remained popular in Scandinavia, Germany, and Eastern Europe, the belief in its prophetic power disappeared. Only in Britain was the oracular power of the goose maintained, if unconsciously, by playing a wishing game with the wishbone. The game was exported by the British to America, South Africa, and Australia. In all these places, the wishbone, especially from the Christmas bird, is dried, then snapped apart by two people pulling on either end. The tradition of linking little fingers to form a makeshift wishbone and wishing grew out of the same custom.

Chicken with Forty Cloves of Garlic

Forty cloves of garlic may sound like a lot but the garlic loses its bite as it slowly braises in the stock with the chicken. The garlic softens, becoming mild and creamy. I have no idea why the magic number seems to be forty, but a few cloves more or less won't alter the flavor very much. The cooked garlic slides easily out of its skin and is eaten as a spread on toasted baguette slices.

1 chicken, about 4 pounds (1.8 kg)
1 lemon
2 thyme sprigs
2 rosemary sprigs
2 flat-leaf parsley stems
2 bay leaves
Kosher salt and freshly ground black pepper
¼ teaspoon paprika
1 tablespoon olive oil
40 garlic cloves, unpeeled
1½ cups (375 ml) Poultry Stock (page 130)
1 teaspoon cornstarch
Toasted baguette slices

1. Preheat the oven to 400°F (200°C). Dry the chicken well. Cut the lemon in half and set one half aside. Rub the chicken inside and out with the other half, then place the lemon in the chicken's cavity along with 1 sprig each of the thyme, rosemary, and parsley and 1 bay leaf. Season the chicken inside and out with salt and pepper, then truss. Using a small sieve, dust the chicken with the paprika.

2. In a Dutch oven or flameproof casserole, heat the oil over medium-high heat and brown the chicken well on all sides. Add the garlic cloves and the remaining herbs. Pour over the chicken stock and bring to a boil, then cover and braise in the oven for 1 hour, basting every 20 minutes with the stock.

3. Remove the lid and continue to cook for another 10 minutes, or until the thigh juices run clear when pierced and the internal temperature registers 165°F (73° C) on an instant-read thermometer. Transfer the chicken and the garlic to a platter and keep warm, loosely covered with aluminum foil.

4. Strain the cooking liquid into a small saucepan and skim off the fat, then bring to a boil and reduce to 1 cup (250 ml). Mix the cornstarch with 1 tablespoon water, whisk into the sauce, and bring to a boil, whisking. Check the seasoning, and add about 1 tablespoon juice squeezed from the remaining lemon half.

5. Carve the chicken and serve with the garlic cloves, sauce, and toasted baguette.

For larger birds such as chickens and turkeys, begin by pulling one leg away from the body and cutting down through the hip joint. Don't worry about leaving the "oysters" attached to the backbone—they are the cook's treat. Cut the leg in two through the joint between the thigh and drumstick. The meat on the leg and the thigh can be sliced by cutting parallel to the bone. Repeat with the other leg. Next, remove the wings and cut them in two.

To carve the breast, begin at the wishbone end and, one side at a time, slice diagonally down through the meat. (If the wishbone was removed before cooking, this will be easier.)

For geese and ducks, the tendons holding the legs and wings together are stronger. You will need more force to cut the legs and wings from the bird. When carving, slice each side of the breast parallel to the breastbone to yield long thin slices.

Herb-Glazed Poussins

Colin Faulkner, who took the black-and-white photographs for this book, made this dish for me. That evening he let his imagination fly with what was at hand and the result was delicious. You can follow the recipe exactly or use your own combination of herbs. Keep in mind that this is a glaze, not a sauce, so it will be thick and syrupy, with just enough to coat the birds. Serve the birds whole or cut them in half before serving, to make them easier to eat.

4 poussins or small Cornish hens, about 1 pound (450g) each
Kosher salt and freshly ground black pepper
2 lemons
4 garlic cloves
4 large tarragon sprigs
5 tablespoons olive oil
1 tablespoon rosemary leaves, chopped
½ cup (125 ml) dry white wine
3 tablespoons maple syrup, or to taste
1 teaspoon Dijon mustard
1 tablespoon chopped sage
1 tablespoon thyme leaves

1. Pat the birds dry and season them inside and out with salt and pepper. Cut 1 of the lemons into quarters, and squeeze the juice from the other one. Place 1 lemon quarter inside each bird along with 1 garlic clove and 1 tarragon sprig. Truss the birds and place in a dish or on a platter.

2. Mix 3 tablespoons of the oil with 2 tablespoons of the lemon juice and the rosemary, and pour over the hens, turning so they are well coated. Season them with salt and pepper, and leave to marinate at room temperature for 20 minutes.

3. Preheat the oven to 400°F (200°C). Pour the remaining 2 tablespoons olive oil into a roasting pan and add the birds, breast side up, along with the marinade. Roast, basting them every 10 minutes with the pan juices, for 35 to 45 minutes, or until golden and the thigh juices run clear when pierced; the temperature of the thigh should register 165°F (73°C) on an instant-read thermometer.

4. Transfer the birds to a warmed platter, breast side down, and keep warm, loosely covered with aluminum foil. Discard the fat from the roasting pan, set pan over medium-high heat, add the white wine and bring to a boil, deglazing the pan by scraping up the browned bits from the bottom. Boil to reduce the wine by half, add the maple syrup, mustard, and any juices from the birds and continue to boil until syrupy. Taste the glaze, adding a little more lemon juice or maple syrup if necessary. Remove from the heat and add the herbs.

5. Place the birds, either whole or cut in half, on dinner plates, and brush with the glaze.

Variation

○ Chicken, capon, and turkey can all be substituted in this recipe. This is enough marinade and glaze for a 4-pound (1.8-kg) chicken. Increase the recipe by half again for a capon and double it for a small turkey. Don't forget to increase the roasting time as necessary.

THE BIGGEST WISHBONE

○○

The biggest wishbone of all is in Chicago's Field Museum of Natural History, and belongs to Tyrannosaurus Sue. Sue's is one of the most complete *Tyrannosaurus rex* skeletons discovered. She's big at 42 feet (12.6 m) long and old, some sixty-seven million years old. But it's not her size or age that impresses, it's the fact that Sue has a furcula. She is the first *T. rex* ever found with a wishbone. This gives credence to the theory that birds evolved either directly from dinosaurs or from a common ancestor. (By the way, no one really knows if Sue is female; she is named after Sue Hendrickson, who found her.)

Poached Chicken with Seasonal Vegetables

Chicken was once a luxury item and the subject of promises of kings and presidents from Henri IV of France to President Herbert "A chicken in every pot" Hoover. This is a classic dish that crosses cultures, and is infinitely adaptable depending on the vegetables used. I have suggested a spring/summer combination, but if you make this in autumn/winter, try celeriac (celery root), parsnip, and rutabaga. Stay away from potatoes, though, which would break up and cloud the stock. If you fancy adding a green vegetable—favas, green beans, or Brussels sprouts—cook it separately and add it at the end. As well as changing the vegetables, play around with the herbs and seasonings. Adding fresh ginger and lemongrass gives the dish an Asian twist. Serve the broth first, then the chicken and vegetables if you'd like, or keep the broth for the next day and add the diced left-over chicken and vegetables to it. The size of the chicken and the amount of vegetables will depend on the size of your pot. Once cooked, the chicken is difficult to remove from the pot without losing a wing or two. To make it easier, before placing the chicken in the pot, tie a double strip of cheesecloth around it with a knot over the breast to form a handle.

1 chicken, about 4½ pounds (2 kg)
Kosher salt and freshly ground black pepper
6 cups (1.5 l) Poultry Stock (page 130)
4 leeks, trimmed
1 bay leaf
1 onion
1 clove
4 carrots, halved
4 turnips, peeled and halved
1 celery heart, halved
4 garlic cloves
¼ teaspoon black peppercorns
3 large flat-leaf parsley stems
2 tarragon sprigs
1 tablespoon grainy mustard
1 shallot, finely chopped
1 tablespoon white wine vinegar
3 tablespoons olive oil
3 tablespoons chopped flat-leaf parsley
2 tablespoons chopped chives
1 tablespoon chopped tarragon
1 tablespoon chopped chervil, optional
Coarse sea salt

1. Pat the chicken dry and season it inside and out with salt and pepper. Truss the bird and tie a length of cheesecloth around it, if using (see the headnote), then place it in a large stockpot. Pour over the stock and add enough water to almost cover the chicken, up to 6 cups (1.5 l). Add 1 teaspoon salt and bring slowly to a boil.

2. Meanwhile, prepare the vegetables: Tie the leeks together in pairs, and attach the bay leaf to the onion, using the clove as a pin.

3. Once the stock begins to boil, reduce the heat so that it barely simmers and skim well. Add the leeks, onion, carrots, turnips, celery, garlic, peppercorns, parsley stems, and tarragon sprigs and simmer gently, uncovered, for 1 hour, or until the chicken is cooked. To check, pierce the thigh with a skewer; the juices should run clear or the temperature of the thigh should register 165°F (73°C) on an instant-read thermometer.

4. Transfer the chicken and vegetables to a warmed serving platter. Remove the cheesecloth (if you used it) and string from the chicken and leeks. Keep warm, loosely covered with aluminum foil. Strain the cooking liquid. Let stand for a few minutes to allow the fat to rise to the top then skim off the fat and discard.

5. Place the mustard and shallot in a small bowl. Whisk in the vinegar and then the olive oil. Add ½ cup (125 ml) of the strained cooking liquid. Stir in the fresh herbs and season with salt and pepper. Carve the chicken and serve with the vegetables, sauce, and coarse sea salt.

WHAT DID HOOVER REALLY SAY?

Politicians and kings have always made promises to win power and favor with the people. While there is no way to check what Henri IV of France really said, Herbert Hoover's presidential archives are quite adamant about what he said. He is often quoted as saying "a chicken in every pot and a car in every garage."

Many campaign slogans were put forward during Hoover's 1928 presidential campaign: "Vote for Prosperity," "Who but Hoover?" But the archives claim he never said "a chicken in every pot." The phrase originated in an advertisement placed by the Republican National Committee. It claimed that Hoover would continue the policies of Harding and Coolidge. They had "reduced hours and increased earning capacity, silenced discontent and put the proverbial chicken in every pot and a car in every backyard to boot."

Yes, you can get away without doing it, but trussing gives the bird a nice compact shape and makes it easier to turn and move around in the roasting pan. Truss after seasoning the bird with salt and pepper and placing any other seasonings or stuffing in the cavity. First, tuck the neck flap under the bird and bend the wings back, under the bird, using the tips to hold the flap in place. Or, if the wing tips have been removed, secure the flap with a metal skewer or toothpick, and then turn the bird on its back. Take a piece of string at least 4 feet (1.3 m) long and place it under the tail. Cross the two ends of string above the bird and then loop them around each leg. Pull tightly to bring the tail and legs together, then tie a knot. Turn the bird on its breast. Take one end of the string, leaving the other end loose, and pull it across the leg, then loop it around the wing, through the space formed by the wing tip across the neck flap, and then through and around the other wing. Tie the ends of the string together in a knot on the side of the bird, and cut off any excess string.

Guinea Hen with Raspberries

The guinea hen is a West African relative of the chicken and partridge, originally from Guinea. It has a gamey taste and can dry out easily because it has little fat. Cooking the bird in a covered pot and adding fat solves that problem, and raspberries match its stronger flavor. The raspberries inside the bird will tint the bird's juices red: don't let this fool you into thinking that it needs more cooking.

1 guinea hen, about 3 pounds (1.35 kg)
Kosher salt and freshly ground black pepper
2 cups (250 g) raspberries
2 tablespoons (30 g) unsalted butter, softened
3 thyme sprigs
½ cup (125 ml) port
1 tablespoon raspberry jam or jelly
1 tablespoon red wine vinegar

1. Preheat the oven to 425°F (220°C). Pat the bird dry and season it inside and out with salt and pepper. Set ½ cup (62 g) of the raspberries aside and place the rest inside the hen. Truss it, then smear the skin with the softened butter.

2. Place the hen and the thyme in a Dutch oven or flameproof casserole. Pour in 1 cup (250 ml) water, cover, and place in the oven. Cook for 1 to 1¼ hours or until the thigh juices run clear when pierced with a skewer or an instant-read thermometer inserted into the thigh reads 165°F (73°C). Transfer the hen to a platter, breast down, and cover loosely with aluminum foil.

3. Skim off the fat from the cooking juices and bring to a boil over medium-high heat. Add the port, raspberry jam or jelly, and vinegar and bring back to a boil, then boil for 3 to 5 minutes, until reduced to ⅓ cup (75 ml). Add any juices from the resting hen and check the seasoning. Strain the sauce through a sieve into a sauceboat and add the remaining raspberries.

4. Remove the trussing string, from the guinea hen. Carve and serve with the sauce.

Roasted Duck with Peaches and Cardamom

Duck is commonly paired with fruit, and too often it's oranges or cherries, which can be overly sweet and taste like dessert. This duck is roasted with peaches and cardamom and then served with more peaches that have been poached separately in a light cardamom syrup. Rather than sweet, the peaches add a surprising acid touch, which complements the rich meat of the duck. Do make sure your cardamom is not old; the seeds should be black and highly aromatic when you crush the pods. There is no need to peel the peaches that go in the duck or the roasting pan. As for the poached peaches, it's up to you.

1 duck, about 4 pounds (1.8 kg), neck reserved
1 tablespoon vegetable oil
1 small onion, diced
1 small carrot, peeled and diced
1 celery stalk, sliced
2 garlic cloves, crushed
Kosher salt and freshly ground black pepper
6 large peaches
14 green cardamom pods, crushed
¼ cup (50 g) sugar
1 cup (250 ml) Poultry Stock (page 130)

1. About 8 hours before you plan to cook the duck, pat it dry and place on a plate, uncovered, in the refrigerator to help dry the skin.

2. One hour before roasting, remove the duck from the refrigerator. Preheat the oven to 425°F (220°C).

3. Pour the oil into a roasting pan and brush or rub a light film of oil over the bottom of the pan. Scatter the onion, carrot, celery, and garlic in the pan. Using a needle or pin, prick the skin of the duck all over. Season the duck inside with salt and pepper, then trim off the wing tips and reserve. Rub the skin with about 1 teaspoon salt.

4. Cut 4 of the peaches into wedges and discard the pits. Place as many peach wedges as will fit comfortably inside the duck—about 2 peaches—along with 4 cardamom pods. Truss the duck. Add the remaining peach wedges, along with the wing tips, the neck, and 6 cardamom pods to the roasting pan. Season them and the vegetables very generously with pepper. Put the duck on its side on top of the vegetables and roast for 10 minutes.

5. Turn the duck on its other side and roast for 10 minutes, then turn the duck on its back and roast for another 10 minutes.

6. Spoon off any fat that has accumulated in the roasting pan. Reduce the oven temperature to 350°F (175°C) and continue to roast for another hour, or until the juices from the thigh are slightly pink when pierced with a skewer or the thigh temperature registers 180°F (82°C) on an instant-read thermometer.

7. While the duck is roasting, put the sugar, 1 cup (250 ml) water, and the remaining 4 cardamom pods in a small saucepan. Bring to a boil, stirring to dissolve the sugar, then boil for 1 minute without stirring. Remove the pan from the heat, cover, and set aside.

8. About 30 minutes before the duck is cooked, halve the remaining 2 peaches, remove the pits, and place them in a small baking dish. Pour over the cardamom syrup. Cook the peaches, uncovered, in the oven for 20 to 25 minutes, or until tender.

9. When the duck is cooked, transfer it to a platter, breast side down. Remove the trussing string, then cover loosely with aluminum foil and let it rest, while you prepare the sauce.

10. Discard the fat from the roasting pan, leaving the vegetables and peaches in the pan. Place it over high heat, add the stock, and bring to a boil, deglazing the pan by scraping up the browned bits from the bottom. Continue to boil until the sauce reduces by half.

11. While the sauce is reducing, carve the duck. Add any juices from the duck to the sauce. Strain the sauce, pressing hard on the vegetables and peaches to extract all the flavor. Check the seasoning. Serve the duck with the peach halves and the sauce.

TIPS Goose works well in this recipe.

To peel peaches, drop them into boiling water for a minute, then transfer to ice water. The skins will slip off.

Grilled Quail with Sage Butter

Quail qualifies as fast food. Farm-raised quail are tender, requiring only a short time in the marinade. If they are spatchcocked, they cook in about fifteen minutes. Ask your butcher to do this, or do it yourself (see page 149). Sage is a good match for any poultry, and especially quail. Fresh sage can be soft and furry, but when you fry the leaves in butter, they crisp right up, improving their texture and flavoring the butter at the same time.

4 quail, about 6 ounces (170 g) each, spatchcocked (see the headnote)
¼ cup (60 ml) olive oil
1 garlic clove, sliced
Kosher salt and freshly ground black pepper
16 fresh sage leaves
4 tablespoons (60 g) cold unsalted butter, diced
½ lemon
4 large slices country-style bread
Fleur de sel

1. Remove the wishbones (see page 153) from the quail, then pat dry. Place on a cutting board, skin side up, and, using your palm, press down on each bird to break the breastbone: you will hear it crack. Fold the neck flap under each bird and secure in position with the wing tips by bending the wings under the bird. Place the birds in a single layer in a shallow dish.

2. Mix the olive oil and garlic, and season with salt and pepper. Finely shred 4 of the sage leaves and add them to the oil. Pour the oil mixture over the quail, turning the birds to coat. Let marinate at room temperature for 1 to 2 hours.

3. While the birds marinate, prepare the sage garnish and butter. Heat a small frying pan over medium heat, when hot, add the remaining 12 sage leaves and the cold butter. Cook the leaves, turning until crisp and dark green, about 4 minutes.

4. Transfer leaves to paper towels to drain, and quickly pour the sage butter into a glass measuring cup to cool. If your butter becomes too cold (it should be liquid), reheat it gently while the quail cook.

5. Preheat the grill to medium. Squeeze a little lemon juice over the quail, place them skin side down on the grill, and cook for 8 minutes, giving the quail a quarter-turn at 4 minutes. Then turn the quail over and cook for another 8 minutes, or until just cooked; they should still have a touch of pink when pierced at the breast.

6. Transfer the quail to a platter, pour 2 tablespoons of the sage butter over them and let them rest for 5 minutes, loosely covered with aluminum foil.

7. While the quail are resting, turn the grill to high. Brush the bread with the remaining flavored butter and grill lightly on both sides.

8. Place a piece of grilled bread on each plate, put the quail on top, and pour over any remaining butter. Garnish with the crispy sage leaves, sprinkle with fleur de sel, and serve.

Spatchcocking

Small birds require more work to eat, but if they are spatchcocked or the wishbone is removed, it will be easier. To spatchcock a bird means to split and flatten, or butterfly, it. The French call the result en crapaudine, *meaning in the form of a toad. Somehow, to the imaginative French eye, the flattened bird resembles a toad. By flattening the bird into a uniform thickness, it cooks more evenly, making it easier to grill. While small birds are most often prepared this way, you can also spatchcock a chicken. The backbone is removed and sometimes the wishbone, then the bird is pressed so that the breastbone snaps and it lies flat.*

Alsatian-Style Pheasant

Like most farm-reared birds, pheasants are not as gamey as their wild brethren. Nonetheless, they are delicious. Roasting can make pheasant dry, so a better method is braising to keep it moist. Sauerkraut is a popular accompaniment for game, especially in Germany, but here it is simply braised cabbage, which doesn't overpower the pheasant. With the braised cabbage, one bird can feed four people.

1 **Savoy cabbage**
Kosher salt
1 **pheasant, about 3 pounds (1.35 kg), neck and liver reserved**
Freshly ground black pepper
2 **tablespoons duck fat or vegetable oil**
2 **onions, sliced**
1 **tablespoon sugar**
½ **cup (125 ml) semi-dry Riesling**
5 **ounces (150 g) slab (side) bacon, rind removed and diced**
2 **sweet apples such as Fuji or Gala, peeled, cored, and sliced**
2 **tablespoons Cognac**

1. Remove 4 large outside leaves from the cabbage and set aside. Quarter the cabbage, remove the core, and finely shred enough cabbage to make 8 cups (2 l).

2. Bring a large pot of salted water to a boil, and fill a large bowl with ice water. Drop the whole cabbage leaves into the boiling water and blanch for 4 to 5 minutes, or until soft. Transfer them to the ice water. Once cold, drain on paper towels. Add the shredded cabbage to the boiling water and blanch for 2 to 3 minutes, or until soft. Drain in a colander and refresh under cold running water. Squeeze as much moisture out of the shredded cabbage as possible. Set aside.

3. Pat the pheasant dry. Season inside and out with salt and pepper, then truss it. Heat the duck fat in a Dutch oven or flameproof casserole over medium-high heat. Brown the bird and the reserved neck on all sides, then transfer to a plate. Lower the heat, add the onions and sugar to the pot, and cook, stirring until the onions begin to caramelize. Add the wine and bring to a boil, deglazing the pot by scraping up the browned bits from the bottom. Add the shredded cabbage, the bacon, and apples, cover, and cook over medium-low heat for 15 minutes.

4. Meanwhile, preheat the oven to 425°F (220°C). Dice the reserved pheasant liver.

5. Remove the lid from the pot, increase the heat, and cook, stirring, until all the moisture has evaporated. Remove from the heat, add the Cognac and diced liver, and season with salt and pepper. Push some of the cabbage mixture out to the sides of the dish to make a nest for the pheasant. Add the pheasant, breast side up, and cover with the 4 blanched cabbage leaves, then the lid. Place in the oven and cook for 50 minutes to 1 hour, or until the temperature in the thigh registers 180°F (82°C) on an instant-read thermometer. Let stand for 5 to 10 minutes.

6. Remove the pheasant from the pot, cut off trussing string, carve, and serve with the cabbage.

OTHER WISHBONES

○○○○○○○○○○○○○○○○○○○○○○○○○○○○○○○○○○○

Wishbone and *merrythought* have other meanings as well. Merrythought is the name of a wishbone-shaped bookbinding tool used in the late fifteenth and the sixteenth centuries.

During the 1970s a popular North American football formation was called the wishbone. In this play, the two fullbacks and the quarterback form a wishbone shape to pass the ball around the opposing defensive line.

Roasted Squab with Fresh Figs

Squab is a fancy word for pigeon. Unlike the birds that pollute our cities, however, these pigeons are specially bred and killed before they can fly, making them quite tender. Even farm-raised squab often have a touch of the liver flavor that game lovers crave. Keep the meat on the pink side, and make sure to let the birds rest before serving. A sharp steak knife is ideal for eating these birds—and encourage your guests to use their fingers to pull them apart. The squab I buy come with their heads and feet still attached, which I remove before roasting. If yours come the same way, ask your butcher to remove them for you, but take the pieces with you, then add them to the pan when you roast the birds to intensify the sauce. I also remove the wishbones (see page 153) from these birds before cooking. It's a simple job, if a bit fiddly, and makes them easier to eat. Use green or purple figs or a mixture; it's your choice.

4 squab, about 12 ounces (350 g) each, trimmed
Kosher salt and freshly ground black pepper
10 fresh figs
2 large oranges
4 thyme sprigs
3 tablespoons vegetable oil
1 cup (250 ml) Poultry Stock (page 130)

1. Preheat the oven to 450°F (230°C). Pat the squab dry and season inside and out with salt and pepper. Cut 2 of the figs into quarters. Using a vegetable peeler, remove 4 large strips of zest from 1 orange. Place 2 fig quarters, a strip of orange zest, and a thyme sprig inside each bird. Truss, or just tie the legs and the tail together, then fold the neck flap under, securing it by tucking the wings under the bird.

2. Heat the oil in a large ovenproof frying pan over medium-high heat. Brown the birds on all sides. Turn the birds on their backs, place in the oven, and roast for 25 minutes, or until the temperature in the thigh registers 155°F (68°C).

3. While the squab roast, juice the zested orange. You need 1 cup (250 ml) juice; if necessary, squeeze the second orange. Trim the remaining 8 figs and cut them into quarters.

4. Remove the pan from the oven, transfer the cooked birds to a warm platter, breast side down, and cover loosely with aluminum foil. Let them rest for 10 minutes. Meanwhile, *remembering that the pan handle will be very hot,* discard the fat from the pan. Add the stock and juice, and bring to a boil, deglazing the pan by scraping up the browned bits from the bottom. Reduce the heat, add the figs, and cook until they start to soften, 3 to 5 minutes. Transfer the figs to a plate and cover to keep them warm. Continue to cook the sauce until reduced to about ½ cup (125 ml); strain.

5. Remove the strings from the birds and place them, with the figs, onto plates. Spoon over the sauce.

This is a fiddly job, but worth the effort, especially with smaller birds. Feel around with your fingers in the neck of the bird to locate the wishbone. Using a small knife, cut through the meat to expose both forks of the bone. Cut through where the top of the bone joins the breastbone, and then pull the bone toward you to free the wishbone from the collarbone.

PERSIAN WISHBONES

In Iran, there is game played with wishbones that has elements of the British tradition. A bet, usually involving a service or money, is made before the wishbone is broken. The winner, in order to receive the service or sum demanded, is required to say, "*Yadam*" (I remember, in Persian) each time the loser hands him anything at all. If he forgets, the game is over. A winner with a good memory can keep the game going for days or weeks. A crafty loser, on the other hand, will try every trick he can think of to end the game. For example, he may pretend to drop something, hoping that the winner will instinctively grab it and forget to say *yadam*.

Chicken with Morel Cream Sauce

Although I prefer to buy whole chickens, it's hard to pass up the deals on chicken thighs and legs. In this recipe I use both dried and fresh mushrooms to intensify the flavor. Morels, a spring mushroom, love cream. When they are out of season, replace them with cremini (brown button) mushrooms.

Morels need careful handling because their honeycomb-textured caps trap sand and their hollow insides are popular with insects. Rinse fresh ones well under cold, running water and cut them lengthwise in half to clean. After soaking the dried ones, strain the liquid, carefully discarding the debris at the bottom of the bowl.

½ ounce (15 g) dried morels
8 bone-in chicken thighs
Kosher salt and freshly ground black pepper
1 tablespoon vegetable oil
½ tablespoon (7 g) unsalted butter
1 cup (250 ml) dry sherry
1 cup (250 ml) heavy (35 %) whipping cream
5 ounces (150 g) fresh mushrooms, preferably morels
Chopped flat-leaf parsley for garnish

1. Rinse the dried morels and place them in a small bowl. Pour over ¾ cup (175 ml) boiling water and allow them to soak for 30 minutes.

2. Pat the chicken thighs dry and season with salt and pepper. In a large heavy frying pan, heat the oil and butter over medium heat. When the butter begins to foam, add the chicken skin side down and cook, turning once, until golden on both sides, about 5 to 8 minutes total. Transfer the chicken pieces to a plate and discard the fat from the pan.

3. Pour the sherry into the pan, *being careful* it doesn't catch alight, and bring to a boil, deglazing the pan by scraping up the browned bits from the bottom. Continue to boil until the sherry is reduced by half. Meanwhile, remove the morels from the bowl, then carefully strain the soaking liquid through a fine sieve; discarding any sand in the bottom of the bowl. Add the mushroom liquid and cream to the pan, bring to a boil, and boil for 3 minutes.

4. Cut the soaked morels lengthwise in half or quarters, depending on their size. Add to the cream mixture, along with the chicken thighs, and cook, uncovered, for 15 minutes, turning the thighs halfway through.

5. Meanwhile, clean the fresh morels and cut them lengthwise in half or into quarters, depending on their size. (If using cremini, thickly slice them.) Add the mushrooms to the pan, cover, and cook for another 15 to 20 minutes, or until the chicken is cooked. The sauce should just coat the chicken, so check during the last 5 minutes of cooking and uncover the pan if the sauce is still too liquid.

6. Sprinkle with parsley and serve.

Chicken with Riesling

While coq au vin, made with chicken and red wine, is well known and delicious, chicken and white wine are also a perfect match. A famous chicken dish was cooked for Napoleon's supper after he defeated the Austrians at the battle of Marengo in northern Italy. His chef supposedly whipped it up from the meager leftovers, which included chicken, white wine, and mushrooms. As I'm not on a battlefield, I have more choices. I add tomatoes and use a dry Riesling, but any dry white wine will work. You can use legs, as here, thighs, or a chicken cut into serving portions. If you can't find small button mushrooms, quarter larger ones.

3 pounds (1.35 kg) chicken drumsticks (about 10)
Kosher salt and freshly ground black pepper
2 tablespoons vegetable oil
1 tablespoon (15 g) unsalted butter
2 shallots, finely chopped
2 tablespoons Cognac
1 cup (250 ml) dry Riesling
6 plum tomatoes, peeled, seeded, and diced
8 ounces (225 g) small button mushrooms, trimmed
2 tarragon sprigs
¼ cup (60 ml) heavy (35%) whipping cream
2 tablespoons chopped tarragon

1. Pat the chicken dry and season with salt and pepper. Heat the oil and butter in a large frying pan with a lid or a Dutch oven over medium heat. Brown the chicken in 2 batches, 5 to 7 minutes per batch. Transfer the browned pieces to a plate. Discard all but 1 tablespoon of the fat from the pan. Add the shallots and cook, stirring, for 1 minute. Pour in the Cognac, then half the wine, and deglaze the pan by scraping up the browned bits from the bottom of the pan. Add the remaining wine, the tomatoes, and mushrooms and bring to a boil.

2. Lower the heat and add the browned chicken, with any juices, the tarragon sprigs, and ½ teaspoon salt. Cover and simmer for about 20 minutes, turning the chicken once, until cooked through. Transfer the chicken to a plate.

3. Tip the pan and skim any fat off the sauce. Bring to a boil and boil uncovered, for 5 minutes to reduce. Stir in the cream and boil for 3 minutes, or until the sauce thickens slightly. Return the chicken legs to the pan and reheat gently over low heat, turning to coat with the sauce. Check the seasoning, sprinkle with the chopped tarragon, and serve.

Coconut Chicken Curry

The advantage of cooking all chicken thighs, or legs, unlike a cut-up chicken, is that they are done all at the same time. This recipe is in no way authentically Thai, but it is tasty and quick. You can add diced tomato, peas, diced potatoes, or sliced green beans instead of or as well as the red pepper. I must admit that I sometimes make this recipe to use up stray vegetables, but don't overdo it. I like to scatter the finished dish with shredded Thai basil, but any basil, coriander, or even parsley, will do.

8 bone-in chicken thighs, skin removed
1 teaspoon turmeric
2 tablespoons vegetable oil
1 tablespoon Thai red (or green) curry paste
One 13.5-ounce (400-ml) can coconut milk
2 tablespoons fish sauce
2 tablespoons freshly squeezed lime juice
2 teaspoons sugar
1 red bell pepper, cored, seeded, and thinly sliced
Kosher salt
A handful shredded basil leaves, preferably Thai, for garnish
1 lime, cut into wedges

1. Pat the chicken thighs dry and remove any excess fat. Sprinkle with the turmeric.

2. Heat the oil in a frying pan over medium-high heat and brown the chicken thighs on both sides. Transfer the chicken to a plate, and discard all but 1 tablespoon fat from the pan. Add the curry paste and stir, mixing it with the oil, until fragrant, about 30 seconds. Add the coconut milk and bring to a boil, stirring and scraping the browned bits from the bottom of the pan. Stir in the fish sauce, lime juice, and sugar and boil for 3 minutes, stirring occasionally.

3. Lower the heat, add the chicken with any juices, cover, and simmer for 15 minutes. Uncover, turn the chicken pieces, and simmer uncovered for another 15 minutes. Tip the pan and skim off any excess oil.

4. Add the red pepper slices and cook uncovered for another 5 to 10 minutes, or until the chicken is cooked. Check the sauce; it probably won't need any salt, but that will depend on your curry paste.

5. Sprinkle the curry with the basil leaves and serve with the lime wedges.

Duck Legs with Cumin, Turnips, and Green Olives

○○ { SERVES 4 } ○○○○○○○○○○

The popularity of duck breasts means there are lots of duck legs available. Not all of them can end up as confit. Use them in place of chicken, especially with an ingredient that cuts through their richness, such as olives and wine. Cumin seed adds an unusual spice note and, according to Indian authorities, it aids digestion, always a bonus with rich food. Prepare ahead and chill so the excess fat can easily be removed, then reheat the stew in the oven.

4 whole duck legs, about 12 ounces (350 g) each
Kosher salt and freshly ground black pepper
1 tablespoon vegetable oil
1 onion, diced
1 carrot, peeled and diced
1 celery stalk, sliced
2 teaspoons cumin seeds
2 garlic cloves, chopped
2 bay leaves
1 thyme sprig
5 flat-leaf parsley stems
1 cup (250 ml) dry red wine
1 cup (250 ml) Poultry Stock (page 130)
8 small cipollini or other small onions
4 medium turnips
12 large green olives, rinsed

1. Pat the duck legs dry. Prick the skin all over with a pin or sharp needle, then season with salt and pepper.

2. Preheat the oven to 300°F (150°C). In a Dutch oven or flameproof casserole, heat the oil over medium heat. Add 2 of the duck legs, skin side down, and cook for 5 minutes, or until golden brown. Turn the legs and cook until brown on the second side, about 2 to 3 minutes. Transfer to a plate. Repeat with the other 2 legs.

3. Pour off all but 1 tablespoon of fat from the pot (keep this extra fat; it is delicious for cooking potatoes). Add the diced onion, carrot, and celery and cook, stirring, until softened and the onions begins to color, about 5 minutes. Add the cumin seeds, garlic, bay leaves, thyme sprig, and parsley stems and stir until you smell the cumin seeds toasting, about 30 seconds. Pour in the wine, and bring to a boil, deglazing the pot by scraping up the browned bits from the bottom. Boil until the wine is reduced by one-third.

Poultry {157}

4. Add the stock, ½ teaspoon salt, and a good grinding of black pepper and return to a boil. Remove from the heat, add the duck legs, and cover with a damp piece of parchment paper and then the lid. Place in the oven and cook for 30 minutes.

5. While the legs are cooking, bring a medium saucepan of water to a boil. Add the small onions and blanch for 2 minutes, then refresh under cold running water. Peel the onions, leaving enough of the root intact so they will remain whole during cooking. Peel the turnips and cut them into quarters.

6. After the legs have cooked for 30 minutes, remove them from the pot and set aside. Stir the onions and turnips into the sauce, making sure they are submerged in the liquid, then place the legs on top of the vegetables. Cover with the parchment and lid again and place in the oven for 1 hour.

7. Smash the olives with the flat side of a knife blade and remove the pits. After the duck and vegetables have cooked for 1 hour, remove the lid and parchment paper and add the olives. Cook uncovered for 30 minutes longer, or until the duck is tender. Remove from the heat, transfer the duck legs to a dish, and allow to cool separately from the sauce.

8. Cover the sauce and the legs and refrigerate overnight.

9. About 1 hour before serving, preheat the oven to 300°F (150°C). Remove the fat from the sauce and any clinging to the duck legs. Place the legs back in the sauce, cover, and cook for 45 minutes, or until heated through.

10. Using a slotted spoon, transfer the duck, onions, and turnips to a deep serving dish and keep warm, loosely covered with foil. Bring the sauce to a boil and boil to reduce and thicken slightly. Spoon the sauce over the legs and vegetables and serve.

Confit

Southwest France is famous for its foie gras, both duck and goose, leaving plenty of meat once the liver is removed. The duck and goose are traditionally preserved by cutting them into portions, salting and seasoning them, and cooking them slowly in their own fat. Confit of duck generally refers to the legs preserved by this method. You can buy them, vacuum-packed, at many groceries and butchers; the fat is sold separately. The duck legs make a delicious quick meal. Bake them skin side down in a 350°F (175°C) oven for 15 to 20 minutes, or until heated through. Then turn them skin side up and broil them, watching carefully, for 5 minutes, or until the skin is crisp. Serve with a salad of bitter greens, endive or frisée, tossed with Orange Mustard Dressing (page 83), and potatoes cooked in duck fat.

Wings à la Coca-Cola

In a cookbook written by Frédéric E. Grasser-Hermé, the wife of the French pastry chef Pierre Hermé, I found a recipe for a whole chicken cooked in Coca-Cola. Madame Grasser-Hermé claims the source for her recipe was *Le Figaro* food critic François Simon. Her recipe started me thinking. Why not try it with chicken wings?

1½ pounds (675 g) chicken wings
Kosher salt and freshly ground black pepper
Grated zest and juice of 1 lemon
1 tablespoon finely chopped fresh ginger
1 garlic clove, finely chopped
Vegetable oil, for oiling rack
2 cups (500 ml) cola

1. Remove the tips from the wings and reserve for stock. Cut each wing into 2 pieces and season with salt and pepper. In a bowl, mix the lemon zest, juice, ginger, and garlic. Add ½ teaspoon salt, then the wings, and season well with pepper. Stir to coat the wings. Cover and marinate in the refrigerator for 2 hours.

2. Preheat the oven to 400°F (200°C). Line a baking sheet with aluminum foil and top with an oiled metal rack. Pour the cola into the bowl with the wings and stir, then remove the wings from the marinade and place bumpy skin side up on the rack, making sure they do not touch each other.

3. Pour the marinade into a saucepan and bring to a boil. Boil hard for 15 minutes, or until reduced to ½ cup (125 ml). Brush the wings with the reduced marinade (it will still be quite thin).

4. Bake the wings for 10 minutes. Brush them again with marinade, and cook for another 10 minutes.

5. Increase the oven temperature to 450°F (230°C). Brush the wings again and bake for 5 minutes. Brush the wings one final time and cook for another 5 minutes, or until deep brown.

Soy-Glazed Chicken Wings

Baking chicken wings in the oven is a simple method and you can use any glaze or sauce you like. Here is a sweet soy glaze. Or try the hoisin sauce for chicken feet (page 161) on your wings, but double the recipe so you will have enough.

¼ **cup (60 ml) soy sauce**
¼ **cup (60 ml) honey**
1 garlic clove, finely chopped
1 teaspoon finely chopped fresh ginger
¼ **teaspoon five-spice powder**
1½ pounds (675 g) chicken wings
Kosher salt and freshly ground pepper
Vegetable oil, for oiling rack

1. Preheat the oven to 400°F (200°C).

2. Place the soy sauce, honey, garlic, ginger, and five-spice powder in a small saucepan, bring to a boil, and simmer until syrupy, about 5 minutes.

3. Remove the tips from the wings, and reserve for stock. Cut each wing into 2 pieces and season with salt and pepper.

4. Line a baking sheet with aluminum foil and top with an oiled metal rack. Place the wings, bumpy skin side up, on the rack, making sure they do not touch each other. Brush with the soy glaze.

5. Bake the wings for 10 minutes. Brush them with the glaze and cook another 10 minutes.

6. Increase the oven temperature to 450°F (230°C). Brush the wings again and bake for 5 minutes. Brush the wings one final time and cook for another 5 minutes or until dark brown.

Spicy Steamed Chicken Feet

Before you turn the page, I urge you to try these once. They are chewy, sticky, and delicious. Like wings, feet are all about the sauce, but with less meat to eat and more to chew, they really need a hot and spicy or sweet and sticky sauce. Look for chicken feet in Asian markets.

Deep-frying chicken feet is supposed to make them puff but mine just exploded in the fryer, with hot oil spattering all over my kitchen. My method might not be how the best Chinese cooks do it, but it is simpler and a lot less messy. After an initial blanching, the feet are braised in fragrant liquid; the braising liquid can be kept refrigerated and reused, for Soy-Poached Chicken (page 163) or another dish.

The first task, and the least pleasant, is removing the claws, or toenails. Use a pair of kitchen scissors to cut them right off. This is best done in the kitchen sink so that those nail clippings don't fly all over the place.

BRAISING LIQUID
¼ cup (60 ml) soy sauce
¼ cup (60 ml) Chinese cooking wine (Shao Xing)
3 slices fresh ginger
1 garlic clove, crushed
3 large strips orange zest
1 green onion, trimmed and sliced
1 star anise, broken apart
3 tablespoons brown sugar
1 cinnamon stick
1 pound (450 g) chicken feet (about 8 to 12)

SPICY HOISIN SAUCE
3 tablespoons hoisin sauce
2 tablespoons rice vinegar
1 tablespoon brown sugar
1 tablespoon chili-garlic sauce
2 tablespoons finely grated fresh ginger
½ cup (125 ml) finely julienned carrot
1 small celery stalk, thinly sliced

1. Pour the soy sauce and wine into a large saucepan and add 2 cups (500 ml) water. Add the ginger, garlic, orange zest, green onion, star anise, brown sugar, and cinnamon and bring to a boil, then reduce the heat and simmer, covered, for 30 minutes.

2. While the braising liquid is simmering, remove the claws from the chicken feet. Place the feet in a saucepan, cover with cold water, and bring to a boil. Lower the heat and simmer for 3 minutes. Drain in a sieve and rinse under cold water. Cut each foot into 2 or 3 pieces.

3. After the braising liquid has simmered for 30 minutes, add the feet, cover, and simmer gently for 30 to 40 minutes, or until they are easily pierced with a skewer. Let the feet cool in the braising liquid.

4. Drain the feet, reserving the liquid. Place the feet in a single layer on a heatproof plate. Strain the braising liquid, cover, and refrigerate for another use. (The feet can be cooked ahead and refrigerated, covered, for up to 2 hours.)

5. Mix the hoisin sauce, vinegar, brown sugar, chili-garlic sauce, and grated ginger. Pour the sauce over the cooked feet and toss to coat. Scatter the carrot and celery over the feet, then place the plate in a steamer. Cover and steam for 10 to 15 minutes, or until the feet are very soft. Serve hot.

FASHIONABLE BONES

Bone is carved into exquisite jewelry, but wearing just plain bones never caught on. British fashion designer Vivienne Westwood, famous for her unique view of fashion, created a T-shirt in 1972 emblazoned with the word *rock* spelled out with real chicken bones. She had collected the bones from meals ordered from her local take-out restaurant.

Soy-Poached Chicken

The poaching liquid used for braising the chicken feet (see page 161) is also excellent for cooking chicken. You can make it specifically for this recipe or use it after you have cooked the feet in it, when it will be even better. The chicken slowly steeps in the liquid and is infused with its flavors. This chicken is best served at room temperature or slightly chilled, especially in summer.

1 chicken, about 3 pounds (1.35 kg)
Braising Liquid
2 green onions, trimmed and sliced
1 tablespoon julienned fresh ginger
1 small chile, seeded and minced

1. Cut the chicken into 6 pieces (see page 128). Bring the braising liquid to a boil in a large saucepan. Add the thighs and drumsticks and return to the boil, then lower the heat and simmer gently for 5 minutes. Add the chicken breasts and bring back to the boil, then reduce the heat and simmer for another 5 minutes.

2. Remove from the heat, cover and leave the chicken in the hot liquid for 1½ hours, turning the pieces after 45 minutes; by the end of this time, the chicken will be cooked.

3. Remove the chicken from the liquid and place on a platter. Strain the liquid into a glass measuring cup or bowl and let stand for several minutes. Skim off the fat and pour ½ cup (125 ml) of the liquid into a small saucepan (discard the rest) and bring to a boil and stir in the green onions, ginger, and chile.

4. Pour the sauce over the chicken, and serve at room temperature.

Fish

Water covers two-thirds of the earth, yet fish remain a mystery to us. Few of us tackle them whole, preferring to buy boneless fillets, which give us little idea of what the whole fish looks like. This is a shame. It's much more appealing to select whole fish from a bed of ice, or live from a tank, than to choose among several sad fillets on a tray. Whole fish have an intrinsic and dramatic beauty that makes fish markets such fun, yet even some fish lovers are scared away because of their bones. Perhaps if we were more familiar with fish, we wouldn't be put off by their bones.

Lurking uncharted in many fish are small and hard-to-see bones, making whole fish not only challenging but somewhat time-consuming to eat. What use are these bones? Why should we even bother with them?

Buying whole fish actually is easier than shopping for boneless pieces. Whole fish provide clues for judging freshness. Fresh fish looks as if it has just leapt out of the water, bright, shiny, and with all its scales intact. The gills, found only on whole fish, are hidden under flaps below the eyes. They should be bright red. If you can, don't be afraid to check; give the fish a prod with your finger at the same time—its flesh should feel firm and resilient. Moreover, with no exposed flesh, whole fish is less susceptible to bacteria and spoilage. Bones keep the fish moist while preserving its flavor.

To find a good fish market takes your nose and a little knowledge. Sniff and look. There should be no fishy smell evident, and the fish themselves should also pass the freshness tests. They should be displayed on a bed of ice with more ice blanketing them. Make friends with the fishmonger, because preparing and cleaning the fish is his job. He can help you select fish and suggest alternatives, since many fish are interchangeable in recipes. He will also set aside those valuable trimmings, heads, and bones for your stockpot.

Bones not only aid you in selecting your fish, they add flavor and texture to the cooked fish. But to simplify cooking and eating fish on the bone, you need to know where the bones are. To understand a fish's bones, familiarize yourself with its skeleton.

Many criteria are used to classify the thousands of fish in our oceans, lakes, and rivers—firm or flaky, freshwater or ocean, lean or oily. I have organized fish in this book by their skeletons.

Roundfish

Ask someone to draw you a fish, and they'll draw a round fish—it's the archetypical fish. The classification name—round—is misleading. Round fish are not round at all, but tube shaped. These swimming tubes come in various sizes, from large tuna to small aquarium fish. Look carefully at the fish in an aquarium and you'll notice that some of them are round, plump tubes, obviously round fish, while others are very thin flattened tubes—but even these thin ones are round fish. Observe how they swim, that's your clue: all round fish swim in a vertical position. While this maybe useful when fish are in a tank, at the fish market, they're mostly on ice. Look closely at one of those reposing fish, however—how many eyes can you see? If the answer is one, its a round fish, and the other eye is against the ice. Eels, despite their snake-like form, are elongated round fish, and slide comfortably into this classification.

Thick or thin, big or small, all round fish have a similar skeleton. The backbone runs down the center of their tubular bodies. From this, a single set of rib bones extends up, and just behind the head, a double set of rib bones fans down and out to form the cavity that holds the fish's innards. Toward the tail end, these bones become a single set. The flesh of round fish lies on either side, atop these bones, so each round fish yields two fillets. The fillets are thicker at the top of the fish, thinning out where they wrap over the ribs around the cavity. There is another set of bones running along the top of the fish, which support its dorsal fin. And behind the stomach cavity lies a small group of bones that support the anal fin. Many round fish, such as salmon, have another series of small, fine bones, pinbones, jutting at right

There are bone whales, bone sharks, but the most interesting are bonefish. Members of the herring family bonefish are found in tropical waters and are a popular game fish. They are eaten but, as the name suggests, they are full of bones. To make them easier to eat, the fish is stretched to break its bones and then suspended so that the bones fall into its stomach cavity.

Bône is a Mediterranean port town in Algeria that is now called Annaba.

The word *bone* refers to the bow wave of a sailing ship

"See how she leaps . . . and speeds away with a bone in her mouth."
—HENRY WADSWORTH LONGFELLOW, *The Golden Legend*

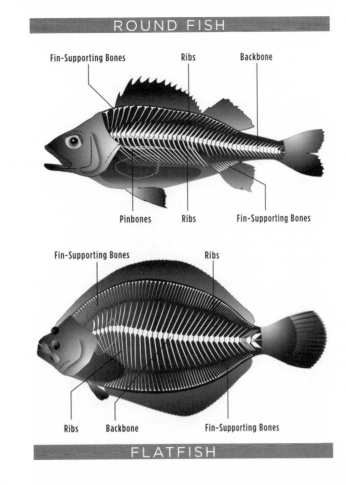

Herringbone is a zigzag pattern that resembles the pattern of herring-fish bones. It describes a pattern of cloth, sewing, bricks, stones, and even skiing.

Bone glass is a milky white glass that contains bone ash.

Bone coal can't be burned like regular coal because of its high ash content.

The word *bonebreaker* describes one of several large birds such as the giant petrel or osprey.

angles from the center of the backbone into their flesh. You will often find these bones running down the center of "boneless" fillets.

Whole, very large round fish are not practical in the majority of kitchens, as few of us have pots or ovens big enough to hold them, but you can still buy these fish on the bone. Large fish are sliced right through the backbone into cross-sections or fish steaks, at least 1 inch (2.5 cm) thick.

Whole small to medium-sized round fish are best cooked with their heads and tails still on. Not only do they look better on the plate, they are easier to handle that way and there are tasty morsels of flesh in the head too.

Flatfish

This small, select group includes two of the finest fish to eat, Dover sole and turbot, plus the more readily available flounder, fluke, dab, plaice, and soles with various names. Flatfish are more accurately named than round fish: their bodies look as if they have been squeezed through a wringer and they are indeed flat. Flatfish swim on their sides, and in the fish market you'll see, at a glance, both eyes are together on the top of the head. Surprisingly, they start life as round fish, happily swimming in a vertical position with one eye on either side of their heads. Then, some genetic memory is triggered and they flip onto their side and begin swimming that way. This dramatic change necessitates that one of their eyes move around from one side of the head to the other, but it results in the fish becoming either sinistral or dextral, as its eyes end up on the left or right side of its head.

With flatfish, the backbone runs down the center of the body from head to tail and the innards are neatly enclosed in the cavity just behind the head. A single set of ribs extends out in both directions from the backbone toward the fins. Another series of small bones lies between the rib bones and the fins. These bones support the dorsal and anal fins. The flesh lies uniformly above and below the rib bones, divided by the backbone, so a flatfish yields four fillets. Larger fish in this group, such as halibut and turbot, are thick enough to be cut like large round fish, through the bone into steaks. Their simpler bone structure and even thickness of flesh mean that flatfish are easier to cook and eat than round fish.

Skate and rays are primitive members of this family. They do not have bones per se but rather a skeleton of flexible, semitransparent cartilage. Usually only their flaps or wings, which contain the most meat, are sold; they are rarely seen whole in the market. A skate wing is a wedge-shaped portion of cartilage sandwiched between two tapering pieces of flesh.

Exceptions

The one exception is the monkfish. Whether for aesthetics or practicality, or both, the monkfish's unattractive head—which totals half of its body weight—is commonly removed when it is caught. All that arrives at the fish market is its tail-like body, containing one long bone, or spinal column. This single bone makes monkfish simple to cook and even simpler to eat. If you do chance upon it with its head, ignore its looks and grab it for your stockpot.

Something else you won't see whole is a frog, as only the hind legs are eaten. Frogs are amphibians, not fish, but I am allowing them to leap into this chapter anyway. Their legs are sold in pairs and each leg has two small bones, like a small bird leg.

While there are hundreds of fish, the focus here is on recipes using fish on the bone and bone-in fish cuts.

A boneshaker was a type of early bicycle without rubber tires. Now, it can refer to an uncomfortable or an amusement park ride. After a boneshaker ride you might need a boneshaker cocktail. It is made with 3 ounces (90 ml) over proof rum, 1 ounce (30 ml) vodka, and 1 ounce (30 ml) clamato juice shaken over ice.

Fish bones must be eaten quite bare and clean in the mouth and removed one at a time between finger and thumb.
—EMILY POST, *ETIQUETTE IN SOCIETY* (1922)

"What's bred in the bone will not go out of the flesh."
—DANIEL DEFOE, *ROBINSON CRUSOE* (1719)

Fish Stock

The choice of bones is the first and most important step in making fish stock. Not all fish bones are equal in the stockpot. Flatfish bones are by far the best, as they contain more gelatin, which will give the stock body and viscosity. A stock made entirely from these bones will set solid when it is cold. All flatfish bones, along with their heads, tails, skin, and any trimmings, can go into your stockpot. All these bits boost the taste; just remember to remove the gills, which would make the stock bitter.

As there are fewer flatfish than round fish, though, their bones are harder to obtain. Seize them when you can and ferret them away in the freezer until you have enough, or make up the difference with round fish bones. How can you tell if the bones of a particular round fish belong in your stockpot? If the fish is white and mild tasting, such as whiting, haddock, or bass, for example, it is just fine. Avoid the bones of any dark, oily, strong-tasting or fatty fish, like mackerel, herring, salmon, bluefish, sardines, and smelt, as they would make your stock strong and oily.

Unlike other stocks, fish stock requires a mere thirty minutes of simmering. The whole process, from soaking the bones to the final straining, shouldn't take much more than an hour. As fish bones yield their essence quickly, though, you must pay attention. Don't leave your fish stock unattended on the back of the stove; if you cook it too long, it can turn bitter.

The recipe can easily be doubled.

2¼ pounds (1 kg) fish bones, preferably from flatfish, heads (gills removed), tails, and skin
3 tablespoons vegetable oil
1 onion, diced
1 leek, trimmed and thinly sliced
1 carrot, peeled and sliced
1 celery stalk, sliced
¾ cup (175 ml) dry white wine
3 flat-leaf parsley stems
2 thyme sprigs
1 bay leaf
6 black peppercorns
Kosher salt, optional

1. Rinse the bones and assorted fish parts well, under cold running water. Break or chop them into 2- to 3-inch (5 to 7.5 cm) pieces (ask the fishmonger to do this, or use kitchen shears). Place the fish bones (and parts) in a large bowl of ice water and leave to soak for 15 minutes. This will leach out any blood from the bones.

2. Heat the oil in a stockpot over medium heat, then add the vegetables and let them sweat (this is a great culinary term to know: you don't want the vegetables to brown, just to cook so they soften and release their liquid—i.e., sweat as we do when we're hot). This should take about 5 minutes; the vegetables will be fragrant and brighter in color.

3. Drain the fish bones and add them to the stockpot. Increase the heat and stir to coat the bones with the oil, then cook, stirring often, for about 3 minutes. You will notice any flesh clinging to the bones beginning to turn opaque. Pour in the wine, bring it to a boil, and then boil for 3 minutes. Add enough cold water to almost submerge the bones, about 6 cups (1.5 l). Toss in the parsley, thyme sprigs, and bay leaf, reduce the heat to medium, and bring slowly to a boil.

4. As soon as the stock comes to a boil, reduce the heat so it simmers. Using a soup ladle, skim off any scum that has risen to the surface (rotate the bowl of the ladle on the surface of the stock to make ripples: these will carry the scum to the edges of the pot and you can then use the ladle to lift it off). Add the peppercorns, and let the stock simmer, uncovered, for 30 minutes, skimming as necessary. Adding peppercorns after the first skimming means there is less risk that you will remove them as you skim; watch out for them, though, as they float close to the surface.

5. Remove the stockpot from the heat. Place a sieve lined with damp cheesecloth or a dampened thin cotton tea towel over a bowl. Ladle the stock, bones, and vegetables into the sieve, pressing down gently on the bones to extract all the juices. Discard the debris left in the sieve, and cool the stock quickly by placing it in a larger bowl or sink filled with ice water; stir occasionally as it cools. When you taste the stock, you will notice that something is missing—the salt. Once it is added, the flavor will sparkle. But it was deliberately left out so that you can reduce the stock without any fear that it will become too salty. If you are not reducing the stock (see page 171) add about 1 teaspoon salt.

6. Refrigerate for 6 hours or overnight to allow the fat to rise to the top of the stock and the debris to sink to the bottom. Remove the fat before using (and discard the debris at the bottom of the bowl). Divide the stock into 1-cup (250-ml) quantities and refrigerate for up to 3 days, or freeze for up to 6 months.

Concentrated Fish Stock

If your freezer space is tight, reduce your stock following the method for Concentrated Brown Stock (page 14).

6 cups (1.5 l) unsalted Fish Stock (page 169)
Kosher salt

○○

The reduced stock will become syrupy and turn the color of grapefruit juice.

FISH BONES AND THE ARTIST

○○

Many artists have painted fish, but Pablo Picasso used his leftover fish bones to create a work of art. The well-known photographer David Douglas Duncan captured this creative moment in a series of photographs. In the first images, Picasso is seen devouring his *sole à la meunière*, a whole sole sautéed in butter (see page 189). As he sucks the last morsels of flesh from the bones, inspiration strikes. He leaves the table, rushes to his studio, and returns with a piece of wet clay. Taking the sole skeleton, he presses it into the clay, making several fossil-like imprints. He then cuts out two of these X-ray fish. Next he dabs paint onto the edge of a large unfired platter and presses the two fish cut-outs onto its rim. After firing, the platter emerges from the kiln decorated with one emerald and one blue fish skeleton.

Fish bones have inspired other artists as well. Photographer Irving Penn created an image, "Fish Bones on a Plate," a frugal lunch that appeared in the October 1993 edition of *Vogue* magazine. A small sardine, head still attached but no flesh left on its bones, shares a plate with a half-eaten olive and some crumbs of bread. Curiously, the sardine hasn't been cooked—its bright, glistening eye gives this away. No doubt Penn decided the fish was more photogenic raw.

Fish Consommé

Fish consommé is the quickest of all consommés to prepare, but the least popular, which is as a shame, because it is delicious and can be served hot or cold, simply or dressed up with a garnish.

6 cups (1.5 l) Fish Stock (page 169)
1 leek, white part only, chopped
4½ ounces (125 g) skinless white fish fillet, chopped
2 egg whites
1 tablespoon dry white vermouth
Kosher salt

1. Place the cold stock into a large saucepan and heat it just until it liquefies. Remove the saucepan from the heat.

2. Place the leek and chopped fish in a food processor and process until finely chopped. Add the egg whites and 2 tablespoons water and blend until well mixed. Stir this mixture into the stock and bring to a boil over medium-high heat, stirring constantly with a spatula or wooden spoon, scraping the bottom of the saucepan to prevent the egg white from sticking. As the liquid approaches a boil, it will appear to curdle; don't panic, that is what you want. As soon as the stock begins to boil, stop stirring, and remove the saucepan from the heat. The whites will form a congealed mass, which will puff up and then crack as the steam escapes.

3. Reduce the heat to very low, and return the saucepan to the heat, making a hole in the egg white mass with a spoon to allow the steam to escape. Simmer very gently—you want to see small bubbles of steam break the egg white mass—for 20 minutes. Remove the saucepan from the heat and let stand for 5 minutes.

4. Line a sieve with a double thickness of damp cheesecloth or a dampened thin cotton tea towel and place over a bowl. Using a skimmer or large slotted spoon, carefully lift off as much of the egg white mass as you can and set it aside in another bowl. Ladle the consommé into the sieve and allow it to drip slowly through the cloth. As you get closer to the bottom of the saucepan, you might notice that the clear consommé is being muddied by bits of egg white. Don't worry, just add it to the sieve. Check the bowl with the egg white debris and pour any liquid that has escaped from it into the sieve. Allow the liquid to drip slowly through the sieve; don't be tempted to press on the egg white, as that would cloud the consommé.

5. You will have about 5 cups (1.25 l) clear consommé in the bowl and a mess of congealed egg white to discard. Add the vermouth to the consommé and season with about ¼ teaspoon salt. Serve hot, or allow it to cool, then chill and serve cold. If you serve the consommé cold, you will probably need to boost the seasoning, as cold dulls the flavor.

Consommé Garnishes

Most garnishes for hot fish consommé should be added just before serving. Place them in the warmed soup bowls and ladle the hot consommé over. The exception is saffron, which is added to the hot stock in the saucepan.

- Finely chopped herbs, such as chives, flat-leaf parsley, coriander, and dill

- Shucked oysters, sliced cooked fish, or cooked shellfish such as shrimp or lobster

- Small cooked pasta

- Finely sliced or diced cooked vegetables

- Saffron: Place the threads in a clean saucepan over medium heat and toast for 30 seconds, or until fragrant; add the fish consommé, and serve.

SINISTRAL AND DEXTRAL FISH

As noted earlier, flatfish begin life as round fish, then gradually transform, with one of their eyes moving around to the other side of their heads, so both are on the same side. Those with eyes on the left are called sinistral. This group includes turbot and brill. The dextral, or right-eyed fish, include flounder, halibut, plaice, and lemon and Dover sole. The placement of their eyes allows them to turn in only one direction, dextral fish to the right and sinistral to the left. Nature sometimes plays a cruel trick and a fish can suffer from reversal. This means that its eyes move the opposite way to the norm, resulting in, for example, sinistral rather than dextral flounder. This poor fish is doomed to swim in the opposite direction to all its relatives.

Tidal Pools

Aspic was traditionally used to preserve whole poached salmon or sliced meats that sat on buffet tables. By protecting the exposed surfaces, aspic prevented the food from drying out. Clear and sparkling, it looked great, but it was often tasteless and rubbery.

The best aspic is a well-flavored, savory jelly made from clarified stock. Clarified stock will set in the refrigerator, but it is not quite firm enough to remain solid at room temperature or use in molds, so extra gelatin is added. Setting layers of cooked seafood and vegetables in molds yields pretty and delicious results, but that is too fussy for me. I prefer to make this cold appetizer based on a dish from Australian cook and food writer Stephanie Alexander. The idea is to turn each soup bowl into a tidal pool; the selection of ingredients is up to you. Cooked shrimp, cooked baby clams in the shell, chunks of cooked fish, for example—keep in mind it is a jellied soup with garnish, so choose only three or four things for each bowl—plus cooked seaweed, if you can find it. If you can't, use blanched shredded green onion or blanched chives. Only a small amount of gelatin is added to the consommé. This is a perfect cold dish for a hot summer night.

1. Pour ¼ cup (60 ml) water into a small custard cup and sprinkle over 2 teaspoons of gelatin. Leave for 3 minutes so the gelatin can soften. Meanwhile, warm 5 cups (1.25 l) Fish Consommé (page 172) in a saucepan so that it liquefies.

2. Bring 1 inch (2.5 cm) of water to a boil in a small saucepan. Remove from the heat, place the custard cup in the hot water, and leave the gelatin to melt. Once it is transparent, stir it into the warm consommé. Pour this mixture into a large glass measuring cup.

3. Pour a thin layer of consommé, about ¼ cup (60 ml), into each of six shallow soup bowls, and refrigerate until almost set but still sticky. Refrigerate the remaining consommé.

4. Remove the bowls from the refrigerator and arrange your choice of ingredients on top; you can dip them into the consommé in the measuring cup to help them stick. Then refrigerate the bowls and the consommé again.

5. When the remaining consommé is very cold and beginning to set, remove it and the bowls from the refrigerator and spoon in the jelling consommé to cover the seafood and seaweed. This will give you an uneven surface like a tidal pool. Refrigerate for up to 3 hours.

6. Remove the soup bowls from the refrigerator 30 minutes before serving, so the jelly can soften.

Variation

○ To try making a mold, increase the gelatin to 1 tablespoon to start. Place ¼ cup (60 ml) of the consommé in a small mold or custard cup and refrigerate until set. Unmold to see if it holds its form (the set of the final consommé will depend on the amount of gelatin released by the fish bones). If it holds its shape you can proceed to make molds; if it doesn't, add extra gelatin ¼ teaspoon at a time until you obtain the right set (you want the mold to support itself but not be rubbery).

∘ Pour a thin layer of consommé into six 1 cup (250 ml) molds. Refrigerate until almost set but still sticky. Refrigerate the remaining consommé.

∘ Remove the molds from the refrigerator and place small pieces of cooked fish or shellfish on top; you can dip them into the consommé in the measuring cup to help them stick. Then refrigerate the bowls and the consommé again.

∘ When the remaining consommé is very cold, thick but still liquid, remove it and the molds from the refrigerator and pour in the consommé to cover the fish and seafood and fill the molds. Refrigerate until set.

∘ Unmold onto plates and serve with a salad.

FISH BONE SUPERSTITIONS

ooooooooooooooooooooooooooooooooooooooooooooo

Fish scales serve their owners well but are messy and annoying for the rest of us. However, some people believe that they are a portent of money. Each New Year's Eve, we continue my husband's family tradition of placing a few (well washed, of course) fish scales in our wallets. I can't promise this works, but I'm yet to be reduced to singing for my supper. The scales, however, probably bring me more embarrassment than cash. I usually forget about them and then in mid-January, I have to explain why my paper money has fish scales stuck to it.

Many fishermen are superstitious about where and when to catch fish. Before the technology of sonar detectors, those whose livelihood depended on fish followed many complicated rituals and taboos. Some thought the way you ate your fish was crucial to the success of your future catch, and that you must always begin eating the fish from the tail, working your way toward the head. If you attacked the head of the fish first, you risked turning the school of fish away from the shore and there would be no catch.

Even more disastrous was to turn your fish over while eating it: that symbolized the capsizing of the fishing boat. This fear is still held by fisherman from China to Central Europe, who, when eating fish, carefully lift the bone out rather than flipping the fish.

Fish Soup

Fish soups, made in every French ocean port and riverside town, are a way to use up fish too small or bony to sell. Bouillabaisse is perhaps the most famous, but it is only one of many soups. My soup is closer to *soupe de poisson*, made with whole fish, complete with bones, heads, and skin. After they are cooked, everything is pureed and strained, leaving just the soup with its intense flavor.

The greater the variety of fish, the more complex the flavor of the soup. I look for small, often cheaper, fish. When choosing the fish, the same rules apply as with stock avoid the oily ones, and make sure all the innards and gills are removed.

In France, fish soups are often served with the traditional accompaniments of croutons, grated cheese, and *rouille*, garlic-and-red-pepper-flavored mayonnaise. Not a big fan of flavored mayonnaise in my soup, I've replaced it with a garlicky sweet potato puree. This delivers the garlic hit as it melts into the soup and thickens it slightly.

3 tablespoons olive oil
1 onion, sliced
1 carrot, sliced
1 leek, white part only, sliced
1 fennel bulb with leaves, chopped
1 head garlic, separated into cloves but not peeled
Kosher salt
1 large orange
1 tablespoon coriander seeds, crushed
5 coriander sprigs, plus 2 tablespoons chopped coriander
1 large rosemary sprig
2 bay leaves
1 chile pepper, such as serrano, halved and seeded
6 pounds (2.7 kg) whole ocean fish (such as red mullet, butter fish, porgy, sea bream, and/or whiting), cleaned
¼ cup (60 ml) Pernod
One 28-ounce (796 g) can whole tomatoes
6 cups (1.5 l) Fish Stock (page 169)
Freshly ground black pepper
Toasted baguette slices
Sweet Potato Garlic Rouille (recipe follows)

1. Heat the oil in large stockpot over medium heat. Add the onion, carrot, leek, fennel, garlic, and 1 teaspoon salt and cook for 10 minutes, or until the vegetables soften.

2. Meanwhile, remove the zest from the orange using a vegetable peeler. Add to the vegetables, along with the coriander seeds, coriander sprigs, rosemary, bay leaves, and chile pepper.

3. Juice the orange, cut the fish into 3-inch (7.5 cm) sections, and rinse well under cold running water. Add the fish to the pot, pour in the orange juice, Pernod, and tomatoes with their juice. Add the fish stock and bring to a boil, stirring so nothing sticks to the bottom. Boil hard for 3 minutes, then reduce the heat and boil gently, uncovered, for 25 minutes. Let cool slightly.

4. Pass the soup through the medium disk of a food mill into a bowl. This method extracts the maximum flavor by grinding the fish bones against the blade. All the liquid and some solids will pass through the food mill, leaving a dry, pasty debris behind. (To clean out the food mill during the process, turn the blade in the opposite direction and tip out the debris.) You can puree the soup, in batches, in a blender and then press it through a sieve into a large bowl (discard the solids), but the finished soup will lack texture.

5. Pour the soup into a clean saucepan, skim off any fat on the surface, and bring to a boil. Season with about 2 teaspoons salt and black pepper.

6. Serve with slices of toasted baguette and the sweet potato rouille, adding about 1 tablespoon per bowl.

NOTE: This soup separates into 3 layers in the refrigerator: top tomato, middle jelly, and fish extracts on the bottom.

○ Sweet Potato Garlic Rouille

{ MAKES ¾ CUP (175 ML)} *Rouille* simply means rust in French. I call this sweet potato puree a rouille since its rusty orange color qualifies it for the name.

¾ cup (175 ml) cooked sweet potato (1 medium)
3 garlic cloves
½ teaspoon kosher salt
¼ cup (60 ml) olive oil

1. Push the cooked sweet potato through a sieve or ricer into a bowl, for a smooth puree.

2. Finely chop the garlic on a cutting board, then add the salt and crush the garlic using the flat side of the knife to obtain a smooth puree. Whisk it into the sweet potato, along with the olive oil.

Fish Head Curry

Is there any use for oily fish trimmings? Yes, with this Thai-inspired recipe for salmon heads. For a few months after taking a Thai cooking course in Bangkok, I faithfully pounded my own curry pastes, but now I admit to buying them ready-made: not totally authentic, but neither is this dish. Buy two good-sized salmon heads, so you have half a head per person, and have the fishmonger split them in half and remove the gills. There are no real bones but lots of cartilage, so pay attention when you eat this.

2 tablespoons tamarind pulp
2 salmon heads, 3 pounds (1.35 kg), cleaned and split
2 tablespoons vegetable oil
2 tablespoons Thai red curry paste
2 tablespoons fish sauce
1 tablespoon sugar
One 13.5-ounce (400-ml) can coconut milk
1½ cups pea eggplant, trimmed, or 1 Asian eggplant, cut in ½-inch (1-cm) dice
¼ cup (60 ml) julienned fresh ginger
6 green onions trimmed and cut into 2-inch (5-cm) lengths
1 medium tomato, seeded and diced
6 fresh lime leaves
1 hot red chile pepper, thinly sliced, optional
½ cup (125 ml) Thai basil leaves
½ cup (125 ml) coriander leaves

1. Place the tamarind pulp in a bowl and pour over 1 cup (250 ml) boiling water. Leave to soak for 30 minutes.

2. Rinse the fish heads well under cold running water. If they are bloody, soak them in a bowl of ice water for 15 minutes to leach out the blood, then rinse again and drain.

3. Heat the oil in a large deep saucepan over low heat. Add the curry paste and cook, stirring, for about 5 minutes, until the paste is fragrant and beginning to stick to the bottom of the pan. Remove from the heat.

4. Using your fingers, squeeze the tamarind pulp together with the water to make a paste, removing any seeds. Strain through a sieve into the curry paste, then add the fish sauce and sugar. Slowly stir in the coconut milk. Bring to a boil over medium-high heat, then add the pea eggplant, if using, and the ginger, reduce the heat, and simmer for 5 minutes.

5. Add the diced Asian eggplant, if using, and the fish heads, cover and cook for 10 minutes, turning the heads once. Add the green onions, tomato, lime leaves, and hot pepper, if using, and simmer for another 5 minutes, or until the fish is cooked.

6. Just before serving, stir in the basil and coriander leaves.

Whole Fried Whitebait
(page 179)

Grilled Sardines with Gooseberry Sauce
(page 182)

Whiting en Papillote
(page 185)

Skate with Butter and Caper Sauce
(page 193)

Rabbit in Saffron Sauce with Spring Vegetables
(page 216)

Roasted Rack of Venison with
Cape Gooseberry Sauce
(page 224)

Tamarind, Pineapple, and Chile–Glazed Boar Ribs
(page 229)

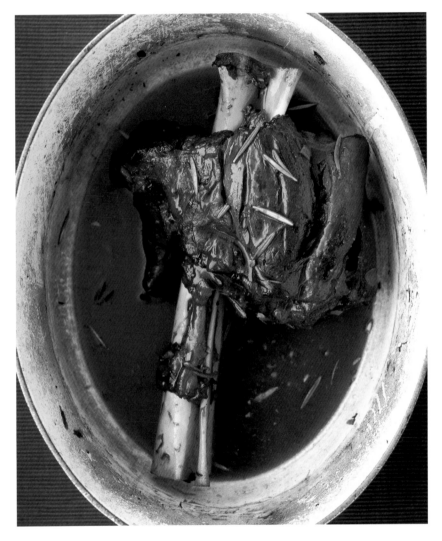

Venison Shank in Rosemary-Wine Sauce
(page 234)

Whole Fried Whitebait

Tiny fish known as whitebait, ranging in size from about 3 to 4 inches (7.5 to 10 cm), are eaten whole, heads, skin, bones, and yes, even their guts. Whitebait is not a species of fish but a catch-all name for very young fish—usually herring, sprats, smelts, or shad. Their bones are so soft that once cooked, they can be eaten whole. Whitebait have a short season, but they are always available frozen.

1 pound (450 g) whitebait
⅓ cup (40 g) flour
½ teaspoon cayenne pepper, optional
Kosher salt and freshly ground black pepper
4 cups (1 l) vegetable oil
Fine sea salt
Lemon wedges
Flat-leaf parsley sprigs, optional

1. Sort through the whitebait, discarding any broken ones, and pat dry. Mix the flour with the cayenne pepper, if using, then season it with salt and pepper. Toss about a quarter of the whitebait into seasoned flour, then transfer the fish to a sieve and shake to remove any excess flour. Place the coated fish on a baking sheet. Repeat with the remaining fish; reserve the remaining flour.

2. Preheat the oven to 200°F (100°C) if you are not planning to eat the fish straight out of the fryer. Line another baking sheet with paper towels. Carefully heat the oil in a deep fryer or in a large deep saucepan to 375°F (190°C).

3. While you are waiting for the oil to heat, toss about a quarter of the whitebait in the flour again, and remove the excess flour with another shake in the sieve. Using a frying basket or large skimmer, add refloured fish to the hot oil; don't try to cook too many at once, or the oil temperature will drop too low and the fish will be soggy. Fry for 2 minutes, or until lightly golden. Drain on the paper towels, sprinkle with sea salt, and keep warm in the oven if not devouring immediately. Repeat the procedure from second flouring to frying with the remaining fish.

Deep-fried Parsley

Deep-fried parsley is a delicious accompaniment to fried foods. Wash some parsley and dry well.

Remove the leaves or tiny sprigs, keeping the stems for stock.

Dry the leaves again, in a towel or in a salad spinner.

When all the fish are cooked, use a frying basket to add a few leaves to the hot oil. This will make a loud noise as the water explodes in the hot oil, since there is always some left on the leaves. The parsley cooks in seconds; remove it immediately, drain on paper towels, and sprinkle with sea salt.

Sardines on Toast

Canned fish was once a luxury, but it has lost much of its appeal and is commonly associated with tough times and poverty. In France, though, where canning began, some cans of sardines have a *millésimé*, or vintage date, stamped on them. These cans are carefully stored for up to twenty-five years. During this time their contents turns into a rich paste that sardine aficionados relish.

Since most of us don't have access to costly vintage sardines, the good-quality hand-packed nonvintage ones deserve our attention. These carefully layered little fish are full of omega-3 oils, minerals, and vitamins and, most important, still have their bones. All of which makes them very good for you.

Sardines on toast with a squeeze of lemon were the fast food of my childhood. The big key attached to the bottom of the tin had to be snapped off. Then you carefully threaded it onto a small tongue of metal and wound open the metal top. This is that childhood dish, improved with experience.

One 3½-ounce (100-g) can good-quality sardines
4 not-too-thick slices country bread
1 tablespoon Dijon mustard
Olive oil
2 teaspoons chopped dill
Fleur de sel or fine sea salt
¼ lemon

1. Preheat the broiler. Carefully remove the sardines from the can, trying to keep them whole. Place them on paper towels to drain.

2. Toast the bread under the broiler: well on one side and then very lightly on the other, so that it is dry but not colored. Spread the lightly toasted sides of the bread with the mustard. Arrange the sardines on top, then drizzle with olive oil. Place on a baking sheet and broil until the sardines are hot and the bread is beginning to darken on the edges, about 1 minute.

3. Sprinkle the toasts with the chopped dill, and then a little salt. Give them a good squeeze of fresh lemon juice, and they are ready to eat.

TIP Serve the toasts with a lightly dressed salad of frisée or arugula.

Sea Bass Baked in a Salt Crust with Fresh Tomato Sauce

ooooooooooooooooooooooooooooooooooooooooooooooooooooooooooooooooooooooooooooooooo { SERVES 4 } oooooooooo

When you are seated on the terrace of the Hotel Cipriani in Venice, sipping an Americano and gazing across the lagoon to St. Mark's Square, life can seem perfect. I was lucky enough to do this once and even luckier to watch chef Renato Piccolotto demonstrate his famous sea bass baked in a crust of salt. This recipe is adapted from that day. I recommend mixing an Americano—pour 1 ounce (30 ml) each Campari and sweet vermouth into a glass over ice, and add a splash of sparkling Italian mineral water and an orange slice—and pinning a postcard of Venice to the kitchen wall before beginning this recipe.

3 ripe plum tomatoes, cored and diced
6 large basil leaves, shredded
1 garlic clove, crushed
Kosher salt and freshly ground black pepper
1 whole sea bass, about 3 pounds (1.35 kg), cleaned but scales left on
1 sprig each rosemary, basil, and sage
3½ pounds (1.6 kg) kosher salt
1 pound (450 g) fine sea salt
12 large egg whites (1½ cups [375 ml])

1. Begin by making the tomato sauce: mix the tomatoes with the shredded basil and garlic in a bowl. Season with salt and pepper, and let marinate at room temperature for at least 2 hours or up to 4 hours. Remove the garlic before serving.

2. Preheat the oven to 375°F (190°C). Remove the fish from the refrigerator. Select a baking sheet, with a lip, large enough to hold the fish with 2 inches (5 cm) space all around. Line the baking sheet with aluminum foil and then with parchment paper. Pat the fish dry and place the herbs in its stomach cavity. In a very large mixing bowl, mix the two salts and egg whites very well, for about 5 minutes; your hand is the best tool for this. The more you mix, the easier the crust will be to cut when it is baked.

3. Put about half of the salt mixture on the prepared baking sheet, spreading it out to create a bed for the fish. Lay the fish on top and cover with the remaining salt mixture, making sure that the fish is entirely buried under a blanket of salt from head to tail.

4. Bake for 35 minutes, or until an instant-read thermometer inserted in the thickest part of the fish registers 130°F (54°C). (If you have a thermometer with a probe, insert it when encasing the fish—or use a metal skewer to make a hole in the crust to insert an instant-read thermometer.) The fish will take about 10 minutes per pound (450 g) to cook. Remove the fish from the oven, break open the crust with a sharp knife, and lift off the pieces of crust to reveal the fish.

5. Remove the skin, any remaining scales, and cut the fish into portions (see page 187). Serve with the tomato sauce.

Grilled Sardines with Gooseberry Sauce

Since green gooseberries are hard to find, I grow them. I love their tartness so much that I am prepared to brave their vicious thorns. The French call green gooseberries *groseilles à maquereaux* to distinguish them from red and white currants, *groseilles*, related fruits. The translation is mackerel currants, an odd name if you don't know that gooseberry sauce was a popular accompaniment for grilled mackerel both in France and England during the seventeenth and eighteenth centuries. Proof, if I needed it, that combining fruit with meats and fish was not invented in the 1970s by the Nouvelle Cuisine movement. Gooseberries are rare and exotic in France today, and their link with mackerel remains mainly in name only.

This sauce is simple to make. I top and tail the gooseberries first, which is easily done with a pair of kitchen scissors so that I have a thick sauce. If you skip this step you will have to puree the sauce at the end and then strain it—more work, and you will have a smooth puree rather than a thick sauce. I serve this sauce with sardines, but it is a perfect foil for any rich oily fish, including both mackerel and bluefish. Follow the instructions for grilling fish (see page 183). Sardines are at their best in the summer, which makes them perfect candidates for outdoor charcoal grilling.

12 ounces/1 dry pint (325 g) green gooseberries, fresh or frozen, topped and tailed
1 tablespoon (15 g) unsalted butter
1 tablespoon sugar
2 green cardamom pods, crushed
Grated zest and juice of 1 orange
Kosher salt and freshly ground black pepper
16 whole sardines, cleaned
1 tablespoon olive oil
Vegetable oil

1. Rinse the gooseberries under cold running water, then drop them into a frying pan large enough to hold them in a single layer. Add the butter, sugar, cardamom, and orange zest and juice and cook, covered, over medium-low heat until the berries become pale and are soft when touched, about 5 minutes. Remove the lid and raise the heat. Continue to cook, stirring, until the sauce is thick and just starts to stick to the bottom of the pan, 3 to 5 minutes. Season with salt and pepper. (This sauce can be made ahead and reheated.)

2. Preheat the grill to high. Rinse and pat dry the sardines and season with salt and pepper and brush with the olive oil.

3. Clean the grill well then brush it lightly with vegetable oil. Place the fish on the grill over high heat for 4 to 5 minutes on each side, or until cooked. Serve hot with the gooseberry sauce. (The sauce can be served hot or at room temperature.)

Variation: Rhubarb Sauce

o If you can't find gooseberries, replace them with an equal amount of trimmed rhubarb. Cut the rinsed rhubarb stalks into ½-inch (1-cm) dice, and use only 1 teaspoon of sugar.

Grilling or Broiling Fish

Grilling fish works if your grill is clean, lightly oiled, and preheated to high before you start. Lower the heat to medium to cook medium to larger fish and be aware that the fish will almost always stick a little no matter what—a fish basket will help solve this. If grilling over charcoal, move your grill rack away from the heat. Broiling fish is simpler and you have more control. Do remember to preheat your broiler. Have the fish cleaned and scaled (mackerel have no scales). Larger fish must be scored to allow the heat to penetrate inside the fish so it cooks more evenly. Make shallow cuts about 1 inch (2.5 cm) apart into the flesh of the fish, 3 to 4 per side. Lightly season your fish with salt and pepper then drizzle with olive oil. To check if the fish is cooked, look inside the fish or insert a small knife into the thickest part of the fish. Fish can overcook easily so test before you think it is done; the fish should be opaque at the bone.

FISH KNIVES

ooooooooooooooooooo

There have always been knives to prepare fish, but special knives to eat them are a more recent invention. Fish knives, along with specific knives for cheese and fruit, began appearing in the seventeenth century. The fish knife is unique in that it doesn't cut: its form is that of an elongated oval with a blunt decorated edge, since cooked fish doesn't require cutting. The fish is just lifted from the bone, and the large surface area of the knife makes this easier. Then you could put this knife, with the piece of fish, directly into your mouth without fear of cutting yourself. These knives became very popular in Victorian and Edwardian times, made from silver so that they didn't affect the taste of the fish.

Grilled Fish with Yellow Tomato Vinaigrette

Fish like snapper, bream, bass, and trout are good on the grill. Simple is best. You can vary the herbs, or use lime instead of lemon. If the fish is fresh, you can't go wrong. Grilled fresh fish needs little more than herbs and seasoning, but if you want to guild the lily try this sauce. It is especially good when made with a yellow tomatoes, as it is less acid.

4 whole fish (see headnote), about 1 pound (450 g) each, cleaned
1 lemon, sliced
4 large fennel fronds
4 large rosemary sprigs
4 large flat-leaf parsley sprigs
4 large thyme sprigs
Kosher salt and freshly ground black pepper
¼ cup (60 ml) plus 3 tablespoons olive oil
Vegetable oil, for oiling the grill
1 medium yellow tomato, cored and diced
1 tablespoon red wine vinegar

1. Preheat the grill to high. Score the fish by making 3 to 4 shallow cuts, ¼ inch (5 mm) deep and 1 inch (2.5 cm) apart, into each side. Place the lemon slices inside each fish, then divide the herbs among them. Skewer together the two flaps of each fish, unless using a grill basket. Season the fish with salt and pepper then brush lightly with 3 tablespoons olive oil.

2. Clean the grill well, then brush it lightly with vegetable oil. Place the fish on the grill, reduce the heat to medium, and grill, turning once, for a total of 10 to 12 minutes, or until just cooked.

3. While the fish is cooking, heat the ¼ cup (60 ml) olive oil in a small saucepan. Add the tomato and bring to a boil, reduce the heat and then simmer for 2 minutes. Add the vinegar, remove from the heat, and season with salt and pepper.

4. Serve the fish hot or at room temperature, with the sauce spooned over.

Whiting en Papillote

I love this way of cooking fish in parchment paper. It's simple, each person has a complete meal in one package, and, dare I say, it, it's low fat. In addition, the presentation is impressive, a puffed package that, once opened (*be careful*, the steam is hot), lets diners enjoy all the aromas of the dish. You can definitely increase this to serve more people, but don't crowd your oven, as the packages need room to puff up.

2 whiting, about 12 ounces (350 g) each, cleaned
2 pieces 15-inch (38-cm) square of parchment paper
4 teaspoons olive oil
2 small new potatoes, sliced ⅛ inch (3 mm) thick
1 medium zucchini, sliced ⅛ inch (3 mm) thick
Kosher salt and freshly ground black pepper
12 cherry tomatoes, halved
10 black olives
4 green onions, trimmed and cut into 1-inch (2.5-cm) lengths
1 egg white, optional

1. Preheat the oven to 400°F (200°C). Remove the fish from the refrigerator.

2. Fold each piece of parchment paper in half to form a crease, unfold, and place on the countertop. Spread one half of each package with 1 teaspoon olive oil. Layer the potato slices on the oiled half of each piece of parchment, centering them and overlapping them ever so slightly. Top with the zucchini slices and season with salt and pepper. Put the fish on top, curling the tail of each back against the body so it fits on top of the vegetables. Scatter over the tomatoes, olives, and green onions, and season again with salt and pepper. Drizzle with the remaining 2 teaspoons oil.

3. Sealing the packages well is the key to getting them puff up. To help, you can brush the cut edges of the paper with a little beaten egg white. Fold the paper over the fish and press down so that the edges meet. To seal, begin at the top of each center fold and make a series of overlapping folds or pleats all the way around; it is important to press down firmly on each fold so that it seals. When you reach the end, fold the seam back on itself and twist to seal.

4. Slide the packages onto a large baking tray and bake until they are puffed, 18 to 20 minutes. Transfer the packages directly to dinner plates. Open them at the table, cutting across the puffed top, and *be careful* of the steam.

Whole Roasted Monkfish (Gigot de Mer)

My West Coast friends tell me that there is usually a monkfish still in possession of its head at Seattle's famous Pike Place Market. The fishmonger attaches a string to it so he can open and close its mouth when anyone, especially children, approach. It never fails to elicit a shriek or two.

Most monkfish is sold without its scary head. Once skinned, the body is shaped like a long isosceles triangle. To the French, this shape recalls a lamb leg, so this monkfish cut is often called a *gigot*. Clarissa Dickson Wright, one of the Two Fat Ladies of the eponymous cooking show, notes that *gigit* is a popular term in Scotland for describing both leg cuts of meat and monkfish.

This recipe, based on one by food writer Sophie Grigson, continues that tenuous connection by treating the fish like a leg of lamb, studding it with slivers of garlic and sprigs of rosemary. It is much easier to carve than a leg of lamb, with only a single central bone. If you have extra rosemary sprigs, place them in the bottom of the roasting pan to make a bed for the fish.

1 whole monkfish tail, about 3 pounds (1.35 kg), skin and membrane removed
4 large rosemary branches
2 garlic cloves, cut into fine slivers
Freshly ground black pepper
½ cup (125 ml) dry white wine
½ cup (125 ml) olive oil
1 small mild onion, thinly sliced
Kosher salt
2 tablespoons chopped flat-leaf parsley

1. With a small sharp knife, make a series of shallow slits all over the top of the monkfish. Take a sprig rosemary from the branch and, using a garlic sliver, push it and the garlic into one of the slits. Repeat the process until all the garlic is used up and the top of the fish is covered with garlic and rosemary; there will be some rosemary left.

2. Season the fish well with pepper, and place in a ceramic or glass dish. Pour over the wine and oil, then scatter over the onion. Cover and refrigerate for at least 3 hours, or up to 12 hours, turning once.

3. Thirty minutes before cooking, remove the fish from the refrigerator. Uncover and season with salt. Preheat the oven to 400°F (200°C).

4. Place the remaining rosemary and any extra branches you have in the bottom of a roasting pan large enough to accommodate the tail comfortably. Lay the fish on top and pour over the marinade, with the onions.

5. Roast the fish, basting every 10 minutes, with the pan juices for 35 to 45 minutes, or until it is just cooked through. The thin end of the tail will cook faster, so cover it with foil about halfway through the cooking time. To check for doneness, pierce the fish at the thick end of the tail, next to the bone.

6. Transfer the fish to a serving platter and keep warm, loosely covered with aluminum foil. Place the roasting pan over high heat, bring the pan juices to a boil, and boil hard for 3 to 5 minutes, until slightly thickened. Stir in the chopped parsley, spoon the sauce and onions over the fish, and serve.

How to Eat a Whole Fish

Once you know where a fish's bones are, eating it is simpler. The following techniques will help you master fish on the bone.

Whole round fish take the most concentration. First, make a cut behind the gill flap, to separate the flesh from the head. Next, cut down along the top of the fish from the head to the tail, then turn your attention to the belly. This was cut open when the fish was cleaned, so simply extend the cut back to the tail. Starting from the tail end, slide your knife between the flesh and the backbone. Keeping the knife against the bones, lift off the fillet—don't despair if it comes off in several pieces. With practice, you'll slide it off in a single piece. With large fish, though, you may want to make a cut down the center of the top fillet through to the backbone so the flesh can be lifted off in sections, which is easier. I like to eat the first fillet as a reward before attacking the rest of the fish. Pay careful attention to the front half of the fillet. No matter how skilled you become, there is likely to be a tiny rib bone or two that has managed to stay attached.

To remove the second fillet, you have two choices, unless you are superstitious (see page 175). Either flip the fish over and repeat the method just described, or lift up the backbone, starting with the tail end, and gently remove it in one piece, to reveal the bottom fillet.

Eating flatfish is simpler. Begin by making a cut down the center of the fish, along the backbone from head to tail. Then run your knife from the backbone along the ribs out to one edge of the fish to remove the first fillet. Repeat in the opposite direction for the second. To remove the other two, flip the fish over and repeat the process.

With round fish steaks, the backbone is exposed in the center of the piece. You'll see bones fanning out in three directions, straight up and then along each side of the flaps of the steak, which formed the cavity of the fish (think an upside-down Y). With these steaks, especially salmon, there can be that pesky row of pinbones that stick out at right angles into the flesh. Your best approach is to eat carefully around the bones.

Flatfish steaks are very little trouble. Locate the backbone in the center of the steak, insert your fork, and twist gently. The bone, with the ribs attached, should lift out.

The best way to learn is to practice, practice, practice.

Cantonese-Style Steamed Fish

Steamed fish is always part of a multicourse Chinese dinner. The Chinese steam the fish whole, as they know some of the best eating is in the head. My friends Karen and Vincent told me how good the steamed fish was at a certain Toronto Chinese restaurant, so we all went to eat it there. As they are regular customers, they arranged for me to see it being cooked. I watched as a live grouper was taken from the tank, killed, prepared for the steamer, and on the table in less than twenty minutes. Here's what I learned: Start with the freshest fish you can, and then follow this simple recipe. My steamer holds only a pound (450 g) of fish, so I serve it as part of a multicourse meal for four people. It also makes a special meal when you find yourself dining alone. I present the cooked fish on a bed of watercress. The heat from the fish and hot sauce cooks the watercress, which provides a peppery contrast to the sweet fish.

1 whole grouper or bass, about 1 pound (450 g), cleaned
3 green onions, trimmed
2 tablespoons vegetable oil
3 tablespoons soy sauce
1 tablespoon Chinese cooking wine (Shao Xing) or dry sherry
2 teaspoons sugar
2 tablespoons julienned fresh ginger
1 bunch watercress, coarse stems removed
1 teaspoon rice wine vinegar

1. Score the fish by making 3 to 4 shallow cuts, ¼ inch (5 mm) deep and 1 inch (2.5 cm) apart, in each side. Place it on a heatproof plate that will fit in your steamer.

2. Slice 2 green onions into 2-inch (5-cm) lengths. In a small bowl, mix 1 tablespoon of the oil, 1 tablespoon of the soy sauce, the wine, and a pinch of the sugar. Pour over the fish and turn it so it is well coated with the mixture. Scatter the sliced green onions and 1 tablespoon of the ginger on top.

3. Place the plate in the steamer basket or rack, then place it over boiling water in a large pot or wok, cover, and steam for 15 to 20 minutes, until the fish is cooked. The flesh will be opaque at the bone.

4. Meanwhile, line a serving platter with the watercress. Cut the remaining green onion into ½-inch (1-cm) lengths. Using a large spatula, transfer the fish to the platter, leaving behind the cooking juices; discard them. Scatter the sliced green onion over the fish.

5. Put the remaining 1 tablespoon oil, 2 tablespoons soy sauce, sugar, ginger, and vinegar in a small saucepan and bring to a boil. Pour over the fish and watercress, and serve immediately.

TIP When using a Chinese bamboo or metal steamer, the plate for the fish should be 1 inch (2.5 cm) smaller than the diameter of the steamer; this allows the steam to circulate.

Panfried Whole Sole

You will need a fish per person and they must fit snugly together in a large frying pan or in two smaller pans. The fish is cooked in butter mixed with oil, so that the temperature of the butter can be increased without it burning.

This classic French way of cooking is called *à la meunière*, which, literally translated, means in the style of the miller's wife, a reference to the flour used to dredge the fish before cooking it. Sole is the traditional fish for this method, but small flounder, fluke, and even round fish like trout work well.

2 whole sole or flounder, about 1 pound (450 g) each, cleaned and skinned
2 tablespoons flour
Kosher salt and freshly ground black pepper
2 tablespoons vegetable oil
4 tablespoons (60 g) unsalted butter
1 lemon, peeled and cut into segments (see page 191)
2 tablespoons chopped flat-leaf parsley

1. Whether you leave the heads on the fish will depend on your frying pan (or you). If it is large enough to hold the whole fish, leave them on. Season the flour with salt and pepper, and dredge the fish in the seasoned flour, shaking off any excess.

2. In a frying pan large enough to hold both fish, or in two smaller pans, heat the oil over medium-high heat then add half of the butter. When the butter sizzles, add the fish and cook for 4 minutes. The fish will be golden brown by this time; turn them over and cook for another 4 minutes, or until the fish are cooked through. Check by inserting a knife into the center of the fish to make sure the flesh is opaque.

3. Transfer the fish to warmed dinner plates and keep warm, loosely covered with aluminum foil. Wipe out the pan, and add the remaining butter, the lemon segments, and parsley. Place over medium heat and cook until the butter begins to foam. Stir the sauce to mix, then pour over the fish and serve immediately.

Variation

∘ Add 1 tablespoon diced oil-packed sun-dried tomato along with the lemon. The tomato adds color and another dimension to the taste.

Eel in Sweet-Sour Fruit Sauce

Eel . . . a fish that evokes prejudices even among the most adventurous of eaters. My first eel swam in a rich red wine stew, which I ate at a restaurant on the banks of the Loire River. Finding a fishmonger who sells fresh eels that he will skin for you is difficult, if not impossible. Poaching the eel first means you can skin it yourself; all you have to do is find your eel. Asian and Italian fish markets are the best source. Buy eels no larger than 2¼ pounds (1 kg) as they will be less fatty and take less time to cook.

This recipe was inspired by one from Michel Troisgros, a son of one of the famous brothers whose restaurant in Roanne, France, became so well known in the 1980s. Michel now has his own restaurant in Paris at the Lancaster Hotel. Matching eel with fruit is a good idea because it cuts through the richness of this fish. If prune plums are not in season, substitute another plum or increase the number of dried ones.

⅓ cup (75 ml) white wine vinegar
2 teaspoons kosher salt
1 teaspoon black peppercorns
1 tablespoon sugar
1 garlic clove, peeled
2 strips lemon zest
2 flat-leaf parsley stems
1 thyme sprig
1 bay leaf
1 eel, about 1 pound (450 g), cleaned, beheaded, rinsed, and cut into 6 sections
6 pitted prunes
1 tablespoon vegetable oil
½ sweet onion, thinly sliced
2 teaspoons flour
6 small purple prune plums, quartered and pitted
½ teaspoon finely grated ginger
Freshly ground black pepper
¼ cup (60 ml) chopped flat-leaf parsley
12 cherry tomatoes, halved

1. Place 4 cups (1 l) water, the vinegar, salt, peppercorns, sugar, garlic, lemon zest, parsley stems, thyme, and bay leaf in a large saucepan and bring to a boil, then reduce the heat and simmer for 5 minutes. Add the largest eel pieces to the pan and simmer for 1 minute. Add the remaining pieces and simmer for 3 minutes, then remove the pan from the heat and let stand for 10 minutes.

2. Remove the eel and let cool slightly; reserve the cooking liquid. Once the eel is cool enough to handle, peel off the skin and remove any fat. (Eel is similar to salmon in that you will be able to see a film of fat covering the flesh once the skin is removed.) Cut the eel into 1-inch (2.5-cm) pieces.

3. Strain the cooking liquid through a sieve. Pour ½ cup (125 ml) over the prunes in a small bowl and leave them to soak. Reserve the remaining cooking liquid.

4. Heat the oil in a large frying pan. Add the onion and cook until it starts to brown. Add the flour and cook, stirring, for 1 minute. Gradually pour in 1 cup (250 ml) of the cooking liquid (discard the rest), bring to a boil, and boil for 3 minutes.

5. Add the prunes, with their soaking liquid, the plums, and ginger and bring to a boil. Reduce the heat, add the eel, and check the seasoning, adding pepper to taste. Add the chopped parsley and tomatoes and cook until heated through.

=========================== *Segmenting Citrus Fruit* ===========┐

Cut a thick slice off the top and the bottom of the fruit to expose the flesh. Stand the fruit upright on a cutting board and, cutting from the top down to the bottom, remove both the skin and the white pith in wide strips, working your way around the fruit. Hold the peeled fruit over a bowl and, with a small sharp knife, cut along either side of each segment to the center to free it from the membranes, catching the juice in the bowl. Once you've removed all the segments, squeeze the juice from the membranes.

Halibut Steaks with Orange Cream Sauce

Braising fish on the bone keeps the flesh juicy. If the halibut steaks are big, have your fishmonger split them. You can substitute other fish steaks as long as they are of a similar weight and, most important, thickness. The green beans match well with the orange sauce. If haricots verts are not available, use regular green beans cut diagonally in half.

Four 1 inch (2.5-cm)-thick halibut steaks, about 7 ounces (200 g) each
1 tablespoon vegetable oil
1 tablespoon (15 g) unsalted butter
3 leeks, white part only, sliced ½ inch (1 cm) thick on the diagonal
Kosher salt and freshly ground black pepper
1 pound (450 g) haricots verts
1 cup (250 ml) Fish Stock (page 169)
1 large orange
½ teaspoon grated lemon zest
⅓ cup (75 ml) sour cream

1. Preheat the oven to 400°F (200°C). Remove the fish steaks from the refrigerator. Heat the oil and butter in a large frying pan over medium-high heat. Add the leeks and cook for 3 minutes, or until beginning to color. Lower the heat, cover, and cook the leeks for 10 minutes, or until soft. Drain in a sieve, place in a bowl, and season with salt and pepper.

2. While the leeks are cooking, clean the haricots verts, blanch them in boiling salted water for 2 minutes, and then drain in a sieve and refresh under cold running water. Drain well.

3. Add the beans to the leeks and toss together. Spread the leeks and green beans on the bottom of a baking dish large enough to hold the halibut steaks in one layer. Season the fish steaks with salt and pepper and place them on top of the vegetables. Pour over the fish stock and cover with aluminum foil. Cook the halibut for 30 to 40 minutes, or until opaque in the center.

4. While the fish is cooking, make the sauce: Finely grate the zest of half the orange and set aside. Using a vegetable peeler, remove the remaining zest, and cut it into matchsticks. Blanch these matchsticks in boiling water for 2 minutes, then drain and refresh under cold running water. Juice half the orange; you should have ¼ cup (60 ml). Mix the juice, grated orange zest, and lemon zest together in a small bowl. Gradually blend in the sour cream, then season with salt and pepper.

5. When the fish is cooked, uncover and garnish with the matchsticks of orange zest. Serve directly from the baking dish, with the sauce on the side.

Skate with Butter and Caper Sauce

Skate wings are usually poached in court bouillon and served with a pan sauce of butter and capers. If you can't find skinned skate, the skin will come off easily once the fish is poached. I prefer salt-packed capers for this dish because they have more flavor, but rinse off all that salt before using them.

⅓ cup (75 ml) white wine vinegar
1 bay leaf
1 small onion, sliced
6 black peppercorns
2 pieces skate wing, 8 to 12 ounces (225 to 350 g) each
Kosher salt and freshly ground black pepper
8 tablespoons (1 stick; 125 g) unsalted butter
2 tablespoons capers, preferably salt-packed, rinsed
3 tablespoons white wine vinegar
2 tablespoons chopped flat-leaf parsley

1. Combine the vinegar, bay leaf, and onion in a large saucepan or a pan large enough to hold the skate, add 4 cups (1 l) water, and bring to a boil. Skim off any foam, add the peppercorns, and simmer for 5 minutes.

2. Place the skate in the pan and poach gently for 10 to 15 minutes, or until it is just cooked. Remove the fish from the court bouillon and drain well. Remove the skin if necessary, and transfer to warmed plates. Season with salt and pepper and keep warm, loosely covered with aluminum foil.

3. Cook the butter in a small frying pan over medium heat until it melts and begins to color. Watch carefully, and use your nose: As soon as it starts to brown and you smell a nutty aroma, remove it from the heat and add the capers and vinegar, swirling to mix. Pour over the fish, sprinkle with the parsley, and serve.

Skate Skin

Skate and ray have thick skin, and the top skin is dark and leathery.
Have your fishmonger remove the top skin and, if possible, the paler underside skin.
The paler underneath skin is not as critical, as it will not mar the presentation of the fish.
If you must buy skate with the skin on, it will lift off easily once the fish is poached.

Skate with Grape Sauce

When in Paris, I often watch a television cooking show hosted by the famous French chef Joël Robuchon. There is no flash or pizzazz, simply carefully demonstrated techniques and dishes that anyone could make. Each week, Monsieur Robuchon invites a different chef, and together, they cook just one dish, explaining every detail right down to the cost per person. Watching this program has given me lots of ideas and made me realize that the simplest dishes are the most delicious. The chef who inspired this recipe is Pascal Auger, a guest on the show.

The skate is sautéed with no preliminary poaching, so make sure your fishmonger removes at least the top skin. Buy similar-sized pieces of skate wing, or select two larger pieces and have the fishmonger cut them in half.

⅔ cup (125 g) seedless green grapes
3 tablespoons capers, preferably salt-packed, rinsed
Kosher salt and freshly ground black pepper
4 tablespoons (60 g) cold unsalted butter, cut into cubes
½ lemon, if needed
4 pieces skinned skate wing, 8 to 12 ounces (225 to 350 g) each
¼ cup (60 ml) olive oil

1. Place the grapes and capers in a small saucepan with ⅓ cup (75 ml) water and heat slowly until the water is very hot, but do not let it simmer. Season with salt and pepper, add the butter, and stir until the butter is almost melted. Remove from the heat. Pour into a blender or food processor, and process until the sauce is emulsified (or very well blended) about 1 minute. Pour the sauce back into the saucepan, taste, and add a few drops of lemon juice if necessary; it shouldn't be sweet. Keep warm over very low heat.

2. Season the skate with salt and pepper. In a frying pan large enough to hold the skate, or two smaller pans, heat the olive oil over medium heat. Add the skate and cook, turning once, until it is golden and the flesh detaches easily from the thickest section of the wing, about 4 minutes per side. Serve with the sauce on the side.

Frog's Legs with Lemongrass and Chile

Eating frog's legs is so closely associated with the French that even today, the English refer to them as froggies, while the French retort with *les rosbifs*. But frog's legs are equally popular in Central Europe, where many of the legs consumed in France are raised, and in Asia, particularly Thailand and Vietnam. This recipe is inspired by the flavors of Vietnam rather than the garlic-and-parsley tradition of Burgundy.

The frog's legs I buy are packaged like shrimp, with a number per pound (450 g) stamped on the box; the legs are sold in pairs, still attached at the tailbone. I used 8-to-12-count frog's legs; once they were prepared, I had about forty pieces. And no, they don't taste like chicken.

2 pounds (900 g) frog's legs
¼ packed cup (50 g) brown sugar
3 tablespoons fish sauce
3 tablespoons vegetable oil
2 stalks lemongrass, the white part, finely chopped
1 shallot, finely chopped
2 garlic cloves, finely chopped
2 red chile peppers, seeded and finely chopped
8 green onions, trimmed cut into 2-inch (5-cm) lengths

1. To separate the frog's legs, cut them away from the tailbone. Cut off and discard the feet and tailbones. Cut each leg in two, like chicken wings.

2. Mix the sugar, fish sauce, and ½ cup (125 ml) water in a small bowl; set aside. Heat the oil in a large frying pan, then add the lemongrass, shallot, garlic, and chile, and cook, stirring constantly, until fragrant, about 2 to 3 minutes.

3. Add the fish sauce mixture to the frying pan, stir, and bring to a boil. Boil for 1 minute, then add the legs and simmer gently for 10 minutes, or until cooked, turning them from time to time to coat with the sauce.

4. Add the green onions and simmer for another 5 minutes, then serve.

Fried Fish Bones

The origin of this dish is the Japanese kitchen, where it is called *senbei*. I had read about it in various sources and my friend, the talented cooking teacher Hiroko Sugiyama, confirmed that it is used as a garnish or snack. These fried bones are crispy, salty, and delicious, the perfect accompaniment to a cold Japanese beer.

You'll have to do the preparation for this recipe yourself; I doubt that your fishmonger will bother with such small fish, but you can always ask. If your filleting techniques are a little rusty, it's a good way to practice. Best of all, leaving a little extra flesh on the bones is a bonus.

1. You will need about 12 fish roughly 6 inches (15 cm) long. I use small whiting, as their heads can be added to the stockpot later and their fillets can be used to reinforce a consommé (see page 172), or headless smelts, which are easy to find. However, the smelt flesh is too overpowering for consommé, so if you use them, broil the fillets on a lightly oiled baking sheet for about 2 minutes per side, brushing with a glaze of soy, sugar, and sake; or simply broil and serve with the gooseberry sauce (see page 182).

2. Using a flexible knife, make the first cut behind the gill flap of each fish, to separate the flesh from the head. Then cut down along the top of the fish until your knife hits the rib bones; keeping your knife against these bones, slice down the length of the fish to remove the fillet, peeling back the flesh. Turn the fish over and repeat on the other side. Chop off the head and tail (reserve for stock, if desired) then cut the backbones in half. Cover and refrigerate the fillets for another dish.

3. Heat 4 cups (1 l) vegetable oil in a deep fryer or a large deep saucepan until it reaches 375°F (190°C). Add a few bones at a time and fry until crisp and lightly golden, 1 to 2 minutes. Remove and drain on paper towels, sprinkle with salt, and serve hot or at room temperature.

4. The first bite might take a leap of faith but, trust me, they're delicious.

FISH BONE LINGUISTICS

A fish bone is a bone is a bone, depending on what language is being spoken. Unlike English, many other languages from Europe to South India have one word for a fish bone and another for animal and bird bones. In France, when I referred to fish bones as *les os*, I was politely corrected. French fish bones are *les arêtes*.

Yet languages are complicated and littered with linguistic booby traps for the unsuspecting. When I was serving the Roast Monkfish (page 186) to my French friend François, I was careful to refer to the fish's *grande arête*. Immediately he corrected me. "*Ce n'est pas une arête, c'est un os.*" It seems that the monkfish is not only an exception when categorizing fish, its bones, at least in France, are an exception too.

English has its fish bone quirks too. Whalebone, the flexible, elastic material that forms the upper jawbone of baleen whales, is really a type of horn. Whales use it to filter their food, but for many of us it is linked to underwear. Since Elizabethan times, whalebone has been used to stiffen dresses, collars, and, most notably, corsets. It is extremely flexible along its length, as well as from side to side, which is why it was so popular in the manufacture of corsets and umbrellas. By the early twentieth century, however, the price of whalebone had become so prohibitive that it was often recycled from discarded corsets and old umbrellas. Eventually whalebone was replaced by the cheaper alternatives of flexible steel and heavy-duty plastic. Corsets made today for the fashion, costume, and fetish markets no longer contain whalebone, although the term *boning* is still used to describe their shaping.

The flexibility of whalebone made it popular with medieval knights, but they weren't wearing corsets. The plumes on their tournament helmets were not always feather, but instead whalebone crafted to resemble plumes. The flexibility and strength of these bone plumes helped deflect their opponent's blows.

Whalebone may not be true bone, but fish scales are. Fish use them as armor. Scales cover the fish in an overlapping flexible shield. Most of these protective scales are transparent, but some are tiny mirrors, which reflect the light. It is these scales that attract our attention in the fish market, but they perform exactly the opposite role when the fish is alive. Their reflective qualities render the fish difficult to see, effectively camouflaging it against any predators.

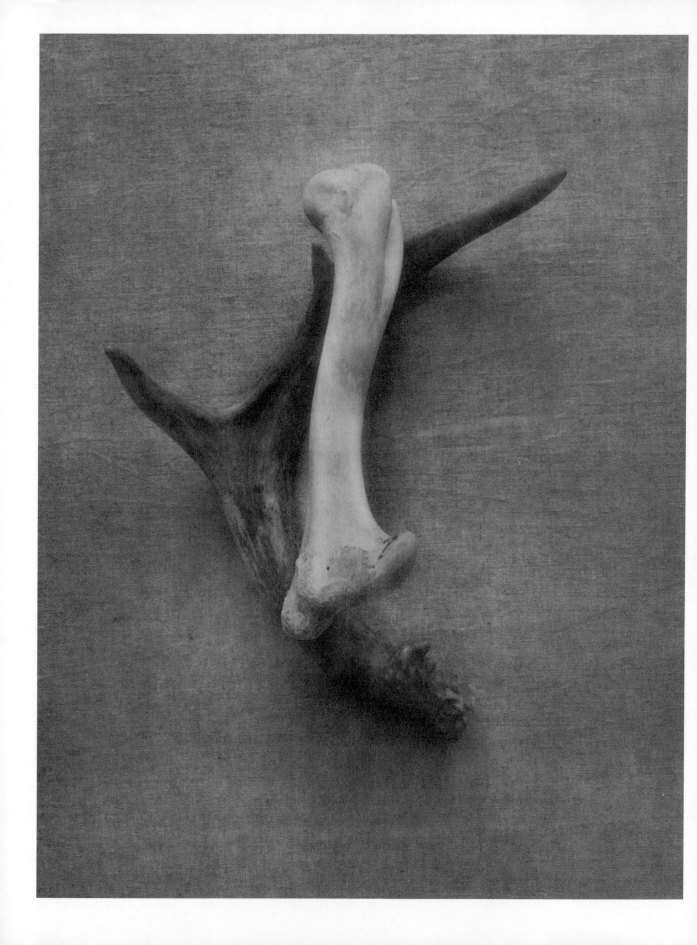

Game

The savvy cook knows that game on the bone has many benefits. A rack of venison, for example, comes with its own built-in roasting rack. And those bones help protect the lean meat while adding flavor. Moreover, the bones enhance the presentation of the dish.

No longer the sole preserve of hunters and their friends, game meat is now more widely available than ever. An increased demand for naturally raised animals has boosted game farming and, in turn, broadened the market for this delicious, healthy meat. Hunters still test their skills in the wild, but the quality of their legally bagged game varies widely. Farmed game, on the other hand, is carefully controlled. The result is meat of consistent quality that makes life easier for the cook.

So why isn't this low-fat, low-cholesterol meat on all our tables? What often deters people from eating game is fear of a gamey taste. However, the flavor of today's farm-raised game and game raised on private preserves is often quite different from that of wild game. The flavor of farm-raised venison, for example, is much milder, closer to beef. I happen to like the livery, gamey accent of animals that forage in a natural environment—it's the reason I eat game—so I look for suppliers who sell free-range game. The animal's diet is one major influence on how it tastes. The aging of game meat is also important, making a good butcher or supplier indispensable. With its range of flavors, today you can certainly buy game that suits your taste.

Game is divided into two main categories, feathered and furred. Feathered game is covered in the poultry chapter. This chapter concentrates on furred game and wild boar. American buffalo, more correctly bison, is often classed as game, but it is so similar to beef that it is can be used in any beef recipe, and I include it the beef and veal chapter.

Larger game animals, such as venison, are butchered like veal and lamb so the cuts are familiar. Rack and leg of venison are impressive pieces of meat, but many less glamorous cuts are overlooked. Ribs, shoulder, shank, and neck are all delicious. When these are cooked slowly, their rich flavor is released and their meat becomes meltingly succulent, while their bones enrich the sauce. Cooking game is no more difficult than cooking any other meat if you remember one important thing—its lack of fat. This lean meat really needs its bones to keep it moist and tender. The addition of some fat, from a marinade, by wrapping it in fat to protect and baste it while it cooks, or by adding a fat like bacon helps too. Game bones make excellent stock that provides the base for soups and great sauces to accompany the meat.

Once you understand where the animal's bones and the meat attached to them are located, you will be able to cook any game cut.

Venison

Venison is the general term for deer meat. The deer family is large and the names often vary from region to region. Among its members are red deer, reindeer, caribou, antelope, elk or wapiti, and moose; farmed venison is typically deer or elk. Despite their range in size, all these animals have the same bone structure. The cuts of meat are the same too, varying only in size, with smaller animals yielding cuts similar to those from lamb and larger ones closer to veal and beef.

The Front End

The front leg, or shoulder, has the shank removed (see "The Extremities") during butchering. Depending on the size of the animal, the leg is sold whole or cut into two pieces. Because the meat in this section consists of several muscles supported by a complicated bone structure, too often this cut is either overlooked or sold boned, but braising is an ideal method for cooking this bone-in cut.

"As fast as his bones would carry him" means to run as fast as possible.

"To be upon the bones of" means to attack.

"Soaked to the bone" is to be completely wet right through.

The funny bone, also called the crazy bone, is that part of the elbow where the ulnar nerve is found. It can refer to one's sense of humor.

"Skin and bones" or a "bag of bones" refers to someone who is very skinny or painfully thin.

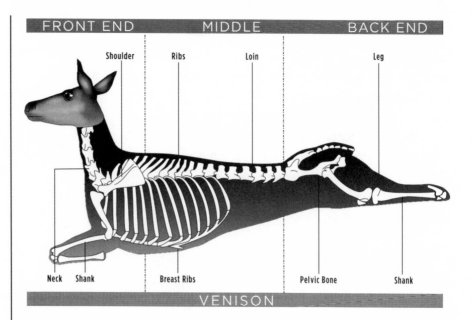

Shoulder   Ribs   Loin   Leg

Neck   Shank   Breast Ribs   Pelvic Bone   Shank

VENISON

The expression "close or near to the bone" has a variety of meanings; it can describe a tactless or offensive remark, or describe someone who is hard up or living on the edge of destitution.

"To cut to the bone" describes removing any frills or excess, and to be left with only the bare minimum.

Lord Timon's mad. I feel't upon my bones.
—WILLIAM SHAKESPEARE, *TIMON OF ATHENS*, Act III, Scene VI

I seem to hear it, muster Gashford in my very bones.
—CHARLES DICKENS, *BARNABY RIDGE*

There is a common warning to tardy dinner guests that is quoted worldwide: Those who come late for dinner will find only the bones, or for the latecomer the bones.

The Middle

The muscles in this part of the body do the least work, so it has the most tender meat. The rack of venison is the most popular cut from this section. Have your butcher remove the chine bone, so that it will be easy to carve, and french the bones (see page 108) for presentation. The whole rack is ideal for roasting, or it can be cut into thick individual rib chops for sautéing or grilling.

Lower down in this section are the ribs that form the animal's chest. These breast ribs are cut into strips 1½ to 2 inches (4 to 5 cm) wide. They have a coating of fat and are perfect for braising like beef short ribs.

Farther toward the leg is the loin. Here the bone splits the meat in two pieces, the loin and the tenderloin. The loin is commonly cut into chops or boned. As with lamb, if this piece is kept whole and not split through the backbone, you have a saddle of venison, an impressive roast that is popular in Europe.

The Back End

Except on large legs, the shank is usually left attached to the leg. The leg is sold whole, and like of leg lamb, it is excellent roasted. On larger animals, the leg may cut into two smaller roasts. The sirloin end, closer to the middle, has a higher portion of meat to bone, but the shank end is easier to carve. When buying a whole leg (or haunch), make sure your butcher removes the pelvic bone.

The Extremities

Venison shanks may come from either the back or front legs. They are sold whole or cut into thick crosswise pieces called venison osso buco. Those from larger animals resemble veal osso buco, but the shanks from small deer can be so small it is better to cook them whole.

Most deer have a small tail, but it is discarded when they are butchered. They have a long neck, which is cut into pieces. These pieces from smaller deer have a similar meat-to-bone ratio as oxtail, and they are perfect for braising. On larger animals, the bone is too dominant, so the neck is cut into smaller pieces to be used for stock

Wild Boar

Wild boar sounds mythic, but it's simply a wild pig. It's butchered like a pig, but the cuts are smaller. Leg of wild boar is the most commonly available cut and is excellent roasted. Depending on your supplier, it will come with or without skin. Boar skin makes delicious crackling, so I always request that it be left on. Wild boar legs are cured to make excellent hams.

My supplier also carries shoulder, rib and loin chops, and spareribs. Spareribs are an ideal way to try this meat without committing yourself to a whole roast. I have also bought wild boar's feet and tails. Although considerably smaller than pig's, they were delicious. Cook them like pig's feet (page 82) and tails (page 86). Wild boar can be substituted for pork in most recipes. Unlike other game, all the wild boar I have cooked has come with a good coating of fat.

Rabbit and Hare

The most readily available small game is the domesticated, or hutch, rabbit. Rabbits are skinned and have no protective layer of fat like chicken and their meat is pale, lean, and mild flavored. They are commonly sold whole, often with the head still attached. Don't be put off by it—have the butcher remove the head and then put it in your stockpot.

Rabbits can be cooked whole but are more commonly cut into 6 or 7 pieces, depending on size (2 forelegs, 2 back legs, and 2 or 3 pieces of saddle). This is easy to do (see page 215), or your butcher will do it. Rabbit can be cooked like chicken, but keep in mind that it is leaner. Hare and wild rabbit have dark, strong-flavored red meat. I have not been able to buy either of these animals ranched or farm-raised. If you wish to cook wild rabbit, try it Flemish-Style (page 214) or Rabbit with Cider and Mustard Sauce (page 220).

For some reason there seem to be hundreds of bones in our garden. Some of them are very old—maybe some two hundred and fifty years old. The farmers in those days were often butchers as well.

—HENRY MOORE

Ne pas faire de vieux os is a French expression describing someone who hasn't long to live.

"Lying was in his very bones," describes a compulsive liar.

"In flesh and bone" means to be physically present.

A bonehead is a stupid person who acts in a boneheaded way. This person could easily pull a boner or make a blunder.

Hare will fare better if treated like venison: roast the saddle, keeping it rare, and serve with Poivrade Sauce (page 211). Or braise the legs following the Venison Osso Buco recipe (page 236).

Game Cooking Temperatures

Because of the range in size of game, particularly venison, your cut may not weigh the same as that specified in the recipe. Use the recipes as a starting point and reduce or increase your cooking time accordingly. With slow-cooked dishes, timing is less critical, as the meat is cooked until it is tender and falling off the bone. Grilled or sautéed meat, though, must be cooked rare or medium-rare. For roasts, check the weight and time per each pound (450 g) roast in the recipes to use as a guide. For the most accurate results, use an instant-read thermometer.

Venison Roasts or Chops

Rare	130°F (54°C)
Medium-rare	135°F (57°C)

Wild Boar

	160°F (71°C)

Be sure to let the meat rest before carving, and remember that during this time the temperature will rise by 5°F (2°C).

Game Stock

Venison bones are the most readily available game bones. You can mix and match all types of venison bones and even add some rabbit bones if you don't plan to make a separate stock with them (see page 207). You can also make up the weight by adding a few veal bones.

The bones and vegetables are first roasted in the oven to give a rich brown stock. There's no need to peel the vegetables, just rinse them. The onion skin will add color to the stock. You can make a white stock by skipping the initial roasting, but I find a dark stock is much more useful because it reinforces game's strong flavors.

2 carrots, sliced
1 large onion, unpeeled, cut into wedges
1 celery stalk, sliced
4½ pounds (2 kg) game bones and trimmings, cut into 2- to 3-inch (5- to 7.5 cm) pieces
1 large tomato, halved
6 garlic cloves
1 bay leaf
3 thyme sprigs
3 flat-leaf parsley stems
¼ teaspoon black peppercorns
6 juniper berries, crushed
Kosher salt, optional

1. Preheat the oven to 425°F (220°C). Scatter the carrots, onion, and celery over the bottom of a large roasting pan. Rinse the bones well under cold running water, pat bones dry, and place them on top of the vegetables.

2. Roast, turning the bones once or twice, for 1 hour, or until they are well browned.

3. Using tongs, transfer the bones and vegetables to a large stockpot. Discard any fat from the roasting pan. Add 2 cups (500 ml) water to the pan and bring to a boil over medium heat, deglazing the pan by scraping up the browned bits from the bottom. Add this liquid to the stockpot, along with the tomato, garlic, bay leaf, thyme, and parsley. Pour in 10 cups (2.5 l) cold water, or enough to cover the bones, and bring slowly to a boil. As soon as the stock begins to boil, reduce the heat so that it simmers. Using a soup ladle, skim off any scum that has risen to the surface (rotate the bowl of the ladle on the surface of the stock to make ripples: these will carry the scum to the edges of the pot, and you can then use the ladle to lift it off). Add the peppercorns and juniper berries and simmer, uncovered, for 5 hours, skimming from time to time.

4. Strain the stock through a sieve into a large bowl. Discard the debris left in the sieve and cool the stock quickly by placing the bowl in a larger bowl or a sink filled with ice water; stir occasionally as it cools. When you taste this stock, you will notice that something is missing—the salt. Once you add it, the flavor will sparkle. But it was deliberately left out so that you can reduce the stock, if desired, without any fear that it will become too salty. If you are not reducing the stock (see page 206), add about 1 teaspoon salt.

5. Refrigerate the stock for 6 hours, or overnight, to allow the fat to rise to the top of stock and the debris to sink to the bottom. Remove the fat before using (and discard the debris at the bottom of the bowl). Divide into 1 cup (250 ml) quantities and refrigerate for up to 3 days or freeze for up to 6 months.

"I FEEL IT IN MY BONES"

○○○

To many people, bones represent the essence of all living things, and they believe that bones have special mythic powers. From the images in the Bible, particularly in the book of Ezekiel, to the Australian aborigine's belief in the power of pointing the bone, bones have always resonated strong images of doom. The giant in the fairy tale Jack and the Beanstalk threatens Jack with, "I'll grind your bones to make my bread." This intuitive belief in the power of bones is with us all, revealed when we utter, "I feel it in my bones."

"To point the bone" is an Australian expression, meaning to finger someone or expose their guilt. Its origin is the Aboriginal belief that by pointing an animal or human bone at someone, they could cause their death. The ritual was always performed in full public view, and that was part of its success. The accuser would point a bone at someone and utter a curse. So strong was the belief by everyone in the bone's power, the effect was usually almost instantaneous. The victim would become physically ill, often fainting. The rest of the tribe would shun him, and, isolated and ostracized, he stopped eating and waited to die. Despite the practice being challenged and shown to be ineffective by British settlers, pockets of belief survived, and the custom continued; deaths from bone pointing were reported as recently as 1980. The power of the bone, of course, lay not in the bone itself but in the victim's belief in its power, and that was what killed him.

In parts of Africa, bones are used to solve disputes rather than kill. Skilled practitioners throw a selection of bones in the air. They decipher the future or find answers to specific questions in the way the bones fall.

While most of us dismiss the power of bones as superstition, who among us doesn't have a lucky number or talisman? The rabbit's foot (although originally it was more likely a hare's foot) has a long history as a lucky charm. Revered for their reproductive prowess, rabbits and hares symbolized fertility, plentiful crops, and many children, all of which equaled prosperity. Their innate good luck was enhanced by their speed and the animals' ability to outrun their predators. So, the logic went, if you carried a piece of this lucky animal, its luck would rub off on you. But not just any rabbit's foot would bestow good luck—it had to be the left hind foot. Why? It's true that the hind legs touch the ground before the front ones, and they are more powerful, but the preference for the left foot remains a mystery.

Concentrated Game Stock

If your freezer space is tight, reduce your stock following the method for Concentrated Brown Stock (page 14).

6 cups (1.5 l) unsalted Game Stock (page 204)
Kosher salt

○○

The reduced stock will become syrupy and turn the color of stout.

Rabbit Stock

I keep the rabbit's head, bones, and the trimmings in the freezer until I have enough to make a stock. I make only a small amount to use when cooking rabbit. This is a white stock and it could also be used with game birds or instead of poultry stock.

2¼ pounds (1 kg) rabbit bones cut into 2 to 3 inch (5 to 7.5 cm) pieces
1 small onion, quartered
1 carrot, sliced
1 small celery stalk with leaves, sliced
2 green leek tops, sliced
1 thyme sprig
2 to 3 flat-leaf parsley stems
5 black peppercorns
Kosher salt, optional

1. Rinse the bones well under cold running water and place them in a large saucepan with the onion, carrot, celery, leek, thyme, and parsley. Pour in 6 cups (1.5 l) water and bring to a boil. As soon as the stock begins to boil, reduce the heat so that it simmers. Using a soup ladle, skim off any scum that has risen to the surface (rotate the bowl of the ladle on the surface of the stock to make ripples: these will carry the scum to the edges of the pot and you can use the ladle to lift it off). Add the peppercorns and simmer, uncovered, for 3 hours, skimming from time to time.

2. Strain the stock through a sieve into a bowl. Discard the debris left in the sieve and cool the stock quickly by placing the bowl in a larger bowl or sink filled with ice water; stir occasionally as it cools. When you taste the stock, you will notice that something is missing—the salt. Once you add it, the flavor will sparkle. But it was deliberately left out so that you can reduce the stock if desired, without any fear that it will become too salty. If you are not reducing the stock (see page 206), add about ½ teaspoon salt.

3. Refrigerate the stock for 6 hours, or overnight, to allow the fat to rise to top of the stock and the debris to sink to the bottom. Remove the fat before using (and discard the debris at the bottom of the bowl). Divide into 1-cup (250-ml) quantities and refrigerate for up to 3 days or freeze for up to 6 months.

Game Consommé

A dark golden crystal-clear broth infused with the intensity of game, this is a great consommé. It is perfect by itself as a first course, but you can dress it up by using the garnishes suggested at the end of the recipe. I like to keep consommé on hand in the freezer—it makes an impressive opener for a special dinner party.

6 cups (1.5 l) Game Stock (page 204)
1 small leek, trimmed and chopped
1 small carrot, peeled and chopped
3 flat-leaf parsley stems
6 ounces (175 g) diced or ground venison
2 egg whites
Kosher salt

1. Place the cold stock in a large saucepan and heat it just until it liquefies. Remove the saucepan from the heat.

2. Place the leek, carrot, and parsley in a food processor and process until finely chopped. Add the meat, egg whites, and 2 tablespoons water and blend until well mixed. Stir this mixture into the stock and bring to a boil over medium high-heat, stirring constantly with a spatula or wooden spoon, scraping the bottom of the saucepan, to prevent the egg white from sticking. As the liquid approaches a boil, it will appear to curdle, don't panic, that is what you want. As soon as the stock begins to boil, stop stirring, and remove the saucepan from the heat. The whites will form a congealed mass on the surface, which will puff up and then crack as the steam escapes.

3. Reduce the heat to very low and return the saucepan to the heat, making a larger hole in the egg white mass with a spoon to allow the steam to escape. Simmer very gently—you want to see small bubbles of steam break through the hole in the egg white mass—for 45 minutes. Remove the saucepan from the heat and let stand for 5 minutes.

4. Line a sieve with a double thickness of damp cheesecloth or a dampened thin cotton tea towel, and place over a bowl. Using a skimmer or large slotted spoon, carefully lift off as much of the egg white mass as you can and set aside in another bowl. Ladle the consommé into the sieve and allow it to drip slowly through the cloth. As you get closer to the bottom of the saucepan, you might notice that the clear consommé is being muddied by bits of egg white. Don't worry, just add it to the sieve. Check the bowl with the egg white debris and pour any liquid that has escaped from it into the sieve. Allow all the liquid to drip slowly through the sieve; don't be tempted to press on the egg whites, as that would cloud the consommé.

5. You will have about 5 cups (1.25 l) clear consommé in the bowl and a mess of congealed egg white to discard. Season the consommé with about ¼ teaspoon salt. Serve hot, or allow to cool, then chill and serve cold. If you serve the consommé cold, you may need to boost the seasoning, as cold dulls the flavor.

Consommé garnishes

Chopped herbs, matchsticks of cooked root vegetables

Try the Liver Dumplings (below) or simply stuff wonton wrappers with a fine dice of well-seasoned cooked game.

◦ Liver Dumplings

{ MAKES 12 TO 15 WONTONS } One snowy winter's day, my friend Miriam e-mailed from deepest Pennsylvania suggesting liver dumplings as a garnish for my consommé. I had some rabbit livers on hand, but you could use chicken livers—or even better, foie gras. These dumplings are wrapped in wonton skins and steamed separately, rather than cooked in the consommé; this ensures that the consommé remains crystal clear.

1 rabbit or chicken liver (about 2¼ ounces [66 g])
¼ cup (20 g) fresh bread crumbs
1½ teaspoons finely diced shallot
2 teaspoons marjoram leaves
1 tablespoon beaten egg
Kosher salt and freshly ground black pepper
12 to 15 wonton wrappers

1. Remove any fat and membranes from the liver, then dice it. Place the bread crumbs, shallot, and marjoram in a food processor and pulse until well blended. Add the diced liver and egg, and season with ⅛ teaspoon salt and a few grindings of pepper. Pulse until blended, stopping to scrape down the sides of the bowl as needed.

2. To test for seasoning, take a small spoonful of the mixture and drop it into gently simmering water. Simmer for 2 minutes, then taste for the seasoning and correct it if necessary. Refrigerate the remaining mixture, covered, for 30 minutes or up to 2 hours.

3. Place 1 teaspoon of the liver mixture onto the center of each wonton wrapper. Brush the edges with water and seal, pleating the edges, if desired.

4. Steam the wontons on an oiled steamer rack for 10 minutes. (You can steam the wontons ahead, then cover them with plastic wrap and refrigerate. Bring them to room temperature before using.) Transfer them to warmed soup bowls and ladle over the hot consommé.

Game Soup

Since this soup isn't clarified, it's less fussy than consommé. If you have game stock stored in your freezer, it is quick and easy to prepare. You can vary the vegetables as you wish, adding more carrots, for example, or some parsnip. Pieces of diced cooked game or even small pasta, such as conchiglie, or orecchiette, are other possible additions, but do not omit the mushrooms and Madeira; together, they enhance the soup's gamey flavor.

1 tablespoon olive oil
1 small onion, sliced
1 small carrot, peeled, halved, and thinly sliced
1 small turnip, peeled, cut into 6 wedges, and thinly sliced crosswise
1 small potato, peeled, cut into 6 wedges, and thinly sliced crosswise
2 celery stalks, sliced
3 cups (750 ml) Game Stock (page 204)
3 medium cremini (brown) mushrooms, thinly sliced
½ teaspoon kosher salt
Freshly ground black pepper
2 tablespoons dry Madeira or Marsala
Chopped flat-leaf parsley for garnish

1. Heat the olive oil in a large saucepan over medium heat. Add the onion and carrot and cook gently for about 5 minutes, or until softened. Add the turnip, potato, and celery, then pour in the stock and bring to a boil. Reduce the heat so that the soup simmers gently, cover, and cook for 7 to 10 minutes, or until the vegetables are just cooked. (The soup can be made ahead up to this point. Let cool, then cover and refrigerate. Bring to a simmer before proceeding.)

2. Stir in the mushrooms and salt. Simmer for 1 to 2 minutes to cook the mushrooms, then add the pepper and Madeira. Ladle the soup into bowls and sprinkle with the parsley.

Game Jus and Poivrade Sauce

With game stock on hand, you can make two easy sauces. Jus is simply a concentrated sauce made by reducing the stock. By thickening this jus and adding Cognac and red currant jelly, you turn it into poivrade sauce, traditionally served with game. The jus can be prepared ahead, or even frozen. It is perfect to serve with a simple sautéed or grilled venison chop or the roasted rack of venison (page 224).

1 tablespoon vegetable oil
1 tablespoon finely diced shallot
1 tablespoon finely diced celery
1 tablespoon peeled and finely diced carrot
2 cups (500 ml) Game Stock (page 204)
3 juniper berries, crushed
10 black peppercorns, crushed
½ teaspoon red wine vinegar
Kosher salt and freshly ground black pepper

FOR POIVRADE SAUCE
¾ teaspoon arrowroot
1 tablespoon Cognac
1 tablespoon red currant jelly

1. Heat the oil in a small saucepan over medium heat. Add the vegetables and cook until softened and fragrant. Pour in the stock, add the juniper berries, and bring to a boil. Lower the heat and simmer for 20 minutes, or until the stock is reduced by half.

2. Add the peppercorns and continue to simmer for 10 minutes. Strain the sauce through a sieve into a clean saucepan, pressing on the vegetables to extract all the flavor. Add the vinegar and season with salt and pepper.

3. To finish the sauce, once you have cooked the roast or whatever meat you are serving the sauce with, set the meat aside and keep warm, loosely covered with foil. Pour off any fat from the pan used for the meat, add the strained liquid to the pan, and deglaze the pan by scraping up the browned bits from the bottom. Bring to a boil, then strain the jus through a sieve and correct the seasoning if necessary.

4. For the poivrade sauce, mix the ¾ teaspoon arrowroot with 1 tablespoon Cognac and whisk it into the sauce after deglazing. Bring back to a boil, whisking constantly, then remove from the heat, strain through a sieve, and stir in 1 tablespoon red currant jelly.

Marinades

Marinades add flavor to meats and can provide the basis for a sauce. With game, they add much-needed fat and tenderize the meat. The oil adds the fat, while the wine, being acidic, tenderizes the meat. A simple marinade of olive oil, white wine, and herbs gives game a protective coat of oil and enhances its flavor without overwhelming it. It is good for prime cuts that are to be grilled, sautéed, or roasted; I also use it on milder game like rabbit. For everything else, I use the stronger red wine marinade, which reinforces the game's flavor.

Smaller pieces of meat only need 6 to 8 hours in a marinade, while larger cuts such as legs and shoulders, and those from older animals, benefit from as long as 2 days in the marinade.

○ Olive Oil Marinade

{ MAKES ABOUT ½ CUP (125 ML) } Use this for wild boar chops, leg of venison, and rabbit.

1. Mix ¼ cup (60 ml) dry white wine (or dry white vermouth) with 3 tablespoons extra virgin olive oil and 1 tablespoon *each* thyme and marjoram leaves. Coat the surface of your meat with the marinade and refrigerate.

○ Red Wine Marinade

{ MAKES ABOUT 3 CUPS (750 ML) } In this marinade, the alcohol is burned off to stop it from cooking the surface of the meat. The theory is that this then allows the flavor of the wine to penetrate the meat more easily.

1 bottle (750 ml) dry red wine
2 carrots, diced
1 onion, sliced
1 large shallot, sliced
1 celery stalk, sliced
1 garlic clove, crushed
3 flat-leaf parsley stems
1 large rosemary sprig
1 thyme sprig
1 bay leaf
4 large juniper berries, crushed
¼ teaspoon black peppercorns
¼ cup (60 ml) red wine vinegar
3 tablespoons olive oil

1. Pour the wine into a large saucepan and bring it to a boil, then reduce the heat so the wine bubbles gently. Tip the saucepan slightly away from you and, using a long match, *carefully* light the wine and let the wine burn. Once the flames die out, light the wine again. Continue lighting the wine until it no longer burns. Pour it into a glass measuring cup and leave it to cool; there will be about 2½ cups (625 ml).

2. Place the carrots, onion, shallot, celery, garlic, parsley, rosemary, thyme, bay leaf, juniper, and peppercorns in a large nonreactive container, and add your meat. Mix the vinegar and oil with the cooled wine and pour over the meat, turning it to coat. Cover and refrigerate, turning the meat from time to time.

BONE TOOLS

ooooooooooooooooooo

Killing game for meat left man with plenty of bones for making tools. Large leg bones were especially useful. Reindeer tibias were sharpened and used to remove the hides of animals, and tubular cannon bones (the bones between the hock and the fetlock) were employed to scrape the remaining flesh off the hides. The knuckle of the cannon bone forms a natural handle, and teeth were notched into the other end.

Early man extracted the rich, nutritious marrow from such bones by smashing them with rocks. That left him with splintered bone pieces with very sharp edges, quickly recognized as useful weapons, and these bones became the first crude spears.

As civilization progressed, man replaced his bone tools with metal ones, but often kept bones as decorative items or features. Even today, many knives, especially hunting ones, have carved bone handles, and we can buy bone-handled cutlery for our dining tables.

Flemish-Style Rabbit

The beer in this recipe hints at its country of origin, Belgium. The prunes counteract any bitterness from the beer, while the bacon adds the necessary fat to keep the rabbit moist. The combination is delicious.

This is one of the first rabbit dishes I ever cooked for company and it is a good way to introduce timid guests to rabbit. Buy the slab (side) bacon, rather than sliced, so that you can dice it yourself. Rabbit doesn't taste like chicken, it tastes like rabbit, but this recipe could be made with chicken pieces. (And you can, of course, use rabbit in your favorite chicken recipes.)

1 rabbit, cut into 6 or 7 pieces
3½ ounces (100 g) slab (side) bacon
12 shallots or small pickling onions
Kosher salt and freshly ground black pepper
3 tablespoons vegetable oil
12 medium mushrooms, quartered
2 cups (500 ml) lager beer
1 cup (250 ml) Rabbit Stock (page 207) or Poultry Stock (page 130)
12 large pitted prunes
2 large garlic cloves, unpeeled
5 flat-leaf parsley stems, plus 2 tablespoons chopped parsley
2 bay leaves
1 large thyme sprig
1 tablespoon sugar
1 tablespoon brandy
2 teaspoons cornstarch

1. Preheat the oven to 350°F (175°C). Remove the rabbit from the refrigerator.

2. Cut off the bacon rind and discard, then cut the bacon into ¼ × ½-inch (5 mm × 1-cm) dice. Place in a small saucepan, cover with cold water, bring to a boil, and boil for 1 minute. Drain the bacon in a sieve and refresh under cold running water; set aside.

3. Refill the saucepan with water and bring to a boil. Drop in the shallots and cook for 1 minute. Drain in a sieve and refresh under cold running water, then peel, leaving enough of the root end intact so they will remain whole while cooking.

4. Pat the rabbit pieces dry and season them with salt and pepper. In a frying pan large enough to hold all the rabbit, heat 2 tablespoons of the oil over medium heat. Add the rabbit and brown on both sides. Once the pieces are browned, transfer them to a Dutch oven or flameproof casserole.

5. Add the bacon and shallots to the frying pan, along with the remaining 1 tablespoon of the oil, and cook until the bacon is crispy and the shallots begin to color. Using a slotted spoon, transfer them to the

pot. Add the mushrooms to the pan and cook until they color slightly, then add to the rabbit. Pour the beer and stock into the pan and bring to a boil, deglazing the pan by scraping up the browned bits from the bottom.

6. Pour over the rabbit, and add the prunes, garlic, parsley stems, bay leaves, and thyme. Bring to the boil on top of the stove, then cover the pot and cook in the oven for 1 hour. The rabbit should be very tender; if not, continue to cook it for another 10 to 15 minutes.

7. Transfer the rabbit to a warmed platter. Discard the herbs and, using a slotted spoon, add the shallots, mushrooms, and prunes to the rabbit. Keep them warm, loosely covered with aluminum foil. Remove the garlic cloves from the sauce and set aside.

8. Bring the sauce to a boil and boil hard to reduce it by half. Squeeze the contents of the garlic cloves into a small bowl, and stir in the sugar, brandy, and cornstarch. Whisk this mixture into the boiling liquid and cook for 2 minutes, whisking all the time.

9. Pour the sauce over the rabbit, prunes, and vegetables, sprinkle with the chopped parsley, and serve.

NOTE: The rabbit can be cooked ahead and reheated. Preheat the oven to 300°F (150°C), and reheat the rabbit covered in the sauce for about 20 minutes.

Cutting Up a Rabbit

Cut off the head and neck, if the butcher hasn't already, and set them aside for the stockpot. Remove the liver (you can leave the heart and lungs attached to the ribs). Turn the rabbit onto its stomach and cut the front legs from the rib cage. Cut the rib cage from the body in one piece by slicing through the backbone where the ribs end and the loins begin. The rib cage has little flesh and lots of small bones; split it in two or more pieces and keep for the stockpot, with the heart and lungs. Cut through the backbone at the point where the hind legs join it, and separate the back legs by cutting on either side of the backbone. Finally, attack the meaty midsection known as the saddle. There are thin skin flaps attached to either side of this piece; trim them off. Turn over the saddle so you can see where the kidneys are, then cut the saddle into 2 or 3 equal pieces without damaging the kidneys. Keep all the trimmings for stock.

Rabbit in Saffron Sauce with Spring Vegetables

Rabbit is the only game I associate with spring, because its light, delicate meat matches well with spring-time vegetables. Fava beans, asparagus, and baby carrots in a saffron sauce make this a pretty dish, but you can vary the vegetables to your taste. The rabbit liver is cooked separately and made into a simple spread to accompany the dish.

1 rabbit cut, into 6 or 7 pieces, liver and kidneys set aside
Olive Oil Marinade (page 212)
Kosher salt
12 asparagus spears, trimmed
16 shelled fresh fava beans
12 baby carrots, trimmed
12 small onions, such as like cipollini
Freshly ground black pepper
2 tablespoons olive oil
16 garlic cloves
1 cup (250 ml) dry white wine
A good pinch of saffron threads
3 to 4 flat-leaf parsley stems, plus 1 tablespoon chopped parsley
1 large thyme sprig
1 bay leaf
8 slices baguette, lightly toasted

1. Place the rabbit in a dish, add the marinade, and turn to coat. Cover and refrigerate for 8 to 12 hours.

2. One hour before cooking, remove the rabbit from the refrigerator. (Keep the kidneys and liver refrigerated.)

3. Bring a medium saucepan of salted water to a boil. Add the asparagus and favas and cook 3 to 4 minutes or until tender. Using a slotted spoon, transfer them to a bowl of ice water to cool. Cut the asparagus into 2 or 3 pieces, and remove the skins from the favas by gently squeezing the beans; return the asparagus and favas to the bowl of ice water.

4. Bring the water in the saucepan back to a boil and drop in the carrots. Simmer until just cooked, then drain and refresh under cold running water. Add to the asparagus. Drop the onions into the saucepan and bring to a boil, then reduce the heat slightly and simmer for 2 minutes. Drain and refresh them under cold running water. Peel the onions, leaving enough of the root intact so they will remain whole while cooking. (The vegetables can be all prepared up to 4 hours ahead, keep them refrigerated.)

5. Remove the rabbit from the marinade (reserve the marinade) and pat dry, then season with salt and pepper. Heat the oil in a large frying pan over medium-high heat and brown the rabbit pieces quickly on each side. Transfer the browned pieces to a platter. Reduce the heat, add the onions, and cook, stirring, for 2 to 3 minutes. Add the garlic and the reserved marinade and cook until the onions and garlic begin to stick to the bottom of the pan. Pour in the white wine and bring to a boil, deglazing the pan by scraping up the browned bits from the bottom. Add the saffron and the rabbit pieces, with any juices, then add the parsley stems, thyme, and bay leaf. Cover and cook over low heat for 1 hour, or until the rabbit is tender, turning the pieces from time to time.

6. While the rabbit is cooking, chop the liver. In a small bowl, mix it with the chopped parsley, and season with salt and pepper. Slice the kidneys in half. Keep the liver mixture and kidneys in the refrigerator until ready to use.

7. When the rabbit is cooked, transfer it and the onions to a serving platter and keep warm, loosely covered with aluminum foil. Discard the herbs and bring the sauce to a boil to reduce slightly. Add the asparagus, fava beans, and kidneys and cook for 3 minutes, or until the vegetables are heated through and the kidneys are cooked.

8. Meanwhile, preheat the broiler. Spread the toasted baguette slices with the liver mixture, and broil the toasts until the topping is cooked.

9. Spoon the sauce and vegetables over the rabbit and serve with the toasts.

Herb-Roasted Rabbit

Farmed rabbit does have some fat around its kidneys and on its back and legs, but it is not enough to keep it moist enough while roasting. Wrapping the rabbit in bacon bastes the lean meat and adds flavor, while the herb and bacon stuffing adds both fat and flavor. It is important not to overcook the rabbit, and you will need a long roasting pan for this, since a whole rabbit is not as compact as a chicken. Ask your butcher to remove (and save) the head, heart, lungs, and liver but leave the kidneys attached. The liver is cooked with the rabbit, and you can use the other pieces for stock (page 207).

1 rabbit, liver reserved (see headnote)
Olive Oil Marinade (page 212)
¾ cup (60 g) fresh bread crumbs
1 tablespoon finely chopped shallot
3 tablespoons chopped marjoram
5 bacon slices
1½ cups (375 ml) Rabbit Stock (page 207) or Poultry Stock (page 130)
Kosher salt and freshly ground black pepper
¼ cup (60 ml) white wine vinegar

1. Pat the rabbit dry, place it in a glass dish, pour over the marinade, and turn the rabbit to coat completely. Cover and refrigerate overnight, turning the rabbit from time to time. Finely chop the liver, cover, and refrigerate.

2. Preheat the oven to 425°F (220°C). Remove the rabbit from the marinade (reserve the marinade). Mix the bread crumbs, liver, shallot, and 2 tablespoons of the marjoram in a bowl. Finely dice 1 slice of bacon, and mix it into the bread crumb mixture, along with ¼ cup (60 ml) of the stock. Season with salt and pepper.

3. Spoon the stuffing into the rabbit's cavity, covering the kidneys. Skewer the belly closed with 1 or 2 small metal skewers. With two pieces of string, first tie the back legs together, then the front legs. Season the rabbit with salt and pepper. Wrap the center section of the rabbit in the remaining bacon slices, and wind a long piece of string around the bacon to hold it in place.

4. Put the rabbit on its side in a roasting pan, and pour over the reserved marinade. Roast the rabbit for 10 minutes, basting twice with the marinade. Reduce the oven temperature to 350°F (175°C), turn the rabbit onto its other side, and roast for 15 minutes, basting 3 times.

5. Turn the rabbit onto its back and roast for another 15 minutes, basting 3 times. Turn the rabbit back onto the first side and roast, without basting, for another 15 minutes, or until it is cooked. To check, pierce the thickest part of the thigh with a skewer—the juices should run clear. Transfer the rabbit to a platter and let it rest, loosely covered with aluminum foil, for 10 minutes.

6. Discard any fat in the roasting pan. Pour in the remaining 1¼ cups (310 ml) rabbit stock and the vinegar and bring to a boil, deglazing the pan by scraping up the browned bits from the bottom. Boil hard to reduce the liquid by half. Season with salt and pepper, strain into a sauceboat, and stir in the remaining 1 tablespoon chopped marjoram.

7. Cut the rabbit into serving pieces and serve with the sauce.

BONE CHINA

ooooooooooooooooooooo

An Englishman, Josiah Spode, created bone china toward the end of the eighteenth century. Bone china does indeed contain bones—about fifty percent of its composition, in fact, in the form of calcined bone ash. To make this ash, animal bones are stripped of meat, then heated to 1832°F (1000°C), which alters their structure (and sterilizes them). They are then ground into a powder that is added to the porcelain clay. Bone china is not only stronger, but also less likely to chip than regular porcelain. The biggest advantage of bone china when first introduced, though, was its very white color and translucency. It set the standard for fine English china, and Spode's competitors, the Wedgwood, Minton, and Coalport factories, quickly followed his lead.

Rabbit with Cider and Mustard Sauce

There are many recipes for the traditional combination of rabbit and mustard, but often by the time the rabbit is cooked, there is no mustard taste left; not so here. For offal lovers, the rabbit liver and kidneys are cooked separately and added at the end. Those who don't appreciate them can skip this step: leave the kidneys attached to the saddle section of the rabbit, and keeping the rabbit's liver for the Liver Dumplings (page 209), if desired.

1 rabbit, cut into 6 or 7 serving pieces, liver and kidneys reserved
Olive Oil Marinade (page 212), made with 2 tablespoons marjoram leaves (omit the thyme)
Kosher salt and freshly ground black pepper
¼ cup (60 ml) Dijon mustard
1 cup (250 ml) hard cider
¼ cup (60 ml) heavy (35%) whipping cream
1 tablespoon chopped marjoram
2 cooking apples, such as Rome, Spy, Mutsu
3 tablespoons (45 g) unsalted butter
1 tablespoon sugar
Chopped flat-leaf parsley for garnish

1. Pat the rabbit pieces dry and place them in a baking dish just large enough to hold them in one layer. Pour over the marinade and turn the pieces to coat. Leave at room temperature for 1 hour, or refrigerate, covered, for several hours. If it has been refrigerated, remove the rabbit 1 hour before cooking so that it warms up to room temperature.

2. Preheat the oven 450°F (230°C). Season the rabbit with salt and pepper, then transfer all the pieces except the hind legs to a plate; set these pieces aside. Stir together the mustard, ½ cup (125 ml) of the cider, the cream, and marjoram in a small bowl. Spoon a couple of spoonfuls of this mixture over the legs, and bake for 10 minutes.

3. Add the rest of the rabbit pieces to the dish. Spoon over some more of the cider-cream mixture and bake for 15 minutes. Reduce the oven temperature to 375°F (190°C), turn the pieces over, and baste again with more cream mixture. As you baste, scrape up any darker bits at the edges of the dish. Bake for another 30 minutes, basting and turning the pieces every 10 minutes. Once all the mustard mixture is used, baste with the juices in the dish, again scraping the browned bits from the edges of the dish into the sauce each time.

4. While the rabbit is cooking, peel, core, and quarter the apples, then cut into ¼-inch (5-mm) slices. Melt 2 tablespoons (30 g) of the butter in a large frying pan over medium heat. Add the sugar and apples and sauté until the apples are golden brown. Transfer the apples to a dish. Add the remaining ½ cup (125 ml) cider to the frying pan and bring to a boil, deglazing the pan by scraping up the browned bits from the bottom. Remove from the heat.

5. After the rabbit has cooked for 30 minutes at 375°F (190°F), add the sautéed apples and cider to the dish (set the frying pan aside). Cook for another 10 minutes, or until the rabbit is very tender.

6. Meanwhile, cut the kidneys in half and slice the liver. Season them both with salt and pepper. Heat the remaining 1 tablespoon butter in the same frying pan and sauté the kidneys and liver until just pink.

7. Scatter the kidneys and liver over the cooked rabbit, sprinkle with the parsley, and serve.

BURNT BONES

There are other uses for burnt bones besides china (see "Bone China," page 219). When animal bones are burned with little or no air, several by-products result. Two of them, bone brown and bone black, are finely ground to make artist's pigments. Bone black is also the main ingredient in the ink used for copperplate printing. Bone char or commercial charcoal, is used industrially to remove impurities from liquids and refine sugar.

Burning bones also creates a vile-smelling oil called Dippel's oil, named after a German theologian and alchemist, Johann Dippel (1673–1734). Herr Dippel made a miscalculation while searching for the elixir of life, and discovered this malodorous oil instead. Unfortunately, the oil doesn't prolong life but is still used in sheep dip and to denature alcohol.

Wine-Braised Venison

One misty autumn day in Piedmont, Italy, I ate a rich, satisfying local dish, beef braised in Barolo wine. Now, making this in Piedmont, where Barolo wines are almost affordable, would be one thing, but a visit to my local wine store revealed that while I may drink Barolo on special occasions, I would definitely not be cooking with it. I chose a well-priced Barbaresco, but any hearty red wine will do, and I decided that this was just the right way to cook a bone-in shoulder of venison. This cut can be difficult to carve elegantly, so I cook it ahead and cut it into thick slices when cold, then reheat the slices in the thick wine and vegetable sauce; consequently, it's an ideal dish for entertaining.

1 bone-in venison shoulder, about 5 pounds (2.25 kg)
½ ounce (15 g) dried wild mushrooms
Kosher salt and freshly ground black pepper
3 tablespoons vegetable oil
5 ounces (145 g) slab (side) bacon, rind removed and cut into 4 pieces
2 onions, sliced
2 carrots, peeled and sliced
2 celery stalks, sliced
2 garlic cloves
1 large rosemary sprig
2 bay leaves
5 sage leaves
3 flat-leaf parsley stems
1 thyme sprig
1 long cinnamon stick
Zest of 1 lemon, removed in wide strips
5 cups (1.25 l) Barbaresco or other hearty dry red wine

1. One hour before cooking, remove the shoulder from the refrigerator. Pour 1 cup (250 ml) boiling water over the mushrooms in a small bowl, and leave them to soak. Preheat the oven to 300°F (150°C).

2. Pat the shoulder dry and season with salt and pepper. In a Dutch oven or large flameproof casserole, heat 2 tablespoons of the oil over medium-high heat. Brown the shoulder on all sides, including the bone. Transfer the meat to a plate and discard any fat from the pot.

3. Add the bacon and the remaining 1 tablespoon oil to the pot and cook over low heat for 2 minutes. Increase the heat, add the onions, carrots, and celery, and cook until the onions begin to soften, about 5 minutes, scraping the bottom of the pot frequently.

4. Lift the mushrooms from the soaking liquid and add to them to the pot, along with the garlic, rosemary, bay and sage leaves, parsley stems, and thyme. Strain the mushroom liquid through a fine sieve, discarding any sand or grit, and add the liquid to the pot, with the cinnamon stick and lemon zest. Bring to a boil, deglazing the pot by scraping the browned bits from the bottom.

5. Place the shoulder, bone side up, in the pot. Pour in any juices from the meat, add the wine, and bring to a boil. Cover with a damp piece of parchment paper and then the lid, and braise in the oven for 3 to 3 ½ hours. The meat should be very tender and lift from the bone with only slightest resistance.

6. Transfer the shoulder to a platter. Discard the herbs, cinnamon stick, and zest and let the sauce cool slightly, then puree it with an immersion blender or in batches in a regular blender. Bring the sauce to a boil, skim off the foam, and then boil hard for 10 to 12 minutes to reduce it to 4 cups (2 l). Cool the meat and sauce separately, then cover and refrigerate overnight.

7. The next day, remove any fat from the sauce and the meat. Preheat the oven to 300°F (150°C). Remove the meat from the bones, keeping it in as large pieces as possible. Cut these pieces into thick slices, and place them in a baking dish. Spoon over the sauce.

8. Cover with aluminum foil and reheat gently for about 45 minutes, or until heated through.

Which Piece of the Shoulder?

Whether from pork, lamb, or venison, the shoulder has a complicated bone structure,
with the blade bone, arm bone, and pieces of rib, depending on how it is trimmed.
If you are buying half a shoulder, ask for the piece of shoulder cut closer to the forearm,
away from the neck. There will be fewer bones and more meat.

Roasted Rack of Venison with Cape Gooseberry Sauce

Cape gooseberries were a fruit I used for garnishing as a food stylist, but I didn't really eat them; if they arrived dipped in fondant at the end of the meal in a fancy restaurant, I passed. Then, as I began working on this chapter, I was on the lookout for fruit that complemented or contrasted with the richness of game. With their touch of tartness, Cape gooseberries are perfect. These berries, also called physalis, ground cherries, or golden berries, are a relative of the tomatillo. They appear in specialty stores in autumn, the game season.

If you can't find Cape gooseberries, cook the venison as directed and serve with Poivrade Sauce (page 211). Both these sauces are excellent with the roast rack or leg, or with a simple grilled venison chop. The number of chops in your rack will depend on the type of venison you have; those from smaller deer will probably have about 8, while one from elk might have only 4 chops. And although the elk and venison racks might be the same weight, elk is thicker and can take longer to cook.

1 rack of venison, frenched (see page 108), about 3 pounds (1.35 kg)
Olive Oil Marinade (page 212)
One 3½-ounce (100-g) basket Cape gooseberries (about 20)
1 cup (250 ml) Game Stock (page 204)
Kosher salt and freshly ground black pepper
2 tablespoons port or sweet sherry
2 teaspoons arrowroot

1. The day before you roast the venison, pat it dry and place it bone side down in a shallow dish. Pour over the marinade and turn over the meat to coat. Cover with plastic wrap and refrigerate overnight.

2. One hour before cooking, remove the venison rack from the refrigerator. Preheat the oven to 425°F (220°C).

3. Set 4 gooseberries with the husks aside for garnish, if you like. Discard the husks from the remaining Cape gooseberries, rinse the berries, and cut them in half. Bring the stock to a boil in a saucepan and add the halved gooseberries, then remove from the heat, cover, and let stand until cool.

4. Strain the Cape gooseberries from the stock, and set both berries and stock aside.

5. Place the venison rack in a roasting pan, bone side down, and pour over any remaining marinade. Season with salt and pepper. Roast for 10 minutes, then reduce the oven temperature to 350°F (175°C) and roast for another 30 to 45 minutes, or until the internal temperature registers 130°F (54°C) for rare, or 135°F (57°C) for medium-rare, on an instant-read thermometer. (Estimate 12 to 13 minutes per pound [450 g].) Transfer the rack on a warmed serving platter and let it rest, loosely covered with aluminum foil, for 15 minutes. The internal temperature of the roast will rise 5°F (2°C) as it rests.

6. Discard the fat from the roasting pan, add the strained game stock, and bring to a boil, deglazing the pan by scraping up the browned bits from the bottom. Strain the stock into a small saucepan and add the cooked Cape gooseberries. Mix the port and arrowroot together, add the sauce, and bring to a boil. Remove from the heat and season with salt and pepper.

7. Serve the venison with the sauce, and the gooseberries for garnish, if you reserved them.

ANTLERS

ooooooooooooooo

Antlers are unique bones designed to take plenty of abuse. Although they are no stronger than other bones, they are more flexible because of a lower proportion of calcium phosphate. This makes them ideal as digging tools and spear throwers. A spear thrower is a piece of wood or bone that in effect lengthens the hunter's arm, enabling him to throw his spear faster and farther; made from antlers, these tools were far more durable than when made from wood. Antlers, like other bones, were crafted into needles, awls, fish hooks, and arrow and harpoon heads.

The supple quality of antlers also made them a popular material for combs. The Vikings, skillful craftsmen, are known for their particularly beautiful antler combs, and many examples have been excavated from sites near the city of York in the England.

Coriander-and-Orange-Braised Elk Ribs

Venison ribs are excellent for braising, but they can be difficult to find because of the lack of demand, so order them ahead. Big, meaty elk ribs are perfect for this dish. My ribs were cut into strips 2 inches (5 cm) wide. If your ribs are smaller, adjust the cooking time as necessary, and you may want to skip the final step of cutting them into pieces. Elk ribs can have a coating of fat, so make this early in the morning or a day ahead and refrigerate them so you can remove any excess fat easily. Their flavor also improves with re-heating.

I like combining parsnip and parsley root—it's a visual trick, because they look the same but taste different. You can substitute other root vegetables, such as rutabaga or celeriac, just watch the cooking time—or roast them separately and add them to the ribs for the final glazing.

4 pieces elk ribs, about 3 pounds (1.35 kg)
Kosher salt and freshly ground black pepper
2 tablespoons vegetable oil
1 Spanish onion, cut into 1-inch (2.5-cm) chunks
4 medium carrots, peeled and cut into 3 pieces each
1 celery stalk, diced
1 cup (250 ml) dry red wine
1 orange
1 lemon
1 cup (250 ml) Game Stock (page 204)
1 tablespoon coriander seeds, crushed
2 garlic cloves, crushed
4 parsley roots, peeled
4 parsnips, peeled

1. Preheat the oven to 300°F (150°C). Pat the meat dry, and season with salt and pepper. In a Dutch oven or flameproof casserole, heat the oil over medium heat and brown the ribs, in batches, on both sides. Transfer them to a plate and add the onion, carrots, and celery to the pot. Cook, stirring, for 5 minutes, or until the onion softens slightly.

2. Pour in the red wine and bring to a boil, deglazing the pot by scraping up the browned bits from the bottom. Meanwhile, grate the zest from the orange, then juice it. Add enough lemon juice to the orange juice to make ½ cup (125 ml).

3. Pour the juice and stock into the pot, and add the zest, coriander, garlic, and 1 teaspoon salt. Add the ribs to the pot, along with any juices, making sure they are almost submerged in the liquid. Place the parsley root on top and cover with a damp piece of parchment paper and the lid. Braise in the oven for 1 hour.

4. Add the parsnips, cover with the parchment and lid, and cook for another 1½ hours. Uncover and cook for another 30 minutes, or until the ribs and vegetables are very tender.

5. Transfer the ribs and vegetables to a dish to cool, then cover. Strain the cooking liquid into a glass measuring cup or a bowl and leave to cool. Refrigerate them both until the fat sets, or overnight.

6. Preheat the oven to 300°F (150°C). Remove the meat and vegetables from the refrigerator and take off any fat. Cut the ribs into smaller pieces, and place them in a baking dish with the vegetables. Cover and transfer to the oven to heat through, about 30 minutes.

7. Remove the fat from the sauce and bring to a boil. Increase the oven temperature to 400°F (200°C) and pour the sauce over the ribs and vegetables. Bake uncovered for about 15 to 20 minutes, basting 3 to 4 times, until the ribs are well glazed.

Wild Boar Chops Martini-Style

I had been developing green martinis for a magazine story (the recipe for the martini follows) and had bottles of gin and Chartreuse in my kitchen. Juniper, a natural with game, is a basic flavoring in gin. So, I thought, why not throw in the gin, plus a little of that Chartreuse for an extra herbal boost? Use a premium gin and green Chartreuse, which is more herbal than the yellow one.

6 wild boar loin chops, ½ to ¾ inch (1 to 2 cm) thick
Olive Oil Marinade (page 212)
Kosher salt and freshly ground black pepper
1 tablespoon vegetable oil
1 tablespoon gin
6 juniper berries, crushed
2 tablespoons Chartreuse
½ teaspoon cornstarch
1 tablespoon chervil or flat-leaf parsley leaves, optional

1. Place the chops in a dish and pour over the marinade, turning the chops so they are well coated. Refrigerate for 4 to 6 hours.

2. Thirty minutes before cooking, remove the chops from the refrigerator.

3. Remove the chops from the marinade (reserve the marinade), pat dry, and season with salt and pepper. In a large frying pan with a lid, heat the oil until very hot. Brown the chops for 1 minute on each side, then transfer them to a plate.

4. Discard any fat from the pan, add the marinade, and bring to a boil, deglazing the pan by scraping up the browned bits from the bottom. Add the gin, juniper, and half of the Chartreuse, return the chops to the pan, cover, and cook over low heat for 7 to 10 minutes, or until the chops are just cooked though.

5. Transfer the chops to a plate and keep warm, loosely covered with aluminum foil. Mix the remaining Chartreuse with the cornstarch and add to the pan. Bring to a boil, stirring constantly. Return the chops to the pan, with any juices, and turn the chops to coat with the sauce. Check the seasoning, sprinkle with the chervil, and serve.

The Green Martini

Fill a cocktail shaker with ice. Add 1 ounce (30 ml) Chartreuse and 1 ounce (30 ml) premium gin. Drop in a piece of lime zest and shake well, then strain into a martini glass and garnish with a lime twist.

Tamarind, Pineapple, and Chile–Glazed Boar Ribs

If you can locate a source for wild boar, demand more than just the usual legs and racks from your supplier—ask for ribs. It will make both of you happy. While working on this book, I came across the name of a boar recipe with these ingredients, but no reference to what cut of meat to use or where the recipe originated. I liked the combination of ingredients so much that I just went ahead and created this dish.

Tamarind, the fruit of an Asian tree, has a sour flavor. The pulp can be found compressed into small packages, seeds and all, in Asian markets. After soaking, squeeze the pulp to remove the seeds. The final glazing of the ribs is messy, so if you want to avoid scrubbing your baking dish, line it with aluminum foil first. Note that you must start this recipe a day in advance.

2 racks wild boar ribs, 8 to 10 ounces (250 to 280 g) each
1 ancho chile, stemmed, quartered, and seeded
1 tablespoon tamarind pulp
¾ cup (175 ml) pineapple juice
2 tablespoons brown sugar
¼ teaspoon kosher salt

1. Pat the ribs dry and place them in a shallow baking dish; set aside. Place the chile and tamarind pulp in a small bowl, pour in ½ cup (125 ml) boiling water, and leave to soak for 30 minutes.

2. Remove the chile from the water and put it in a blender, along with the pineapple juice, brown sugar, and salt. Using your fingers, squeeze the tamarind pulp together with the water to make a thick liquid, removing any seeds as you squeeze. Add the tamarind liquid to the blender and blend until smooth; you will have about 1 cup (250 ml) sauce.

3. Strain the sauce through a sieve, then pour over the ribs. Cover and refrigerate overnight, turning the ribs from time to time.

4. One hour before cooking, remove the ribs from the refrigerator. Preheat the oven to 350°F (175°C).

5. Turn the ribs flesh side up and cover the dish with aluminum foil. Bake for 30 minutes, then turn the ribs over (*be careful* when removing the aluminum foil to avoid the steam). Cover and cook for another 30 minutes. The ribs should be cooked by this time—the bones will be exposed and loose. If not, cover and cook for another 10 to 20 minutes, checking often. Increase the oven temperature to 450°F (230°C). Uncover the ribs and baste with the pan juices. Bake for about 10 minutes, basting 3 to 4 times, until the ribs are browned and glazed.

Roast Wild Boar Leg in Sweet-Sour Sauce

Leg of wild boar is not an everyday roast and so it deserves special attention. In this recipe, the leg is first marinated for 2 days and coated with an herb rub before roasting. The marinade forms the base of the sauce, which blends cranberries, caramel, and cocoa to give a rich, deep, sweet-and-sour flavor. Boar legs vary in size; mine have averaged 6 to 7 pounds (2.75 to 3.125 kg) with and without the shank bone. If you've been lucky enough to find a leg with skin on, you can crisp up the crackling while the leg is resting.

1 leg wild boar, 6 to 7 pounds (2.75 to 3.125 kg)
10 juniper berries
Red Wine Marinade (page 212)
Kosher salt
6 sage leaves
1 teaspoon rosemary leaves, chopped
½ teaspoon thyme leaves
2 tablespoons olive oil
¼ cup (40 g) raisins
¼ cup (50 g) sugar
2 tablespoons red wine vinegar
1½ cups (150 g) fresh or frozen cranberries
2 tablespoons (10g) unsweetened cocoa powder
Freshly ground black pepper

1. Pat the leg dry and remove the skin, if any, from the underside of the leg. Turn the leg rounded side up and, using a small sharp knife (a scalpel is great for this job), score the skin: make cuts about ½ inch (1 cm) apart through the skin into the fat, without cutting into the meat. If your leg is skinless, just score the fat without cutting through to the meat.

2. Crush 4 of the juniper berries. Add them to the marinade and pour into a nonreactive container large enough to hold the leg and marinade. Add the leg skin or fat side up (the marinade should come halfway up the leg), then cover with plastic wrap and refrigerate for 2 days. If the leg has its skin, don't turn it; if there is no skin, turn it twice a day. If it has skin, about 12 hours before you plan to cook the leg, remove the plastic wrap and leave the leg uncovered in the refrigerator. This will dry the skin so that it will crisp up better.

3. One hour before roasting it, take the leg out of the refrigerator. Pour off the marinade, and set it aside. Pat the leg dry. Preheat the oven to 425°F (220°C).

4. With a mortar and pestle pound together 2 tablespoons salt, the remaining juniper berries, the sage, rosemary, and thyme leaves. (You can also grind these ingredients in a spice grinder.) Mix in the oil, then rub this paste all over the leg.

5. Place the meat on a rack in a roasting pan and pour in enough water to cover the bottom of the pan. Roast for 20 minutes. Reduce the oven temperature to 350°F (175°C), baste with any juices, and continue to cook, basting the meat every 30 minutes for another 2 to 2½ hours, or until the internal temperature of the leg registers 155°F (68°C) on an instant-read thermometer. Make sure that there is always water covering the bottom of the roasting pan.

6. While the roast is cooking, pour the marinade, with the herbs and vegetables, into a saucepan. Bring to a boil, reduce the heat, and simmer, partially covered, for 1 hour.

7. Strain the reduced marinade through a sieve and discard the herbs and vegetables. Set 1 cup (250 ml) of the liquid aside, and pour the remainder over the raisins in a small bowl. Leave them to soak.

8. Place the sugar and ¼ cup (60 ml) water in a small saucepan and cook over medium heat, stirring to dissolve the sugar; once the sugar is dissolved, stop stirring. Bring to a boil and continue to boil until the syrup turns a light caramel color. Remove the pan from the heat and *carefully* add the vinegar. The caramel will spit and sputter as the vinegar hits it, creating a cloud of fumes. Return the saucepan to low heat and cook, stirring, to dissolve the caramel. Add the cranberries and continue to cook, stirring until the cranberries begin to pop. Set the pan aside.

9. Once the leg is cooked, remove the skin (if you have it) and transfer it to a baking sheet. Place the leg on a warm platter (set the pan aside) and let rest, loosely covered with aluminum foil, for at least 15 minutes. (The internal temperature will rise to 160°F (71°C) as it rests.)

10. Meanwhile, preheat the broiler, then broil the skin, watching carefully, until puffed and golden. Discard the fat from the roasting pan, add the 1 cup (250 ml) reduced marinade, and bring to a boil, deglazing the pan by scraping up the browned bits from the bottom.

11. Strain the liquid into the saucepan with the cranberry caramel, and add the raisins and their soaking liquid. Place the pan over medium heat. Mix the cocoa with 2 tablespoons water and whisk into the sauce. Bring to a boil and simmer until it thickens slightly, then season with salt and pepper.

12. Carve the leg, and serve with the sauce and crackling.

Variations

◦ If you can't get wild boar, try this recipe with a pork roast, adjusting the cooking time accordingly.

◦ This sauce can also accompany the Roast Leg of Venison (page 232) or the Roasted Rack of Venison (page 224). Use the marinade for the sauce, but don't marinate the venison.

Roast Leg of Venison

A roasted haunch of venison is a classic dish. If you plan to cook the whole leg, have the pelvic bone removed by the butcher to make carving easier. If the shank is still attached, make sure the meat is cut around the bone to free the tendons (it's easy to do if the butcher has not done this). Half a leg is often more practical than a whole one. Whichever half you choose (see page 201), the roast needs a good coating of fat to keep it from drying out in the oven. Vintage cookbooks often show beautifully larded haunches of venison. Larding is done with a special needle that allows you to stitch pieces of pork fat into the meat. I own a larding needle, but I have used it only twice; I find it much simpler to wrap the leg in caul fat.

Caul fat is the net that holds the animal's internal organs in place. Although sometimes hard to find, it freezes well. Most caul fat sold is pork and comes in large rectangles, either fresh or salted. The fresh needs only a rinse, while the salted must be soaked in warm water for 30 minutes; pat it dry before using. The advantage of caul fat is that it sticks to itself, making it easy to wrap around the meat. You can substitute thin slices of pork fat, but you will have to tie them in place with string. You could ask your friendly butcher to help.

Roasted venison is best served rare. You can cook it to medium-rare, but no more, or it will be dried out.

½ leg of venison, about 5 pounds (2.25 kg)
1 piece fresh or salted caul fat, rinsed, or thin slices pork fat
Olive Oil Marinade (page 212)
Kosher salt and freshly ground black pepper
Poivrade Sauce (page 211)

1. The day before roasting the venison, pat the leg dry and wrap it in the caul fat (or pork fat). Place in a shallow dish and pour over the marinade, rubbing it into the leg. Cover and refrigerate.

2. One hour before cooking, remove the leg from the refrigerator. Preheat the oven to 425°F (220°C).

3. Season the leg with salt and pepper, and put it in a large roasting pan along with the marinade. Roast for 10 minutes, then reduce the oven temperature to 350°F (175°C), and baste the leg with the pan juices. Continue to roast, basting every 15 minutes, for 1 hour, or until the internal temperature registers 125°F (52°C) for rare, or 130°F (54°C) for medium-rare, on an instant-read thermometer. (Estimate about 12 to 13 minutes per each pound [450 g].) Transfer the meat to a warmed serving platter; if you used pork fat remove it from the roast. Let the leg rest, loosely covered with aluminum foil, for 15 minutes. As the roast rests, its temperature will rise by 5°F (2°C).

4. Discard the fat from the roasting pan. Add the poivrade sauce and bring to a boil, deglazing the pan by scraping up the browned bits from the bottom. Add any juices from the meat and the arrowroot Cognac mixture and return to a boil, whisking constantly. Remove from the heat, strain through a sieve, and stir in red currant jelly.

5. Carve the leg and serve with the sauce.

Variation

- You could also serve the leg with the Cape Gooseberry Sauce (page 224).

Venison Shank in Rosemary-Wine Sauce

Lean and sinewy venison shank, especially from elk, benefits from a day or two of marinating. Braising the shank produces tender, succulent meat, coated with a rich satisfying sauce. (You can also use 2 or 3 smaller deer shanks instead and adjust the cooking time.) The red wine and the rosemary here hold their own with strongly flavored meat.

This recipe reheats well, so make it a couple of days in advance if you like.

1 large venison shank, about 3 pounds (1.35 kg)
Red Wine Marinade (page 212)
1 large rosemary branch, plus 1 teaspoon rosemary leaves
4 ounces (115 g) slab (side) bacon
2 tablespoons vegetable oil
Kosher salt and freshly ground black pepper
1 tablespoon red currant jelly

1. Ask your butcher to make a cut (or do it yourself) around the thinner end of the shank, about 1 inch (2.5 cm) from the end, cutting right through the meat to the bone; this will release the tendons from the bone. Pat the shank dry and place it in a large bowl. Add the marinade, turning to coat. Add the rosemary branch, cover, and marinate in the refrigerator for a day or two, turning from time to time.

2. One hour before cooking, remove the shank from the refrigerator.

3. Preheat the oven to 300°F (150°C). Remove and discard the rind from the bacon, then cut it into ¼-inch (5-mm) dice. Place it in a small saucepan, cover with cold water, and bring to a boil. Drain the bacon in a sieve and rinse under cold running water; set aside.

4. Remove the shank from the marinade and pat dry. Strain the marinade through a sieve, and keep the vegetables and liquid separate.

5. In a Dutch oven or flameproof casserole large enough to hold the shank, heat the oil over medium heat. Season the shank with salt and pepper, then brown it on all sides. Transfer it to a plate. Lower the heat, add the bacon to the pot, and cook until it begins to pop and render its fat. Add the reserved vegetables from the marinade and cook, stirring, for about 5 minutes, or until the liquid boils off and the vegetables begin to stick to the bottom of the pot. Pour in the marinade liquid and bring to a boil, deglazing the pot by scraping up the browned bits from the bottom.

6. Remove from the heat, lay the browned shank on top of the vegetables, and season again with salt and pepper. Cover the shank with a damp piece of parchment paper and then the lid. Place in the oven and braise for 1½ hours.

7. Carefully turn the shank and baste it. Replace the parchment paper and the lid, and cook for another 1½ to 2 hours. Although the meat will shrink quite dramatically from the bone, that does not mean

that it is cooked; cook the shank until the meat is very tender and almost falling off the bone. Carefully transfer the shank to a platter and keep warm, loosely covered with aluminum foil.

8. Strain the sauce through a sieve into a glass measuring cup, let stand. You will have 1½ to 2 cups (375 to 500 ml). Skim off any fat, pour back into the pot then bring to a boil. Boil hard for 5 minutes to reduce the sauce to about 1 cup (250 ml). Add the red currant jelly and rosemary leaves, and check the seasoning.

9. Serve the shank with the sauce.

NOTE: To prepare this dish ahead, transfer the cooked shank to a platter and allow it to cool. Strain the sauce through a sieve into a glass measuring cup; do not reduce it. Once both the shank and sauce are cool, cover and refrigerate them separately. The fat will set on top of the sauce and can easily be removed. Reheat the shank gently in the sauce, covered in a 300°F (150°C) oven. When it is hot, remove and keep warm while you reduce the sauce as above and add the jelly and rosemary leaves.

Venison Osso Buco with Quince and Ginger

Quinces are not a pretty fruit: at first glance, you might mistake them for large, misshapen apples. But these lumpy, greenish-yellow fruit, while impossible to eat raw, transform when cooked, becoming tender and rosy-hued. They have a powerful fragrance that conjures up vanilla, musk, lemon blossoms, and pineapple. Fruit and game are a natural match, and the power of quinces complements strong game well. Fresh ginger emphasizes the quince's aroma and cuts through the richness of the meat.

The term *osso buco* originally denoted thick pieces of veal shank but is now often used to describe the same cut from other animals. If you can't find quinces, you can substitute apples (see the sidebar). The recipe can be made ahead and reheated but don't prepare the gremolata until just before serving.

Four 1½ to 2 inches (4 to 5 cm) thick pieces venison shank, about 12 ounces (350 g) each
2 tablespoons flour
Kosher salt and freshly ground black pepper
2 tablespoons vegetable oil
2 cups (500 ml) Game Stock (page 204)
¼ cup (60 ml) julienned fresh ginger, plus 1 tablespoon plus 1 teaspoon finely diced ginger
2 tablespoons sugar
2 teaspoons grenadine
2 cloves
2 quinces
1 garlic clove, finely chopped
½ cup (125 ml) loosely packed flat-leaf parsley leaves, chopped

○○○

1. Preheat the oven to 325°F (160°C). Pat the shank pieces dry. With kitchen scissors, cut completely through the membrane surrounding each shank piece in two places. Tie a piece of string around each shank to hold the meat in place while it is cooking. Season the flour with the salt and pepper. Dredge the shanks in the seasoned flour, shaking off the excess.

2. In a Dutch oven or flameproof casserole large enough to hold the venison pieces in a single layer, heat the oil over medium heat. Add the venison and brown on both sides, then transfer to a plate. Discard the fat from the pot, pour in the stock, and bring to a boil, deglazing the pot by scraping up the browned bits from the bottom. Add ½ teaspoon salt, then return the venison to the pot. The liquid will come about three quarters of the way up the pieces. Scatter the julienned ginger over the top, and cover with a damp piece of parchment paper and then the lid.

3. Pour 2 cups (500 ml) water into a saucepan, stir in the sugar, 1 tablespoon of the finely diced ginger, the grenadine, and cloves, and bring to a boil. Boil for 1 minute, and remove from the heat. Peel the quinces and cut them into eighths, then cut out the seeds and cores. Place them in a single layer in a baking dish, pour over the syrup, and cover the dish with aluminum foil.

4. Place the venison and quinces in the oven and cook for 1½ hours.

5. *Carefully* remove the lid and aluminum foil to avoid the steam and turn both the venison and quinces. Cover them both again and cook for another 1½ hours, or until the venison and quinces are tender. Transfer the meat and quinces to an ovenproof serving dish with a lip and keep warm, loosely covered with aluminum foil. Reduce the oven temperature to 300°F (150°C).

6. Skim the fat from the venison cooking juices. Remove and discard the cloves from the quince syrup, and then pour it into the venison cooking juices. (There will be about 2 cups [500 ml] liquid.) Bring to a boil and boil hard for 5 to 7 minutes to reduce the sauce to 1 cup (250 ml). Pour it over the venison and quinces, cover, and return to the oven for 10 to 15 minutes to reheat.

7. Mix the remaining teaspoon of the chopped ginger with the garlic and parsley. Serve this gemolata with the venison, and don't forget to enjoy the marrow in the bones.

TIP If you can't buy large pieces of osso buco, cook two smaller pieces per person. Sometimes if the osso buco is sold in packages that include very small pieces, not worth serving, either save the them for stock or cook them along with the bigger ones. You can use their meat for Game Soup (page 210) or in dumplings for consommé (page 209).

===================== *Quinces* =====================

Quinces are becoming more widely available. Try to buy green quinces, free of any marks or bruises. They hold their shape better when cooked. Nestle them in paper towels to keep them from knocking against each other and store them in the vegetable section of your refrigerator; I have kept quinces this way for more than 3 months. They will slowly ripen and turn yellow. Grenadine is added to the cooking syrup in this recipe to ensure a pinky hue to the quinces. If you can't get quinces, substitute cooking apples, such as Rome, Spy, or Mutsu. Apples cook much more quickly than quinces. Instead of baking them, cook them in the syrup on top of the stove, for about 30 minutes or less.

===================== *Venison Neck* =====================

While searching for venison osso buco at the market, I happened across some venison neck. I used it in this recipe for Venison Osso Buco with great success. One of the cheapest venison cuts you can buy, they are delicious and you can use them instead of the venison osso buco, or try them in the Lamb Neck with Anchovies recipe (page 122). With larger animals like elk, though, the neck is better cut into pieces and used for stock.

Bonelogue

The connection between bones and dessert may not be immediately apparent. While marrow bones were a popular dish at English high teas and often served at the end of dinner, a plate of roasted bones is not my idea of dessert. However, both bones and the marrow they contain were and still are important in the dessert kitchen.

Bones yield a natural gelatin, and it is this that thickens stocks and sauces. And by following a series of steps, from a rich stock to consommé, we can make a savory aspic. The gelatin that sets this aspic is the same gelatin we use for desserts. A neutral, flavorless gela-tin is derived by boiling animal feet. Luckily, we don't have to boil up bones or calves' and pigs' feet to make rich coffee mousses, sparkling fruit jellies, and creamy smooth Bavarians. We can buy our gelatin in a package.

Commercial gelatin became widely available in the late nineteenth century. Granulated gelatin is the most readily available form; it is simple and easy to use. It can be bought in bulk or in individual envelopes; each envelope contains ¼ ounce (7 g) gelatin, which is enough to set 2 cups (500 ml) liquid. Gelatin is also sold in thin sheets, each weighing ¹⁄₁₆ ounce (2 g), which are more commonly used in Europe. Both the granules and the sheets must be soaked in cold liquid before using. This step allows the gelatin to soften and swell so that it will dissolve completely on heating. Today there is also a wide variety of sweetened and flavored gelatin products available, all thanks to bones.

While gelatin is the most common, it is not the sole use of bones in the dessert kitchen. Bones also provide the fat to enrich some desserts. Anyone familiar with English cooking will know the importance of suet, the fat that envelops animals' kidneys, in the preparation of steamed puddings. I still make my Christmas pudding using suet. Marrow is also part of this tradition. An important source of digestible fat, marrow was often used instead of butter in desserts in the past. Two old English recipes that are easy to make today using marrow are included here. I urge you to try them—the marrow melts into the desserts, and I defy anyone to detect its presence.

Another way bones play a sweet role is visually. Halloween is the time for all sorts of chocolate and candy skeletons to appear. In Mexico, as in many Catholic countries, the days after Halloween, November 1 and 2, are the most important. First the saints are celebrated, and then the dead are remembered. Mexicans celebrate the festival by making skeletons, bones, and skulls out of sugar. In Italy, there are sweet cookies called *ossi di morto*, bones of the dead, or *ossi da mordere*, bones to chew on. Shaped to resemble bones and skeletons, they are made from a mixture of ground almonds, sugar, and egg white and are traditionally eaten on the Day of the Dead.

So bones can accompany you from the beginning of your meal right through to the end.

There is a French saying that appeals to me (probably because of my food styling background); *Il extrait la moëlle des os.* Literally this means, "He takes the marrow out of the bones." In French, it refers to someone who pays attention to the details.

Beauty is only skin deep, but ugly goes to the bone.
—DOROTHY PARKER

Barley Marrow Pudding

This recipe is based on a medieval recipe recorded by Dorothy Hartley in her book *Food in England*. It is really a rice pudding made with barley, because at the time the recipe was written, that was the readily available grain. The barley is cooked in milk, then enriched with bone marrow. The dish is highly nutritious, and according to Chinese medicine, the combination of barley and bone marrow is an excellent tonic for the body. If you need a pick-me-up, this is the dish for you.

The marrow must be soaked ahead of time in salted water, changed frequently to remove any traces of blood. It must be also very cold so you can finely dice it.

4 cups (1 l) milk
1 cup (200 g) pearl barley, rinsed well
½ cup (100 g) sugar
½ cup (70 g) currants
Pinch of kosher salt
3 tablespoons (30 g) finely diced bone marrow
Finely grated zest of 1 lemon
1 teaspoon vanilla extract (essence)

1. Pour the milk into a medium saucepan and add the barley, sugar, currants, and salt. Bring to a boil over medium-high heat. Lower the heat, cover, and simmer very gently, stirring from time to time, for 15 minutes.

2. Uncover the saucepan and continue to simmer very gently for another 15 minutes, or until the barley is just tender.

3. Remove the pan from the heat and stir in the marrow, lemon zest, and vanilla. Cover the pan and let it stand until barley has completely absorbed the milk. Serve warm or cold.

Marrow Pudding

{ SERVES 6 }

This recipe is adapted from one in Florence White's *Good Things in England*. It is a type of bread and butter pudding, the food of my childhood. However, instead of the buttered bread slices my mother used, it is made with bread crumbs that are enriched with marrow. Good-quality fresh bread crumbs, preferably from an egg bread or brioche, are essential for this recipe. Slice the bread and trim off the crusts, place in a food processor, and process to coarse crumbs. Be sure to soak the marrow in advance to remove any traces of blood.

8 ounces (225 g) fresh white bread crumbs (about 3 cups)
2 cups (500 ml) whole milk
3 ounces (90 g) bone marrow, chopped (about ⅔ cup)
½ cup (80 g) raisins
2 large eggs
⅓ cup (65 g) granulated sugar
½ teaspoon ground cinnamon
⅛ teaspoon freshly grated nutmeg
⅓ packed cup (70 g) brown sugar

1. Preheat the oven to 350°F (175°C). Butter a 9-inch (23-cm) square baking dish. Place the bread crumbs in a bowl. Pour the milk into a saucepan and bring to a boil, then pour over the crumbs. Leave the crumbs to soak for 10 minutes.

2. Stir the marrow and raisins into the bread crumbs. Whisk the eggs with the granulated sugar, cinnamon, and nutmeg in a bowl. Add to the bread crumbs and mix well. Pour this mixture into the baking dish.

3. Place the baking dish in a larger pan and add enough hot water to come halfway up the sides of the baking dish. Bake for 45 minutes, or until just firm in the center.

4. Preheat the broiler to high. Sprinkle the top of the pudding with the brown sugar and broil until the sugar melts. Let cool slightly, and serve.

{ 242 } **Bones**

Bone Cookies

These are called *ossi da mordere* or *ossi di morto* in Italian and in her book *The Italian Baker*, Carol Field describes them as "crunchy chocolate cookies traditionally shaped like bones." She makes them into balls in her recipe, but I wanted bone-shaped cookies, and I wanted white bones. So, I left out the cocoa, formed them into bone shapes, and chilled them for about 1 hour before baking. (The chilling helps them hold their shape.) When they came out of the oven, I had a tray of white bones, still soft and chewy in the center. The amount of egg white needed will vary depending on the humidity in your confectioners' sugar. You want a mixture that is neither crumbly nor too sticky.

¾ cup (125 g) blanched almonds
1½ cups (150 g) confectioners' (icing) sugar
3 to 4 tablespoons egg whites (1 to 2 egg whites)
1 tablespoon milk

1. Line two baking sheets with parchment paper. Place the almonds in a food processor and process to a coarse powder. Add the sugar and process to a fine powder. Pour in 3 tablespoons egg white and process until the mixture forms a stiff paste the consistency of almond paste; add a little more egg white if necessary.

2. Remove the dough from the processor. To shape the cookies, take about 2 teaspoons of dough and roll it into a rope about 3 inches (7.5 cm) long, then shape it into a bone. Place the cookies 2 inches (5 cm) apart on the lined baking sheets. Place the baking sheets in the refrigerator for at least 1 hour or up to 3 hours before baking.

3. Preheat the oven to 325°F (160°C). Remove the cookies from the refrigerator and lightly brush them with the milk. Bake for 15 to 20 minutes, until slightly puffed and just firm to touch. Let them cool slightly on the baking sheets, then, using a spatula transfer them to a cooling rack.

4. When cool, store the cookies in airtight container.

Variation

○ To make chocolate bones, add ¼ cup (20 g) unsweetened Dutch-process cocoa to the food processor with the confectioners' sugar.

Suggested Reading

Aidells, Bruce, and Denis Kelly. *The Complete Meat Cookbook*. Boston: Houghton Mifflin, 1998.

Alexander, R. McNeil. *Bones: The Unity of Form and Function*. New York: Nevraumont Publishing, 1994.

Alexander, Stephanie. *The Cook's Companion*. Australia: Viking, 1996.

Ammer, Christine. *The American Heritage Dictionary of Idioms*. Boston: Houghton Mifflin, 1997.

Andrews, Coleman. "Close to the Bone." *Saveur* no. 10.

Ayrton, Elizabeth. *The Cookery of England*. Australia: Penguin, 1977.

Ayto, John. *The Diner's Dictionary*. New York: Oxford University Press, 1993.

Bittman, Mark. *Fish*. New York: Wiley, 1999.

Bocuse, Paul. *La Cuisine du Gibier*. Paris: Flammarion, 2000.

Boxer, Arabella. *A Visual Feast*. London: Random Century House, 1991.

Child, Julia, Louisette Bertholle, and Simone Beck. *Mastering the Art of French Cooking*, vol. 1. 40th anniversary edition. New York: Knopf, 2001.

Claiborne, Craig. *The New York Times Food Encyclopedia*. New York: Times Books, 1985.

Colwin, Laurie. *Home Cooking*. New York: HarperCollins, 1988.

———. *More Home Cooking*. New York: HarperCollins, 1993.

Conran, Terence, and Caroline Conran. *The Cookbook*. New York: Crown, 1980.

Corriher, Shirley. *CookWise*. New York: William Morrow, 1997.

Daguin, Ariane, George Faison, and Joanna Pruess. *D'Artagnan's Glorious Game Book*. Boston: Little, Brown, 1999.

David, Elizabeth. *Spices, Salts, and Aromatics in the English Kitchen*. Australia: Penguin, 1981.

Davidson, Alan. *The Oxford Companion to Food*. Oxford: Oxford University Press, 1999.

———. *Seafood*. New York: Simon & Schuster, 1989.

De Pomiane, Edouard. *Cooking with Pomiane*. New York: Modern Library Food, 2002.

Fearnley-Whittingstall, Hugh. *The River Cottage Meat Book*. London: Hodder and Stoughton, 2004.

Ferniot, Vincent. *Mon Carnet de Recettes*. Paris: Flammarion, 2002.

Field, Michael, and Francis Field. *Foods of the World—A Quintet of Cuisines*. New York: Time-Life Books, 1970.

Fisher, M. F. K. *The Art of Eating*. New York: World Publishing, 1954.

Fitzgibbon, Theodora. *Food of the Western World*. New York: Quadrangle, 1976.

——. *A Taste of Ireland*. J. M. Dent & Sons, 1971.

Grappe, Jean-Paul. *Gibier à Poil et à Plume*. Montréal: Les Éditions de l'Homme, 2002.

Grasser-Hermé, Frédérick. E. *Délices d'Initiés*. Paris: Noesis, 1999.

Gray, Rebecca. "The Return of Venison." *Saveur* no. 31.

Grigson, Jane. *Charcuterie and French Pork Cookery*. Penguin, 1978.

——. *European Cookery*. New York: Antheneum, 1983.

——. *Fruit*. Penguin, 1983.

——. *Jane Grigson's Vegetable Book*. Penguin, 1981.

——. *The Observer Guide to British Cookery*. London: Michael Joseph, 1984.

Grigson, Sophie, and William Black. *Fish*. London: Headline, 1998.

Hartley, Dorothy. *Food in England*. Boston: Little, Brown, 1966.

Hedgecoe, John, and Henry Moore. *Henry Moore: My Ideas, Inspiration and Life as an Artist*. Stoddart, 1986.

Henderson, Fergus. *The Whole Beast*. New York: Ecco, 2004.

Herbst, Sharon Tyler. *Food Lover's Companion*, 3rd ed. Hauppage, NY: Barron's, 2001.

Hibler, Janie. *Wild About Game*. New York: Broadway, 1998.

Hopkins, Jerry. *Strange Foods*. Hong Kong: Periplus, 1999.

Hopkinson, Simon. *Roast Chicken and Other Stories*. London: Ebury, 1994.

Humphreys, Angela. *Game Cookery*. Trowbridge, Eng.: David Charles, 1993.

Innes, Jocasta. *The Pauper's Cookbook*. Penguin, 1971.

Jamison, Cheryl Alters, and Bill Jamison. *Texas Home Cooking*. Boston: Harvard Common, 1993.

Janson, H. W., ed. *Library of Art, American Painting 1900–1970*. New York: Time-Life Books, 1970.

——. *Library of Art, Picasso 1810–* . New York: Time-Life Books, 1967.

Keller, Thomas. *The French Laundry Cookbook*. New York: Artisan, 1999.

Kiple, Kenneth F., and Kriemhild Coneè Ornelas, eds. *The Cambridge World History of Food*, vols. 1 and 2. Cambridge, Eng.: Cambridge University Press, 2000.

Ladenis, Nico. *My Gastronomy*. London: Headline, 1987.

Lawson, Nigella. *How to Eat*. New York: Wiley, 2000.

Lobels, The. *Meat*. New York: Alpha Books, 1971.

Marrone, Teresa. *Apprêter et cuisiner le gibier*. Trans. from the English by Odette Lord. Montréal: Les Éditions de L'Homme, 2000.

Mathiot, Ginette, *La Cuisine pour Tous*. Livres de Poche, 1955.

McGee, Harold. *The Curious Cook*. San Francisco: North Point Press, 1990.

——. *On Food and Cooking*. New York: Scribner, 1984.

Mieder, Wolfgang. *The Prentice Hall Encyclopedia of World Proverbs*. New York: Prentice Hall, 1986.

Olney, Richard. *The French Menu Cookbook*. Boston: Stoddart, 1985.

——. *Ten Vineyard Lunches*. New York: Interlink, 1988.

Olney, Richard, ed. *The Good Cook Series: Fish*. New York: Time-Life Books, 1981.

——. *The Good Cook Series: Game*. New York: Time-Life Books, 1981.

——. *The Good Cook Series: Pork*. New York: Time-Life Books, 1981.

——. *The Good Cook Series: Variety Meats*. Netherlands: Time-Life Books, 1979.

Paterson, Jennifer, and Clarissa Dickson Wright. *The Two Fat Ladies*. New York: Random House, 1996.

Puck, Wolfgang. *Wolfgang Puck Cookbook*. New York: Random House, 1986.

Ray, Cyril. *The Gourmet's Companion*. London: Eyre and Spottiswoode, 1963.

Reader's Digest. *Les Grandes Recettes de la Cuisine Légère*. Paris: Reader's Digest, 1978.

Rhodes, Gary. *New Classics*. London: Dorling Kindersley, 2001.

Ritchie, Carson I. A. *Bone and Horn Carving*. Barnes, 1975.

Robuchon, Joël. *Ma Cuisine pour Vous*. Paris: Robert Laffront, 1986.

Root, Waverley. *Food*. New York: Simon & Schuster. 1980.

Schott, Ben. *Schott's Food & Drink Miscellany*. New York: Bloomsbury, 2003.

Schneider, Elizabeth. *Uncommon Fruits and Vegetables*. New York: William Morrow, 1998.

Schwabe, Calvin W. *Unmentionable Cuisine*. Charlottesville: University Press of Virginia, 1999.

Slater, Nigel. *Appetite*. New York: Random House, 2000.

———. *Real Cooking*. London: Michael Joseph, 1997.

Stevenson, Burton. *The Home Book of Proverbs, Maxims, Familiar Phrases*. New York: Macmillan, 1948.

Thompson, Anthony Worral. *The ABC of AWT*. London: Headline, 1998.

Time Life Books, eds. *Fresh Ways with Fish and Shellfish*. New York: Time-Life Books, 1986.

Toussaint-Samat, Maguelonne. *History of Food*. Trans. from the French by Anthea Bell. Oxford, Eng.: Blackwell, 1992.

Troisgros, Michel. *La Cuisine Acidulée*. Le Cherche Midi, 2002.

Walker, Harlan. *Oxford Symposium on Food and Cookery 1994: Disappearing Foods*. Blackawton: Prospect Books, 1995.

Wells, Patricia. *Bistro Cooking*. New York: Workman, 1989.

Wheaton, Barbara Ketchum. *Savoring the Past*. New York: Touchstone, 1983.

White, Florence. *Good Things in England*. London: Futura, 1974.

Whiting, Bartlett Jere. *Modern Proverbs and Proverbial Sayings*. Cambridge: Harvard University Press, 1989.

Willan, Anne. *La France Gastronomique*. London: Pavilion, 1991.

———. *La Varenne Pratique*. London: Dorling Kindersley, 1989.

Wolfert, Paula. *The Slow Mediterranean Kitchen*. New York: Wiley, 2003.

Index

Korean pork soup, spicy, 64
Kutna Hora, 48

L

lamb, 91–123
  and barley soup, 97
  carving rack of, 108
  concentrated, stock, 96
  cooking temperatures for, 94
  guard of honor or crown roast of,
    108
  and Jerusalem artichoke soup, 98
  Lancashire hot pot revisited,
    103–4
  locating and choosing cuts of,
    91–94
  mustard oregano glaze for, 111
  olive-crusted, racks, 107–8
  roasted over potatoes, 105–6
  spiced yogurt glaze for, 111
  stock, 95
lamb, leg of:
  carving, 106
  seven-hour, 114
lamb chops:
  with caramelized leeks, 109
  wasabi-coated, 112
lamb neck(s), 119, 121
  with anchovies, 122
  with lettuce and dill, 120–21
lamb ribs, 110–11
  with beans and spinach, 113
lamb shanks:
  cooked in paper with Guinness,
    118–19
  in pomegranate sauce, 115–16
lamb shoulder:
  carving, 106
  with preserved lemon and dates,
    99–100
  ratatouille-style, 101–2
Lancashire hot pot revisited, 103–4
Lee, Vernon, 89
leeks:
  in court bouillon, 60
  in halibut steaks with orange
    cream sauce, 192
  lamb chops with caramelized,
    109
  in poached chicken with
    seasonal vegetables, 142–43

in pork stock, 58
in post-Thanksgiving soup, 136
in poultry stock, 130
lemon:
  in barley marrow pudding, 241
  in breast of veal, 35–36
  in chicken with forty cloves of
    garlic, 138
  in coriander-and-orange braised
    elk ribs, 226–27
  in grilled fish with yellow tomato
    vinaigrette, 184
  in herb-glazed poussins, 140–41
  in lamb chops with caramelized
    leeks, 109
  -mustard bread crumbs, marrow
    topping, 46
  in mustard oregano glaze, 111
  in olive-crusted lamb racks,
    107–8
  in panfried whole sole, 189
  preserved, lamb shoulder with
    dates and, 99–100
  in wings à la Coca Cola, 159
lemongrass, frog's legs with chile
    and, 195
lentils, pig's tails with, 87–88
lettuce, lamb neck with dill and,
    120–21
liver dumplings, for game
    consommé, 209

M

Madeira, roasted veal chops with
    parsnips and, 21
maple tomato glazed ribs, 73
marinades for game, 212–13
marrow, 51
  barley, pudding, 241
  pudding, 242
marrow bones, 51
  in double-bone beef with red
    wine sauce, 22–23
  in four bones in one pot, 37–38
  poached, 45
  roasted, 44–45
  spoons for, 46
  toppings for, 46
martini:
  green, 228
  -style, wild boar chops, 228

Mercer, Johnny, 89
milk:
  in barley marrow pudding, 241
  in marrow pudding, 242
  sauce, caramelized, pork with,
    65–66
monkfish (gigot de mer), whole
    roasted, 186–87
Moore, Henry, 31
mushrooms:
  in chicken with Riesling, 155
  in Flemish-style rabbit, 214–15
  in four bones in one pot, 37–38
  in game soup, 210
  morel cream sauce, chicken with,
    154
mustard:
  and cider sauce, rabbit with,
    220–21
  -lemon bread crumbs marrow
    topping, 46
  in pig's feet, 82–83
  in orange Dijon glaze, 76
  orange dressing, for pig's feet, 83
  oregano glaze, for lamb ribs, 111
  in rack of pork with coffee sauce,
    69
  sauce, 62
  veal shank with sage and, 43
mutton, 94

O

O'Keefe, Georgia, 31
olive oil marinade, for game, 212
olives:
  black, in whiting en papillote, 185
  -crusted lamb racks, 107–8
  green, duck legs with cumin,
    turnips and, 157–58
onions:
  in four bones in one pot, 37–38
  in lamb shanks cooked in paper
    with Guinness, 118–19
  in Lancashire hot pot revisited,
    103–4
  in rabbit in saffron sauce with
    spring vegetables, 216–17
  in seven-hour leg of lamb, 114
orange:
  blood, sauce, osso buco with
    fennel and, 41–42